Images of America
Gladstone

On the Cover: In 1893, Mary Howell rides her bicycle along the north bank of the Clackamas River. Earlier that day, Gladstone celebrated the maiden run of the first electric interurban railway in the United States. Greeted by a cheering crowd, the trolley rolled down Portland Avenue on its way from Portland to Oregon City, crossing the Clackamas River on the new trolley bridge, visible through the trees at left. (Courtesy of the Clackamas County Historical Society and Museum of the Oregon Territory.)

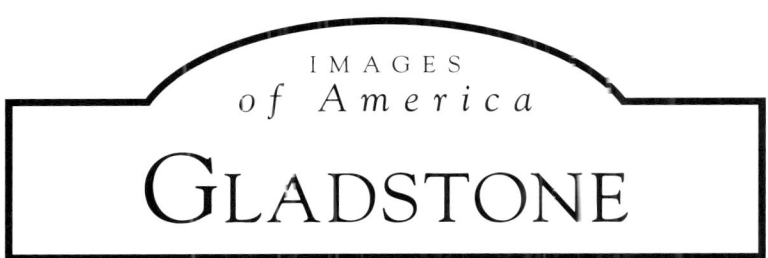

IMAGES of America
GLADSTONE

Kim Argraves Huey

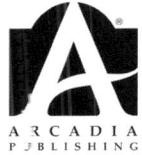

Copyright © 2019 by Kim Argraves Huey
ISBN 978-1-4671-0302-2

Published by Arcadia Publishing
Charleston, South Carolina

Printed in the United States of America

Library of Congress Control Number: 2018960596

For all general information, please contact Arcadia Publishing:
Telephone 843-853-2070
Fax 843-853-0044
E-mail sales@arcadiapublishing.com
For customer service and orders:
Toll-Free 1-888-313-2665

Visit us on the Internet at www.arcadiapublishing.com

To everyone who has ever lived in, loved, or been a part of the town of Gladstone. Enjoy!

Contents

Acknowledgments		6
Introduction		7
1.	First Residents and First Visitors	9
2.	First Settlers	21
3.	First Ferries, Bridges, and Roads	29
4.	First Fairs and a War	47
5.	The First Railroad	57
6.	Judge Harvey Cross, Gladstone's Founder	67
7.	The Coming of Chautauqua	79
8.	Gladstone Becomes a Town	105
Bibliography		126
Index		127

Acknowledgments

I wish to thank all the wonderful people who said yes when I asked for help, needed expertise, or requested photographs. Without you, this book would not be possible: Johna Heinz and the Clackamas County Historical Society and the Museum of the Oregon Territory; Valerie Stinson, office manager of the Gladstone Christian Church; Laura Cray, digital services librarian, Oregon Historical Society; Scott Daniels, reference services manager, Oregon Historical Society; library staff of the State Library of Oregon; Kenn Lentz, Oregon bridge historian; Diane Nickerson Timmons and Amy Timmons, members of the Judge Harvey Cross family, who shared memories, photographs, and historical documents; Lori Anderson, Louise Newland Clark, C. Riddell, and Nancy Stone Brown, for sharing family photographs; Richard Samuels, Oregon Pacific Railroad (OregonPacificrr.com), for his memories and photographs; and Ralph Matile and the members of the "Growing Up In Gladstone" Facebook group, for their helpful suggestions, memories, and historical inspiration.

I also want to thank Devon Huey, photographer; my husband, Ron Huey, and family members Reneé, Shanna, and Laura for supporting and assisting in this project; and members of the Gladstone Historical Society for keeping Gladstone history alive and for cheering me on. And from Arcadia Publishing, a special thank-you to Caroline Anderson for her cheerful guidance through the development of this book, and Jim Kempert, a terrific proofreader.

Last but never least, my deepest appreciation and everlasting gratitude to the late Herbert K. Beals, historian, author, and my dear friend and mentor; without his exhaustive research on the history of Gladstone, this book could not have been written.

Unless otherwise noted, all images in this volume appear courtesy of the Clackamas County Historical Society and Museum of the Oregon Territory. Other photographs appear courtesy of Gladstone Historical Society (GHS), Gladstone Christian Church (GCC), Oregon Historical Society (OHS), State Library of Oregon (SLO), and Kim Argraves Huey (KAH).

INTRODUCTION

Gladstone, Oregon, is located at the confluence of the Clackamas and Willamette Rivers and was once the northern half of the historic town of Oregon City. In 1829, when Dr. John McLoughlin, chief factor of the Hudson Bay Company at Fort Vancouver, crossed the Columbia River and traveled south on the Willamette River in search of the great falls, he passed by the mouth of the Clackamas River and the future site of the town of Gladstone.

Arriving at the falls, now known as Willamette Falls, Dr. McLoughlin claimed two square miles of land where he constructed a mill race, built three employee houses, and opened a store. In 1842, McLoughlin's small fur trapping outpost, which he named Oregon City, became the first permanent settlement in Oregon's Willamette Valley. Two years later, Oregon City became the first incorporated town west of the Rocky Mountains. In 1845, Oregon City was appointed the seat of Oregon's provisional government, and from 1848 to 1851, served as the first territorial capital of Oregon.

The northern boundary of Dr. McLoughlin's land was the Clackamas River, which originates at approximately 4,900 feet on the western side of the Cascade Mountain range. From its origin, the Clackamas River flows westward 83 miles, cutting its course through layers of volcanic rock to create a rugged shoreline. The final two miles of the Clackamas River, before it empties into the larger Willamette River, define the southern and eastern borders of present-day Gladstone. And while Gladstone has some of the Clackamas River's less difficult and more manageable shoreline, it also has one of the most unpredictable and dangerous stretches of water on the Clackamas.

Gladstone's earliest residents were the Clackamas Indians, the once great tribe of the Chinook people who lived in villages on either side of the Clackamas River and controlled the fishing at Willamette Falls. The Clackamas Indians were generally a settled people, living in peace amongst themselves and their neighbors while existing on a diet of mainly fish and some meat. The Clackamas Indians did not engage in traditional agriculture but did routinely harvest naturally growing crops such as nuts, berries, seeds, and roots. They were also traders, dealing extensively in shells, beads, blankets, horses, and furs.

In 1834, when the missionaries arrived in Oregon City, Jason Lee and his nephew Daniel Lee explored the banks of the Clackamas River hoping to establish a Methodist mission and save many native souls. While the Lees found the Indians to be friendly, they had a decisively negative opinion of the terrain along the Clackamas River. Considering the area too inhospitable for settlement, they turned south and explored farther into the Willamette Valley.

When the settlers began arriving, they had an entirely different impression of the Clackamas River. While all of the land surrounding Oregon City was rich and appealing, the wildly beautiful Clackamas River held a near-magical allure for them. Pioneer memoirs recount their first view of the river in almost Edenic terms, describing the Clackamas as "a lovely native stream that gracefully flowed through mostly flat ground comprised of fertile meadows filled with wild flowers, groves of tall firs, and an abundance of other leafy trees."

Looks can be deceiving. While no one would dispute the Clackamas River's scenic wild beauty, in reality, the river hid an unpredictable temperament. With seemingly no more provocation than a spring thaw, the Clackamas River could suddenly release a torrent of raging water that surged into the Willamette River and ravaged everything in its path.

In 1843, Fendel Cason and his family immigrated to Oregon and purchased 640 acres of land along the northern bank of the Clackamas River. Two years later, the Rinearson brothers arrived and filed a 640-acre land claim that adjoined the Cason land on the west. These two land claims became the area of what is now the town of Gladstone.

For the next 50 years, pioneer life around the future Gladstone was an exciting time of firsts, beginnings, innovations, and progress, all of which were accomplished in spite of the occasional neighborhood disagreement and the mayhem caused by the Clackamas River. Yet, it was not the agricultural fairs, military, or the coming of two railroads that distinguished Gladstone from other developing Western towns; rather, it was becoming a permanent site for the singular American phenomenon known as Chautauqua.

In 1874, Methodist minister John Heyl Vincent and businessman Lewis Miller organized a summer religious educational outdoor retreat for the purpose of instructing Sunday school teachers in how to better teach the Bible. The event was so successful that within a few years the annual assembly had taken on the name of its location, "Chautauqua," for Lake Chautauqua, New York, and the curriculum of Bible lessons had expanded to include lectures on literature, science, politics, economics, history, religion, and art. In no time, Chautauqua fever swept the nation and countless towns were recreating the assembly.

In 1883, Harvey Cross, a man of many talents and endless accomplishments, began purchasing parcels of Cason and Rinearson land where he hoped to build the town of Gladstone. On the eastern side of his land, he set aside a 73-acre tract that he named Gladstone Park and later leased as a permanent Chautauqua site. In 1894, Chautauqua arrived.

Offering identical classes, programs, activities, and amenities as the original Chautauqua, the Oregon City Chautauqua at Gladstone Park was an overwhelming success. Crowds numbering in the thousands came and camped for the entire session, with visitors also numbering in the thousands streaming through the main gate daily to hear lectures, enjoy baseball games, and watch the famous people of the time perform on the auditorium's huge stage. Consequently, with a flourishing Chautauqua, Gladstone could not help but be noticed. Many who came to attend the assembly were so impressed with the young community that they decided to stay and become residents.

By the start of the 20th century, Gladstone was experiencing growing pains. No sooner had it passed its first decade than residents were ready to live independently from Oregon City. In 1927, the great Chautauqua ended, but Gladstone was just coming into its own as a town.

One

First Residents and First Visitors

Alexander Henry (1765–1814), a fur trader with the North West Company in Astoria, is believed to be the first European to have encountered the Clackamas Indians, Gladstone's first residents. While earlier fur trappers and traders may have met the Clackamas Indians, they did not chronicle the event as Henry did.

In 1814, while on a company exploration of the Willamette River, Henry's expedition put ashore at the Clowewalla Indian village, located at the south end of the Clackamas Rapids on the Willamette River. Henry's party routinely purchased meat, nuts, seeds, and other food items from local Indians, and it was during such a transaction that several canoes arrived from the Clackamas Indian villages. Henry noted in his journal, "The "Clukerrus [Clackamas] Indians are a numerous tribe, great rogues who live in plank houses, and who go every summer to the [Willamette] falls for the salmon."

The "rogue" description Henry attributed to the Clackamas Indians probably related to the Indians' trading practices. While making it known that they were displeased at having white men settle among them, they also eagerly agreed to bargain. In exchange for the coveted blue beads Henry offered, the Indians returned cleverly disguised inedible food.

In 1830, a mysterious sickness arrived in the Willamette Valley. Continuing intermittently for the next few years, the illness afflicted both the local Indian tribes and the Hudson Bay Company employees and their families. Opinions differ, but considering the symptoms, the epidemic was likely influenza or malaria brought by ships arriving on the Pacific coast from Asia.

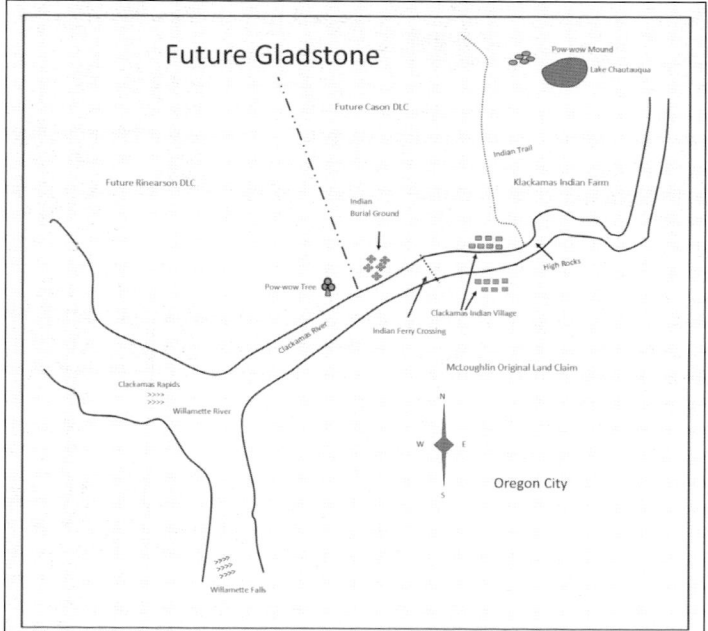

The Clackamas Indians were once a leading tribe of the greater Chinook nation that inhabited the Pacific Northwest. In 1806, when Lewis and Clark visited Oregon, they estimated the Clackamas Indians to number 1,800. Native to Gladstone, the Clackamas Indians lived along both banks of the Clackamas River, which is the southern and eastern border of present-day Gladstone. This map shows the location of their villages.

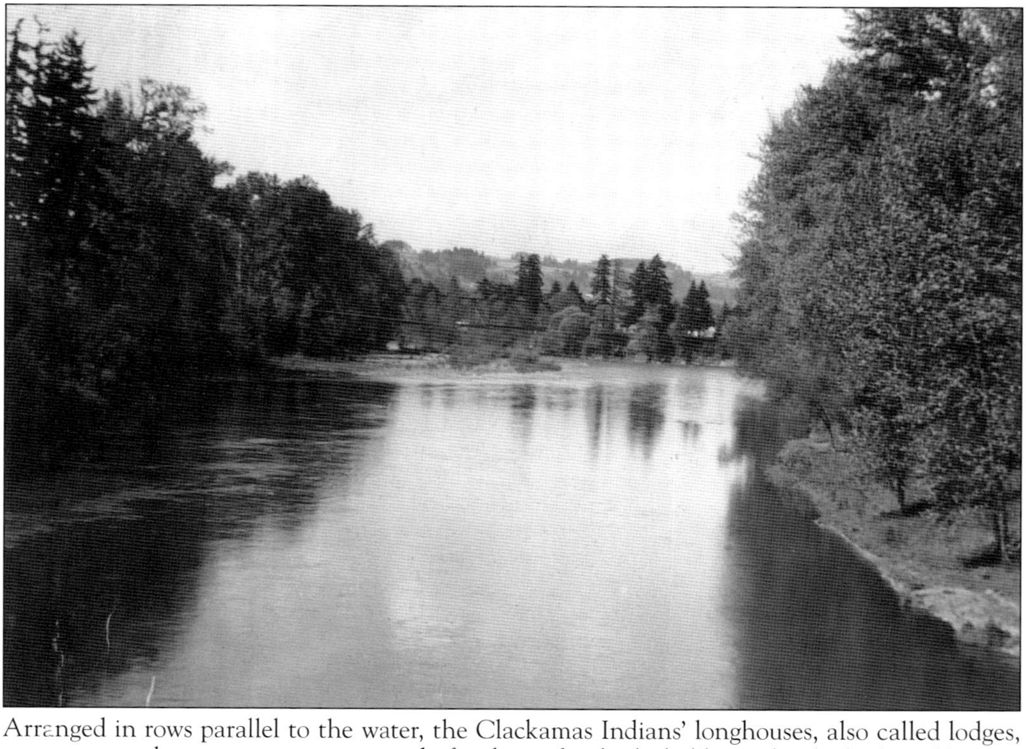

Arranged in rows parallel to the water, the Clackamas Indians' longhouses, also called lodges, were rectangular structures constructed of cedar or fir planks held together by bark and leather straps. As many as 30 family members lived in one longhouse, with the eldest member being appointed chief and governing the other family members. This 1913 photograph, taken facing west, shows the area of the Clackamas River where the longhouses were located.

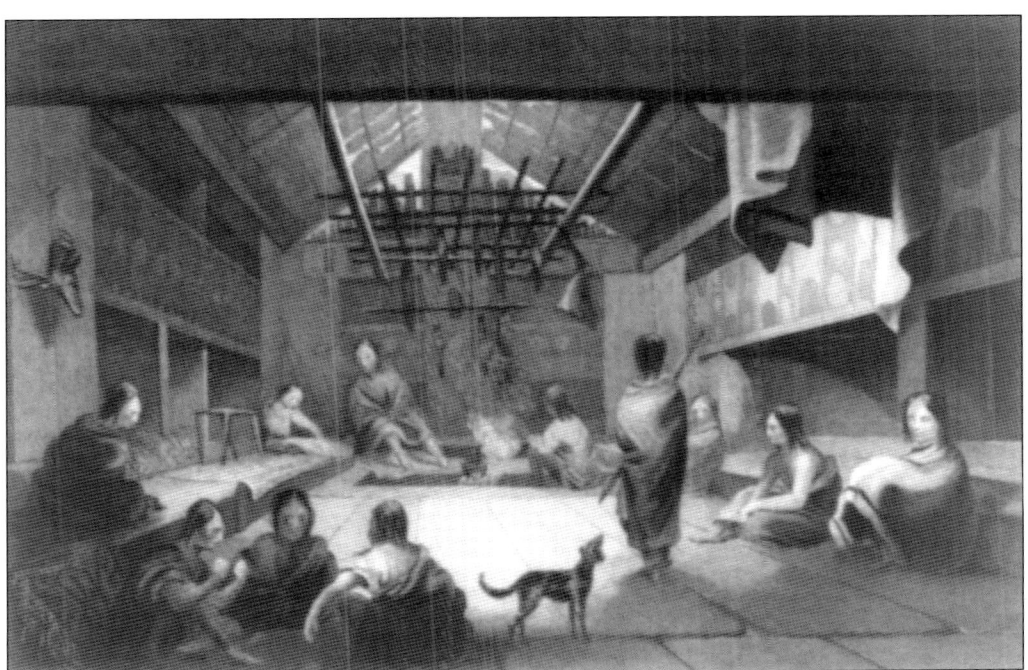

Longhouses measured approximately 60 feet long, 15 feet wide, and 15 feet high, and contained only one room. Inside, shelves lined the long walls and were used for beds, fur, and food storage. Meals were cooked communally over a central fire pit. This 1844 drawing by A.T. Agate shows the interior of a Chinook longhouse. (Courtesy of Richard W. Dodson, Rare Book and Special Collections Division, Library of Congress.)

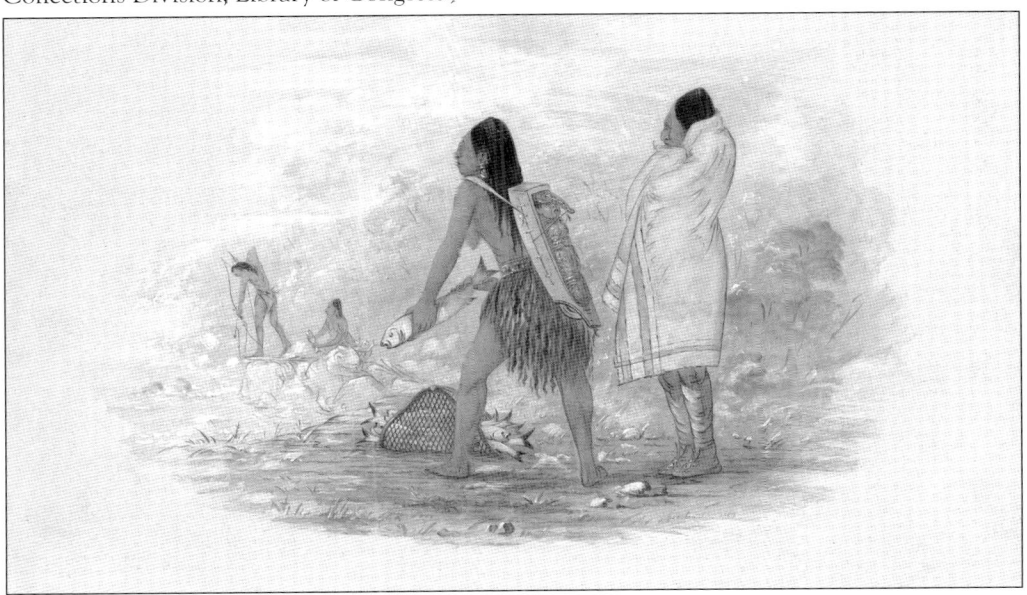

The Clackamas Indians practiced cranial deformation. Using a cradleboard with a moveable wood cover, pressure was applied to a baby's forehead until the head formed a conical shape. A flattened profile, as shown in this 1861 oil painting by George Catlin, signified high social status. (Courtesy of the National Gallery of Art.)

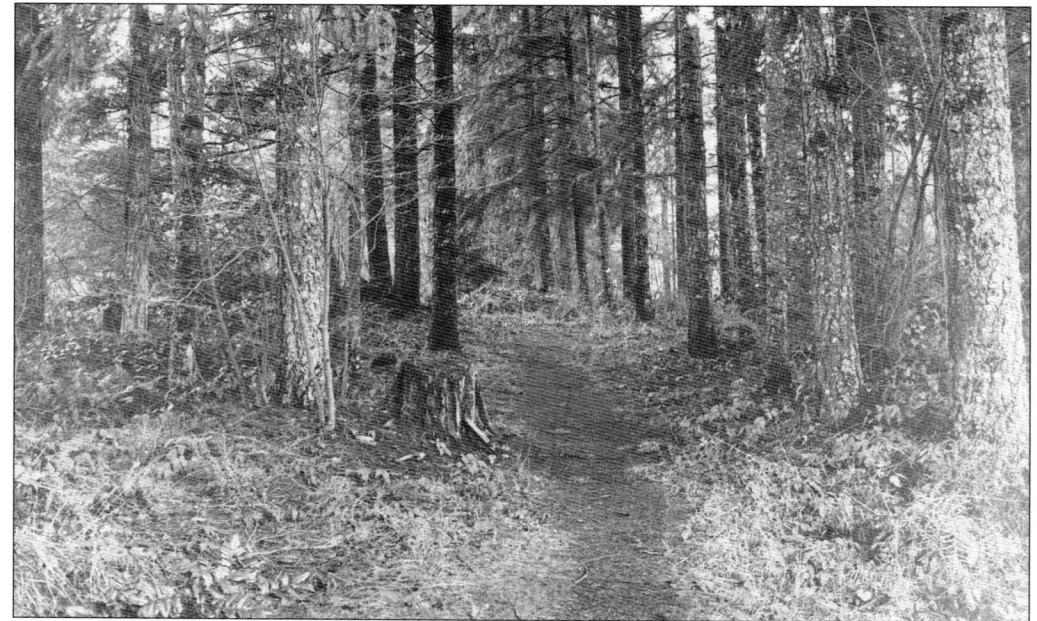

In 1834, Jason Lee and nephew Daniel Lee explored the Clackamas River banks for a suitable site on which to build a Methodist mission. According to Jason Lee's diary, the men became "lost, in a swamp thickly timbered and covered with underbrush." They nearly starved before a party of Clackamas Indians rescued them. Taken in 1895, this photograph of the path leading into Lake Chautauqua shows terrain similar to where the Lees were lost.

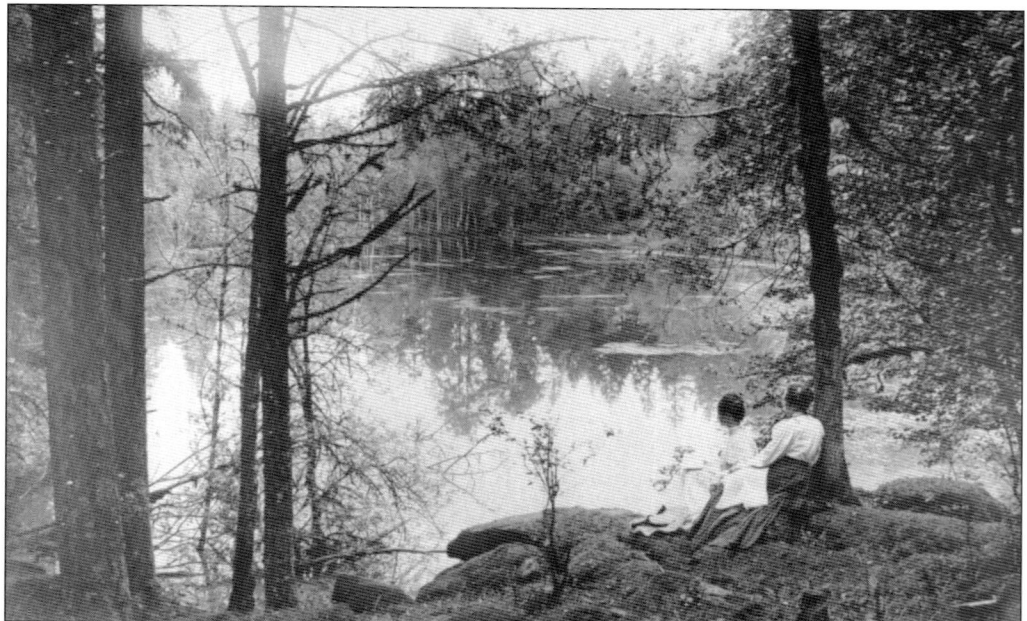

Lake Chautauqua is a volcanic lake approximately a quarter mile north of the Clackamas River in present-day Gladstone Park. Clackamas Indian George described the lake as having "no apparent inlet or outlet and in places no bottom . . . a rock-walled mystery with a motionless surface." In 1908, Marceline Cross Hammond (left) and her mother, Orpha Cross, gaze eastward at Lake Chautauqua.

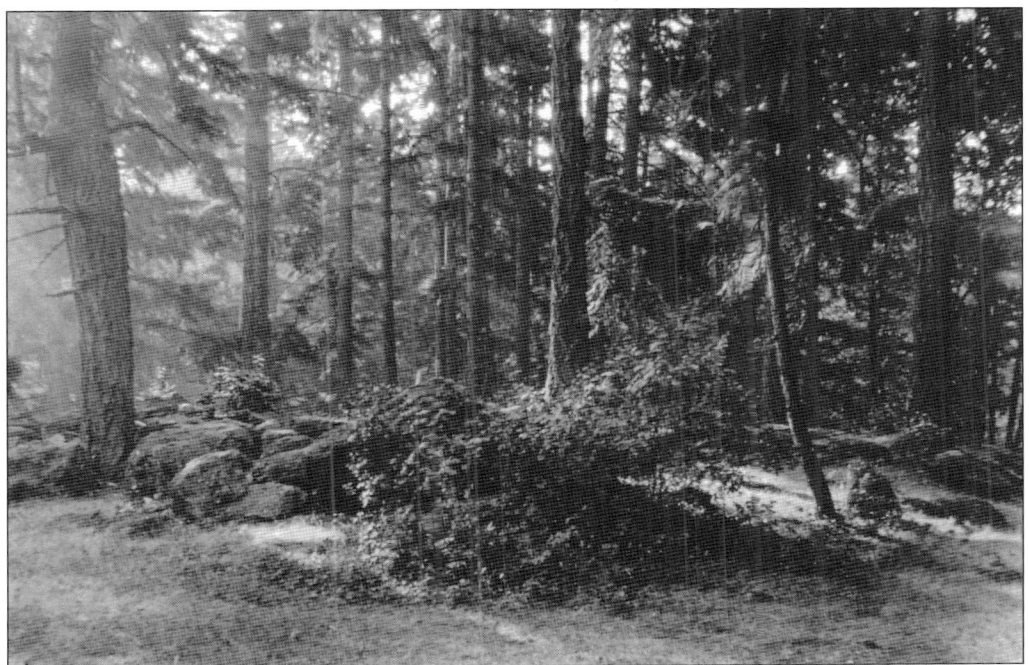

According to Clackamas Chief Jake, the Clackamas Indian tribes once held powwows on a rocky mound near Lake Chautauqua's northeast corner. Later, beads, trinkets, and feathers were discovered in small, natural niches in an adjacent rock wall. The Pow-Wow mound is shown here in 1900.

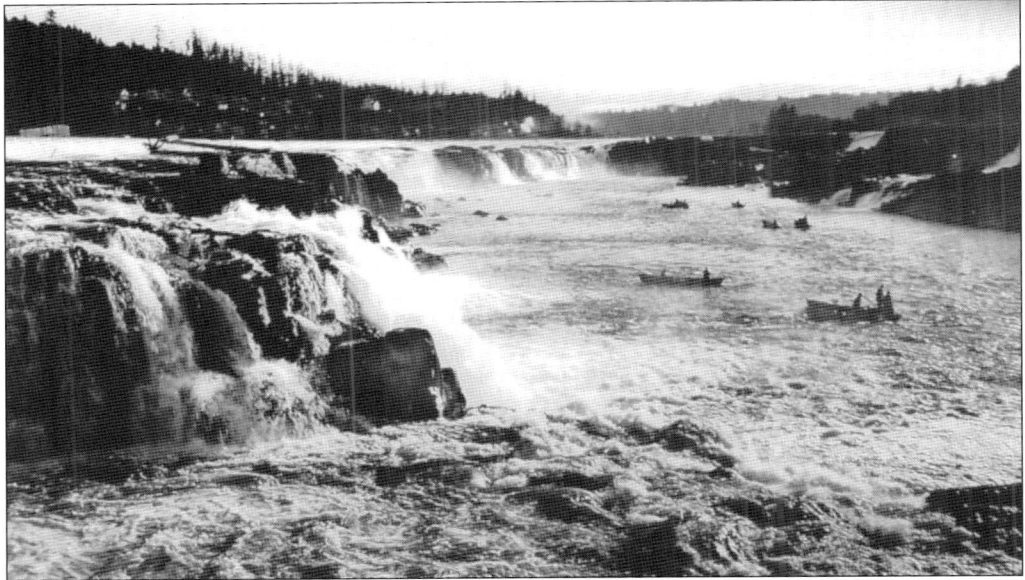

Willamette Falls is the second most powerful waterfall in the United States and is located on the Willamette River at Oregon City. Once controlled by the Clackamas Indians, other area tribes asked permission before fishing in the turbulent waters that were abundant with salmon, steelhead, and lamprey. This 1900 postcard shows Willamette Falls with the Canemah area of Oregon City in the background. (GHS.)

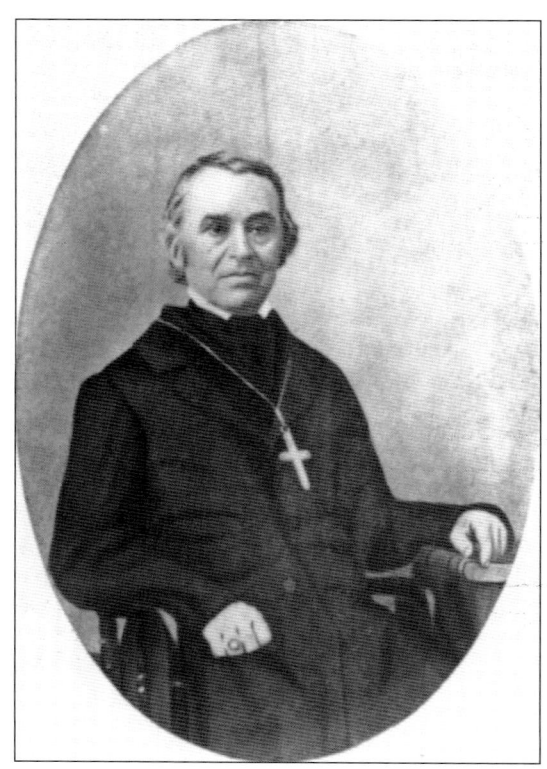

Catholic priest Father Blanchet, left, and Methodist minister Rev. Alvin Waller, below, came to Oregon City to evangelize the Indians and ended up in their own private religious war. Undertaking all manner of devious tricks to convert the Clackamas Indians to their respective religions, their "holy feud" soured the Indians on Christianity. The winter of January 1841 was harsh. The Clackamas River, the Willamette River, and Willamette Falls all froze, leaving the Indians short of food. The following spring, Reverend Waller acquired land on the north bank of the Clackamas River at High Rocks and demanded the Indians learn to grow wheat and vegetables. Thoroughly weary of missionaries, the Indians refused to farm. According to historians, the Catholics had only slightly more converts than the Methodists because the Indians favored their black-robed ceremony over dull prayer meetings and hoeing.

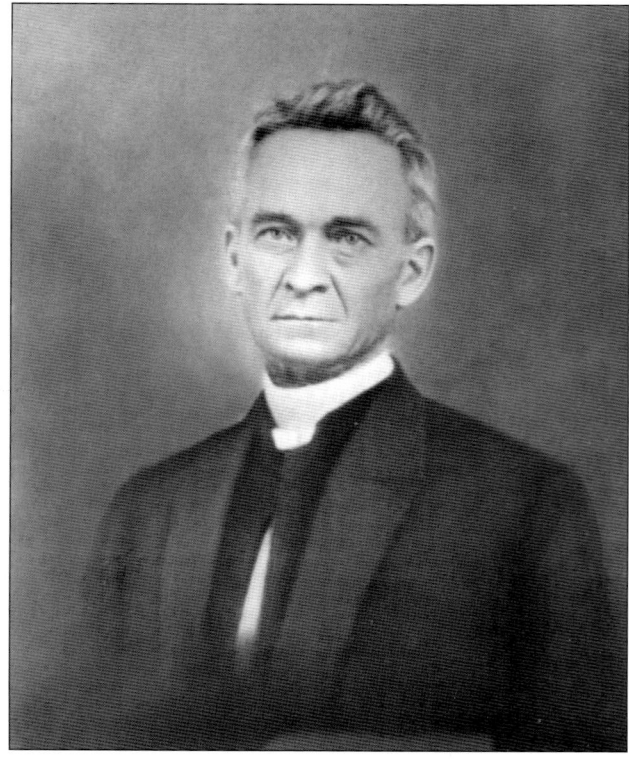

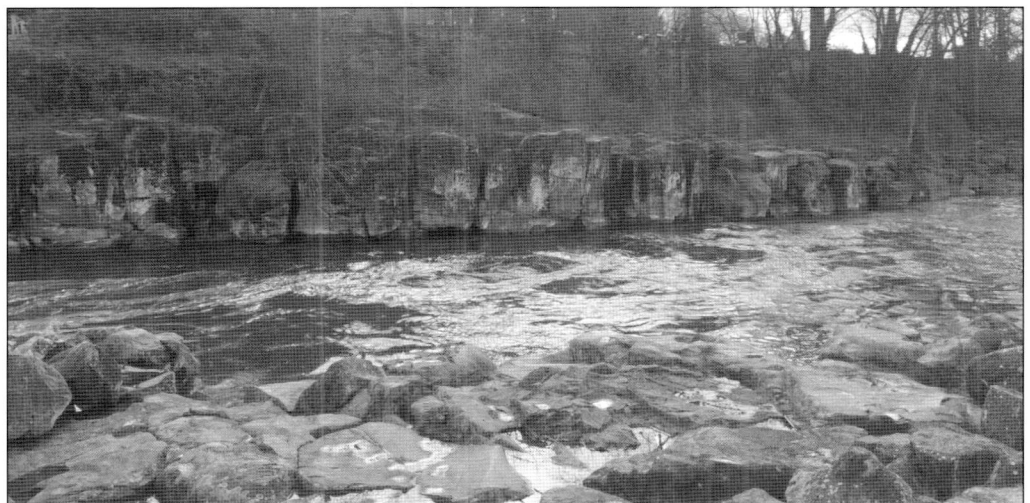

High Rocks, where Reverend Waller planted his "Klackamas Farm," is an area of the Clackamas River 500 feet east of the Clackamas Indian village. Here, the river narrows into a gorge that runs fierce and deep in the winter yet appears deceptively calm and shallow in the summer. Year-round, the dark water is frigid and hides surprisingly strong currents, rocky ledges, and undercut banks. (Courtesy of Devon Huey.)

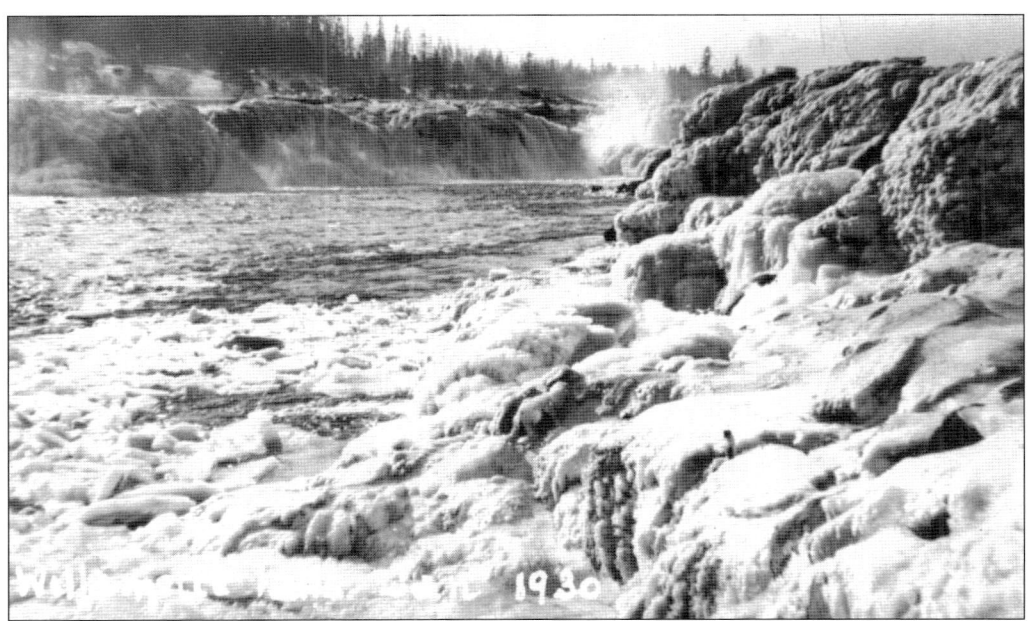

Between 1840 and 1930, the Clackamas River, Willamette River, and Willamette Falls froze solid at least six times, with the rivers becoming hard enough to be walked across. This 1930 photograph of Willamette Falls shows a similar winter to the one the Indians endured in 1841.

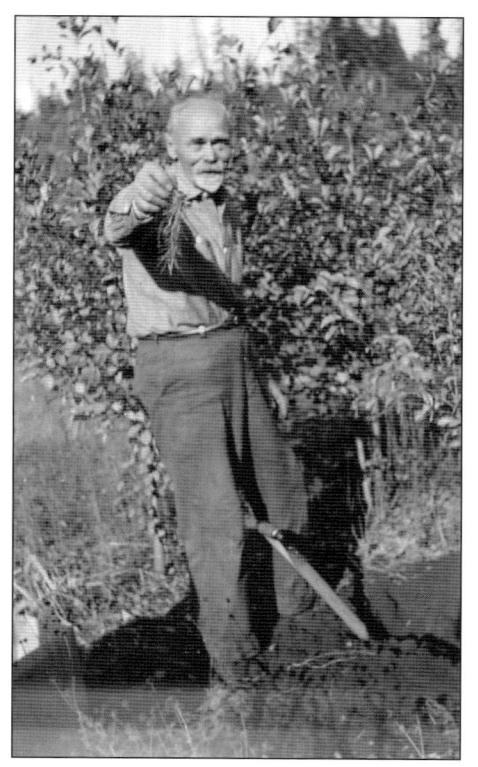

In 1834, John Kirk Townsend of the Wyeth Expedition recorded the sighting of an Indian burial ground along the Clackamas River. However, the burial ground was not discovered until 1910 when Oscar Freytag, Gladstone's first mayor, uncovered Indian skeletons, beads, and trinkets while digging a garden bed. In 1979, an archaeological study of the burial ground revealed more skeletons. At left, in the 1930s, Freytag is seen digging in his garden. Below, in 1895, Mary Howell rides her bicycle along the north bank of the Clackamas River in the vicinity of the Indian burial ground, which is the present-day two-block area of Arlington Street on the north, Harvard Avenue on the east, Clackamas Boulevard on the south, and Portland Avenue on the west. (Left, GHS.)

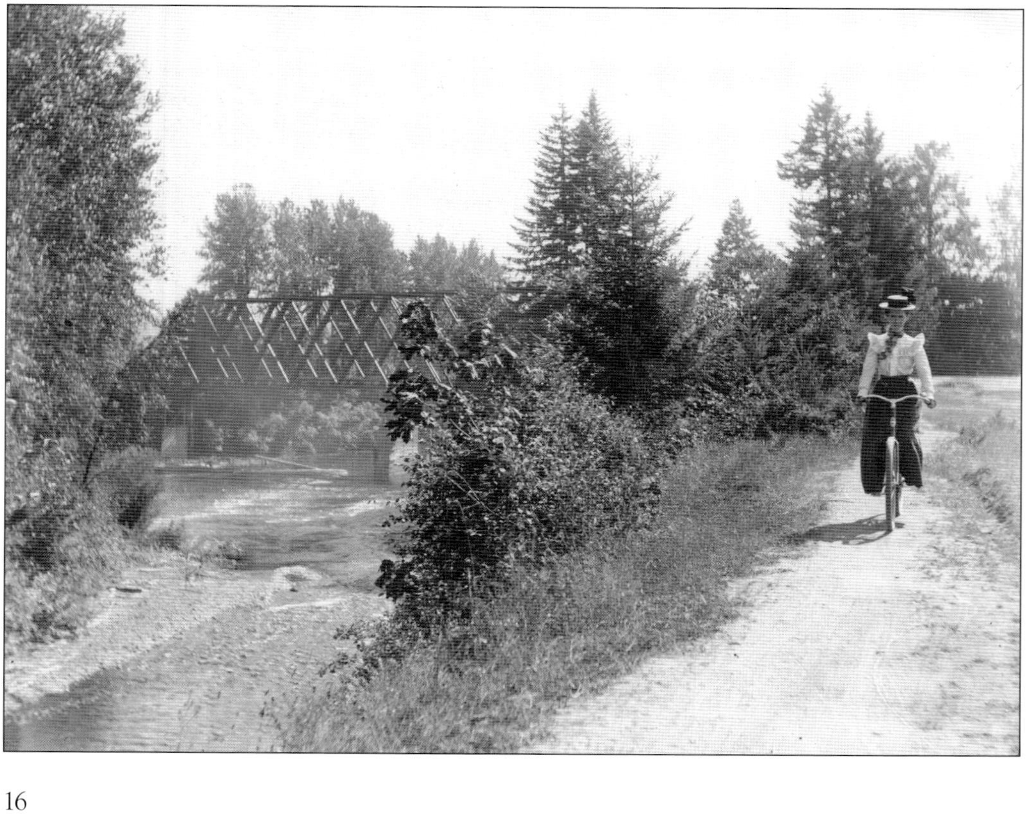

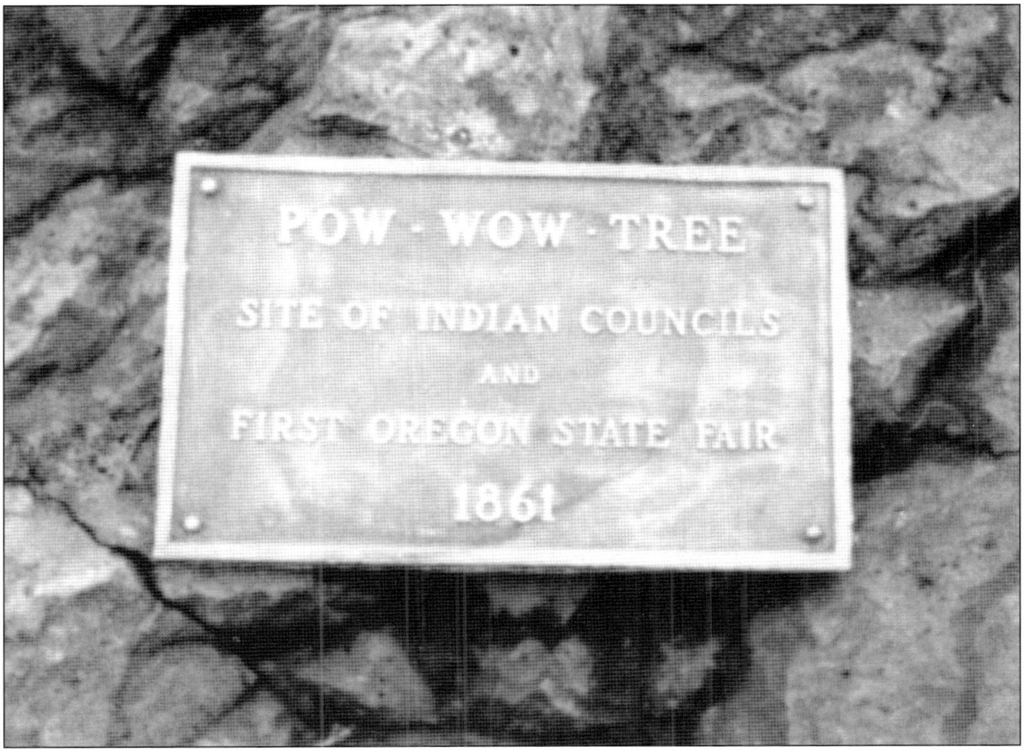

Two blocks west of the burial ground stands the Pow-Wow tree, a bigleaf maple that is Gladstone's oldest resident and most important landmark. Dating to 1790, the Pow-Wow tree still stands where it once served as the centerpiece of the four-acre Clackamas Indian race track, as well as the official site for councils, treaties, ceremonies, and weddings. It also marked the entrance to the first Clackamas County Fair (1860) and the first Oregon State Fair (1861). In 1937, the Girl Scouts held a powwow celebration to honor the Pow-Wow tree with a plaque (above) for its contribution to both Gladstone and Oregon history. At right, the Pow-Wow tree stands on Clackamas Boulevard in 1921, between Bellevue and Beatrice Avenues.

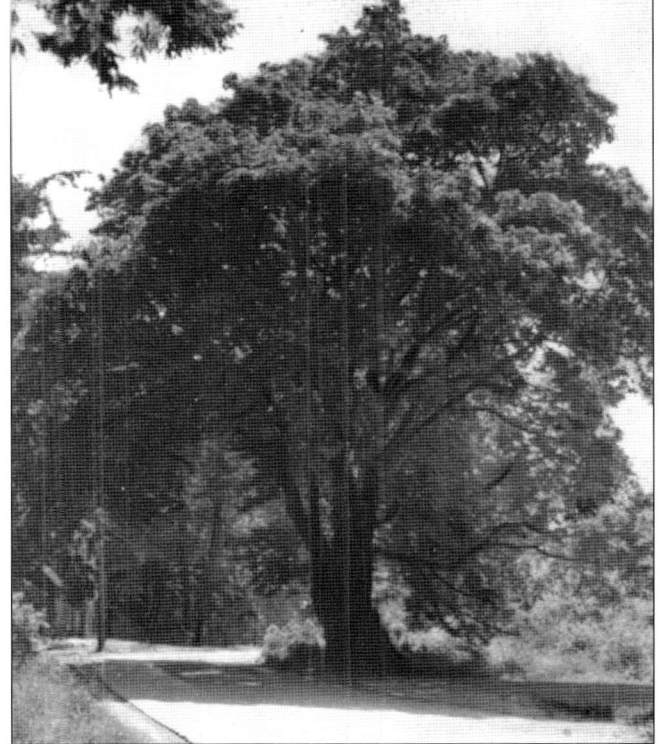

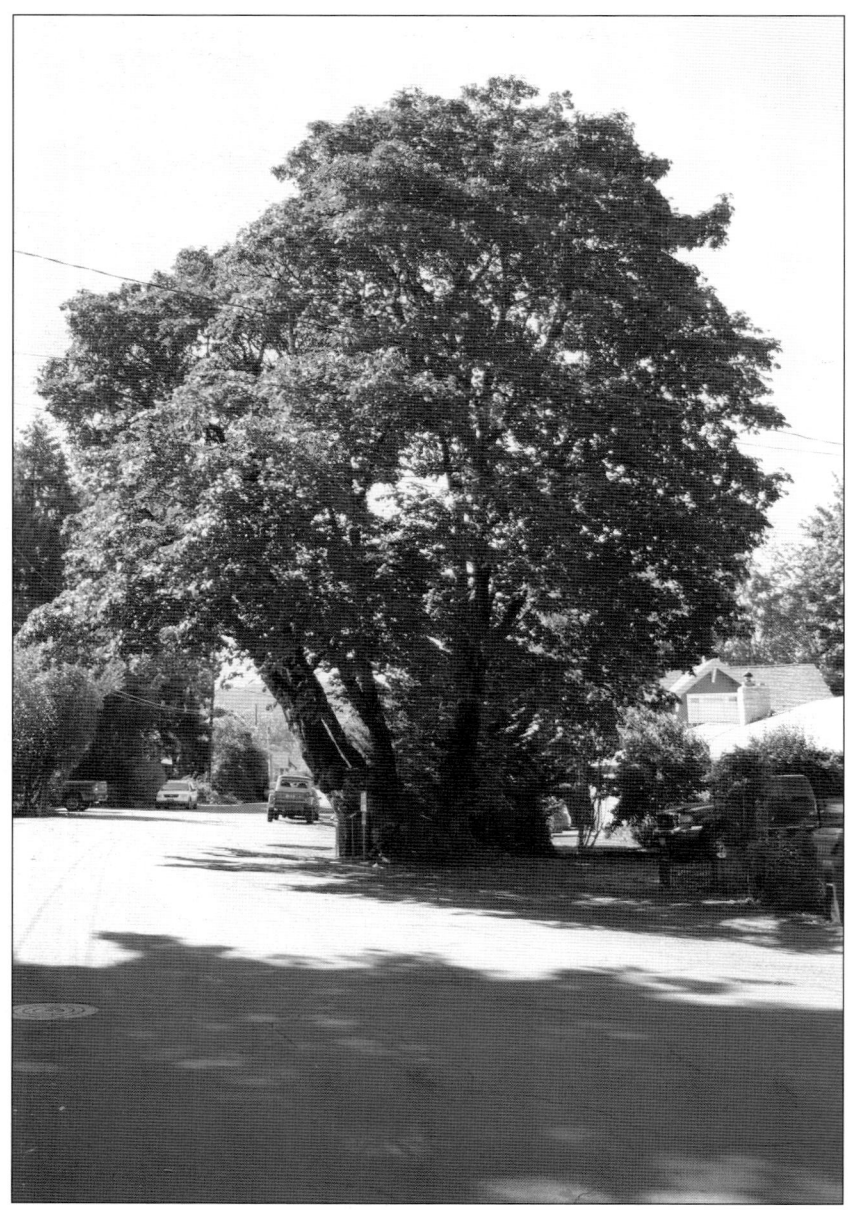

Because the Pow-Wow tree lived during the American Revolutionary period, the International Society of Arboriculture and the National Arborist Association designated it a 1976 bicentennial tree. Also in 1976, the Oregon Travel Information Council named the Pow-Wow tree an Oregon heritage tree. In 2004, the Cultural Landscape Foundation of Washington, DC, placed the tree on the National Historic Tree Register. In 2007, the Pow-Wow tree was selected as a Hero of Horticulture. In the 1960s, due to age, bad weather, and decay, the Pow-Wow tree's vitality waned and measures were taken to save it. In this recent photograph, the nearly 250-year-old tree is shown thriving at its original location. New root sprouts have grown up, and the tree's wide-spreading leafy branches are now supported by numerous sturdy trunks. Next to the Pow-Wow tree's base is the original plaque given to the tree by the Girl Scouts, accompanied by a standing plaque that lists the tree's other honors and awards. (Courtesy of Devon Huey.)

In 1856, a federal treaty relocated the Clackamas Indians to Oregon's Grand Ronde reservation. At about that same time, Capt. Jacob Rinearson, one of Gladstone's first settlers, was engaged in Indian hostilities in the Snake River region of Idaho. During a military operation, he rescued three Shoshoni Indian children. In finding the children homes, one of the boys, named Dave, was adopted by his brother and sister-in-law, Peter and Rebecca Rinearson. Throughout his life, Dave shunned all Indian ways, preferring instead to live and dress as a white man. However, on one occasion, Dave did dress in native costume, as shown in this 1925 newspaper photograph. As the guest of honor at an Indian wedding held at the Clackamas County Fair in Canby, Dave arrived in native blanket, feathered headdress, and strings of beads that had been gathered at the sites of the Clackamas Indian village and the Clackamas Indian burial ground. (GCC.)

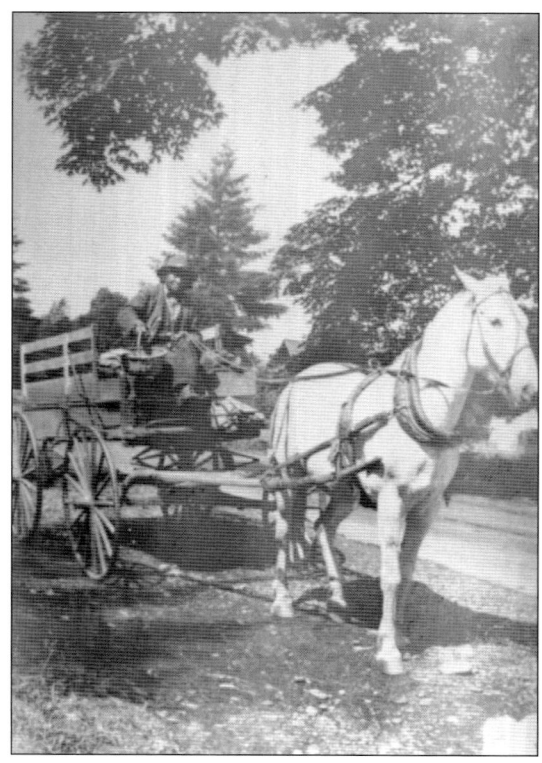

Indian Dave became a beloved figure in Gladstone, earning his living by growing produce and flowers and selling them along the streets of Gladstone. Without any education, Dave was able to keep his own accounts, pay his own debts, and buy his own house, all of which made him extremely proud. Dave loved music, especially jazz, and owned one of the first phonographs in Gladstone. At left, in 1912, Dave passes under the leafy branches of the Pow-Wow tree as he drives his produce cart along Clackamas Boulevard. Dave regularly attended the Gladstone Christian Church. He is seen below in 1912 wearing his Sunday best before the start of a church service.

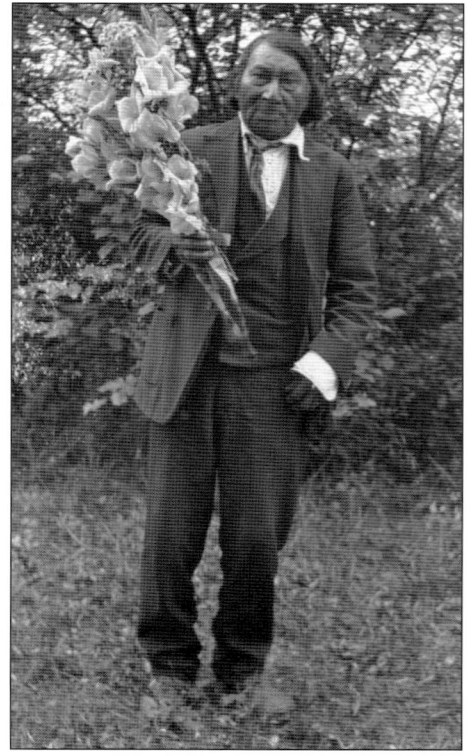

Two

First Settlers

The Westward Migration was well underway in 1842 when Elijah White, a Methodist missionary and physician, brought the first wagon train of more than 100 people to Oregon City. In 1843, the Applegate wagon train arrived with the Fendel Cason family, followed in 1845 by the Hackleman-Buck wagon train bringing brothers Peter and Jacob Rinearson. The Casons and the Rinearsons were Gladstone's first settlers.

Arriving on the same wagon train as the Casons, Charles E. Pickett soon became both the Casons' and the Rinearsons' closest neighbor to the south, settling directly across the Clackamas River from their land claims. For the most part, the Casons and the Rinearsons lived quietly, but Pickett was noisy.

At age 23, Pickett was an aristocratic, well-educated, meddlesome character, consumed with grandiose dreams, possessed of great oratorical ability, and prone to flightiness. He was also a cousin to Gen. George E. Pickett of Civil War fame and an acquaintance of Pres. James K. Polk. Fond of all things political and contentious, Pickett waged war in court on what he believed to be the unfair "Methodist land monopoly" along the south bank of the Clackamas River. He disputed the Methodists' ownership of the acreage that they had wrested and won from Dr. John McLoughlin. Pickett prevailed, and on what Elijah White, now newly appointed sub–Indian agent, pronounced to be ill-gotten ground, Pickett staked out one square mile of unimproved land, built a cabin, and set to work imagining his empire.

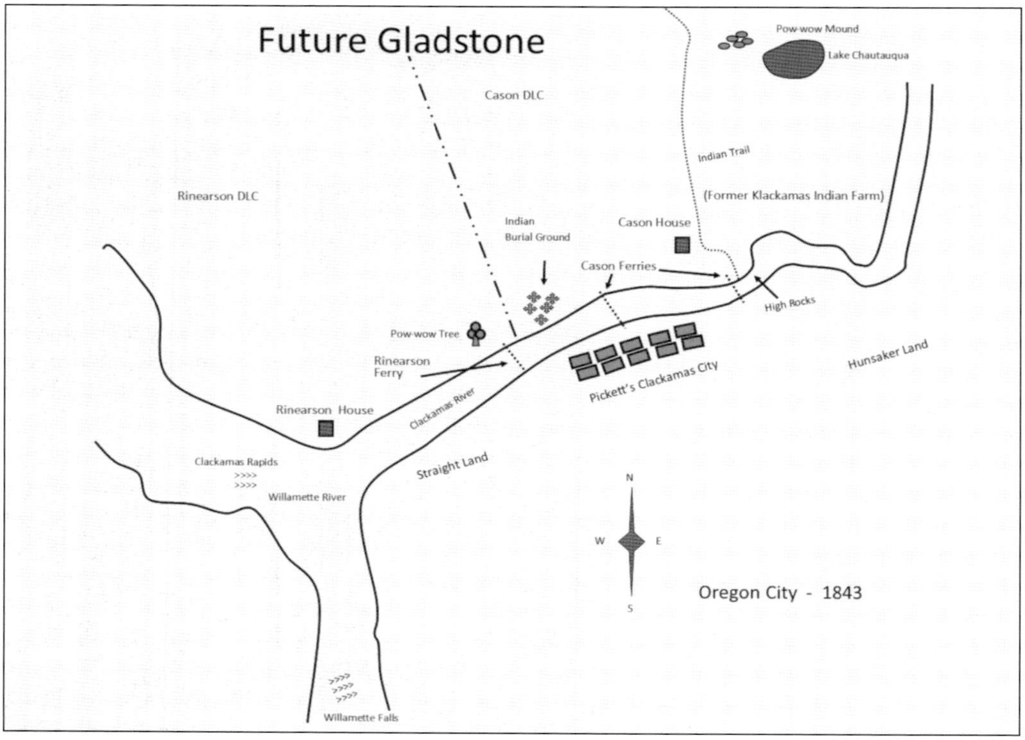

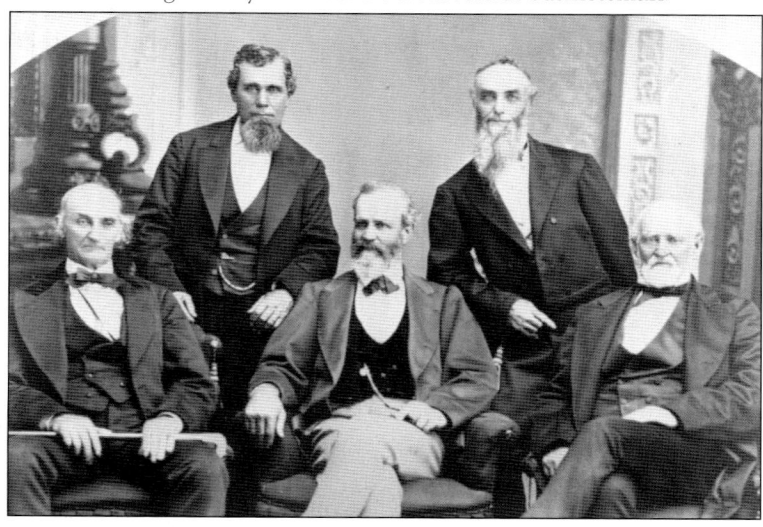

James Robb, a 25-year-old carpenter when he arrived in Oregon City, helped to build the first Protestant church west of the Rocky Mountains. After Reverend Waller's Klackamas Farm failed, Robb purchased the land but never settled on it. The next year, before departing for California, he sold all 640 acres to Fendel Cason, as shown on the above map. Below, during the 1870 Oregon Pioneer Reunion, five members of Elijah White's 1842 wagon train posed for this photograph. From left to right are (first row) Sidney W. Moss, surveyor of Oregon City; Capt. Medorem Crawford, a legislator in Oregon's provisional government; and Asa L. Lovejoy, cofounder of Portland, Oregon; (second row) Francis X. Matthieu, founder of Butteville, Oregon; and James R. Rob, who eventually returned to Oregon City and became a successful businessman.

Fendel Cason, 44, was a gunsmith and his wife, Rebecca Holladay Cason, 38, was a cousin of Ben Holladay of the Pony Express–Overland Stage fame when they arrived on the Applegate wagon train with nine of their ten children. On their newly purchased land, Fendel built the family's first cabin 1,000 feet back from the Clackamas River. Later, Fendel and his son Adoniram (called "Ad") built the family's second house at the same location. Extensively remodeled, the second Cason house is the oldest structure in present-day Gladstone and can be seen on Eighty-Second Drive, between Arlington and Berkley Streets. At right, in the mid-1880s, the Cross family gathers beneath the buckeye tree planted by Fendel. Below, in 1895, a portion of the Clackamas River flows past Cason land.

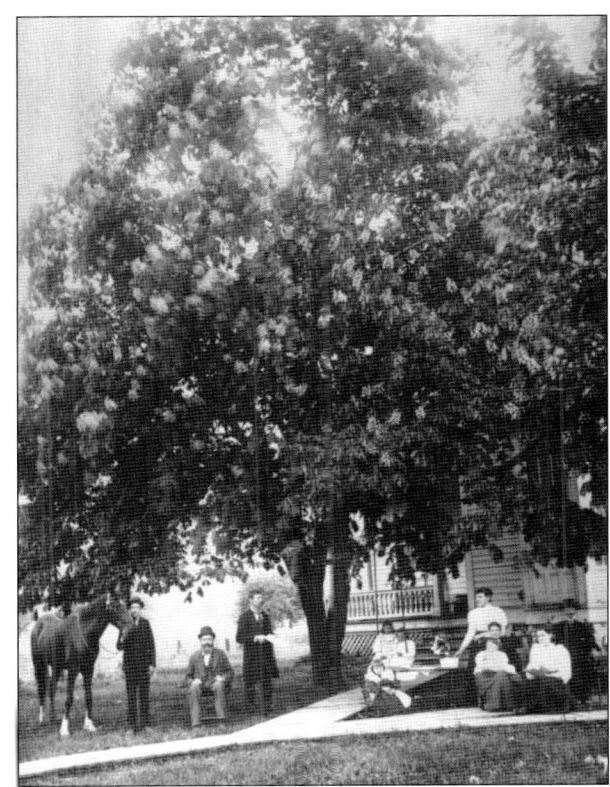

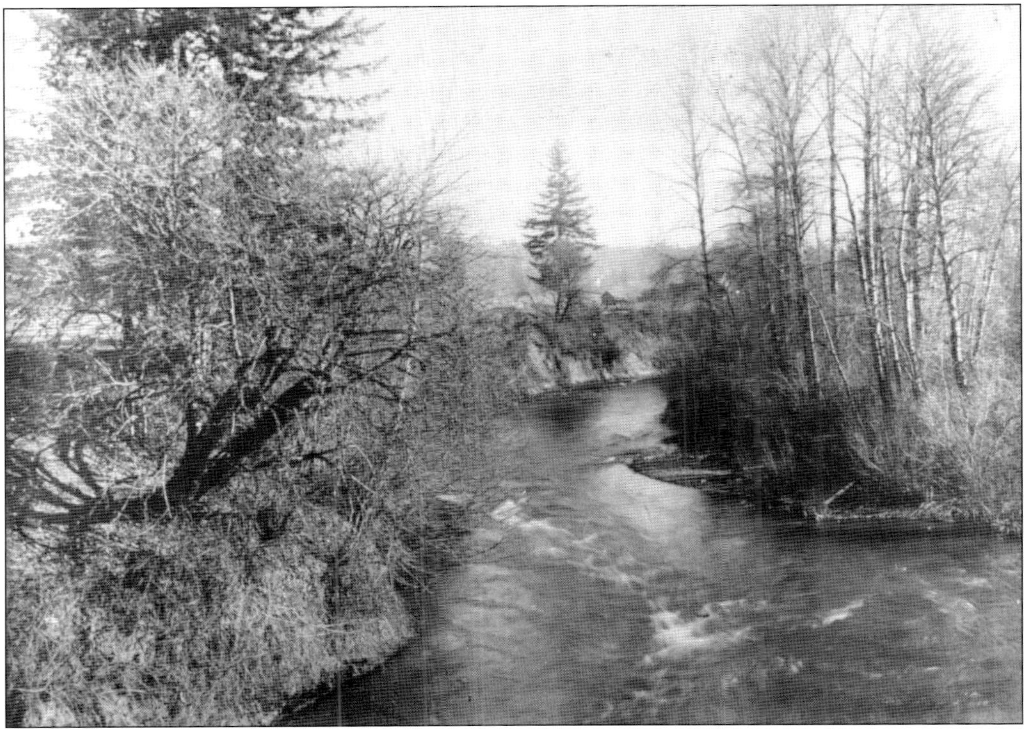

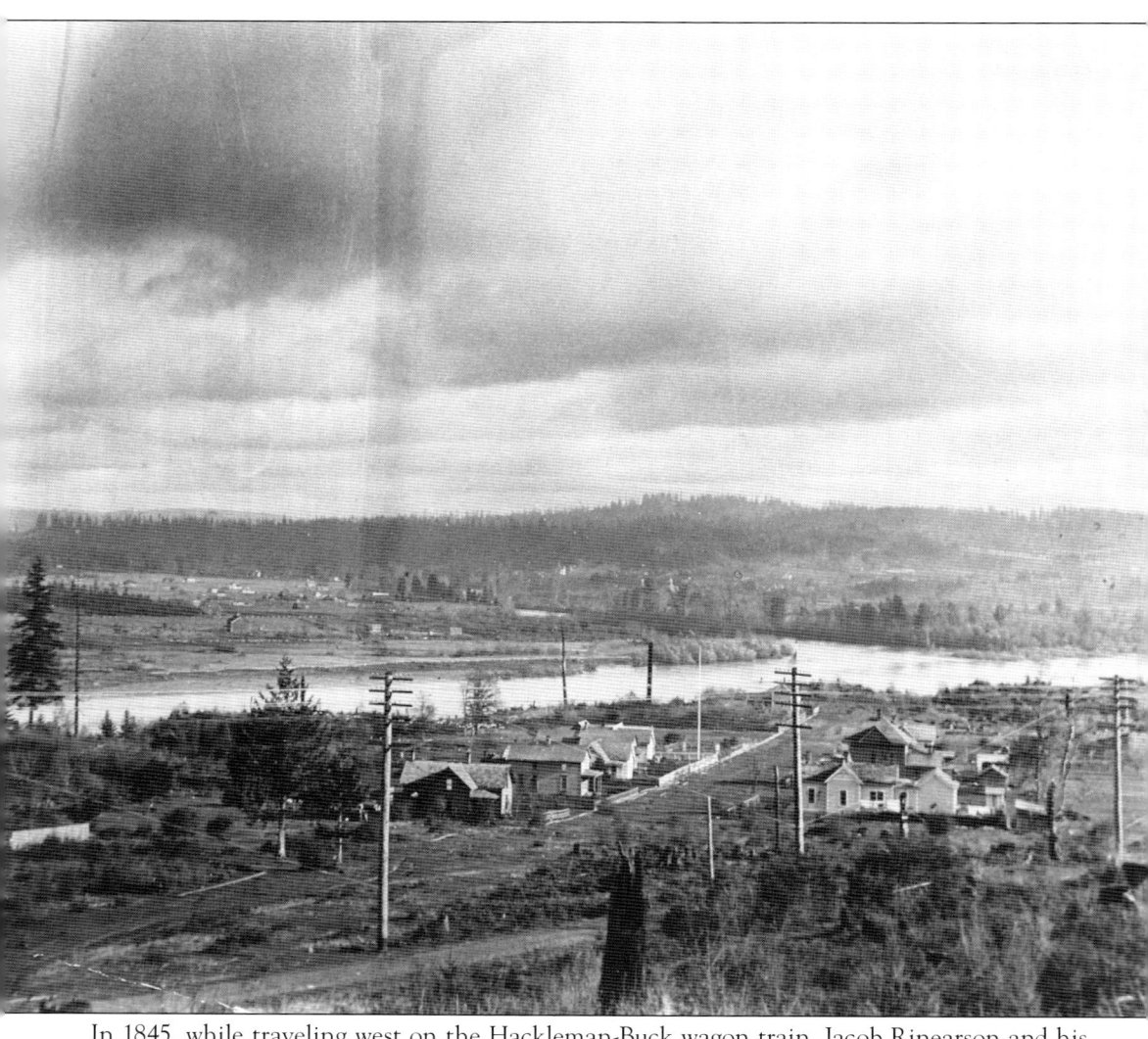

In 1845, while traveling west on the Hackleman-Buck wagon train, Jacob Rinearson and his younger brother Peter both became romantically interested in 17-year-old Rebecca Cornelius, a young woman who was traveling with her family. During the trek, Rebecca married John Scott but was widowed shortly afterward. Two years after the brothers arrived in Oregon and settled on their joint 640-acre land claim at Clackamas Point, Peter proposed marriage and Rebecca accepted. Without ill feelings, Jacob signed over his half of the land claim to Peter and joined the military. As seen here in 1899 facing east, Clackamas Point is the stretch of land north of the confluence of the Willamette and Clackamas Rivers. At center is the Willamette River with the mouth of the Clackamas River at center right. Peter and Rebecca's third house and agricultural buildings can be seen directly above the utility pole in the left foreground. Gladstone is on the north bank (left) of the Clackamas River, and Park Place is on the south bank. Oregon City is farther south on the Willamette River.

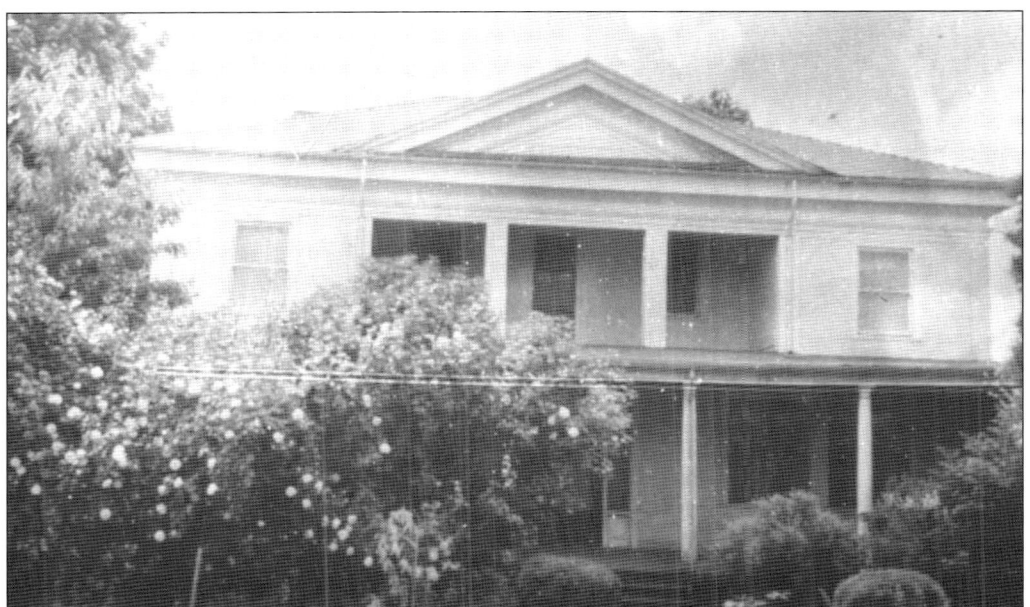

Peter and Rebecca Rinearson built their first cabin too close to the river and lost it in the 1849 Christmas flood. Rebuilding at the same location, they lost their second house in the 1856 flood. As shown above in 1933, Peter and Rebeca's third house was built away from the water and with 22 rooms so that Jacob and his family could live with them. Instead, Jacob joined the First Company of Oregon Riflemen, marched off to the Indian hostilities in eastern Oregon, and never married. After Rebecca died of Cholera, Peter married Isabella Greaves, a Rogue River Indian War widow with four children. Including Peter's seven children, the four that he and Isabella produced, and adopted son Indian Dave, Peter and Isabella raised 16 children. Peter built a fourth house, as seen below in 1906, for other family members.

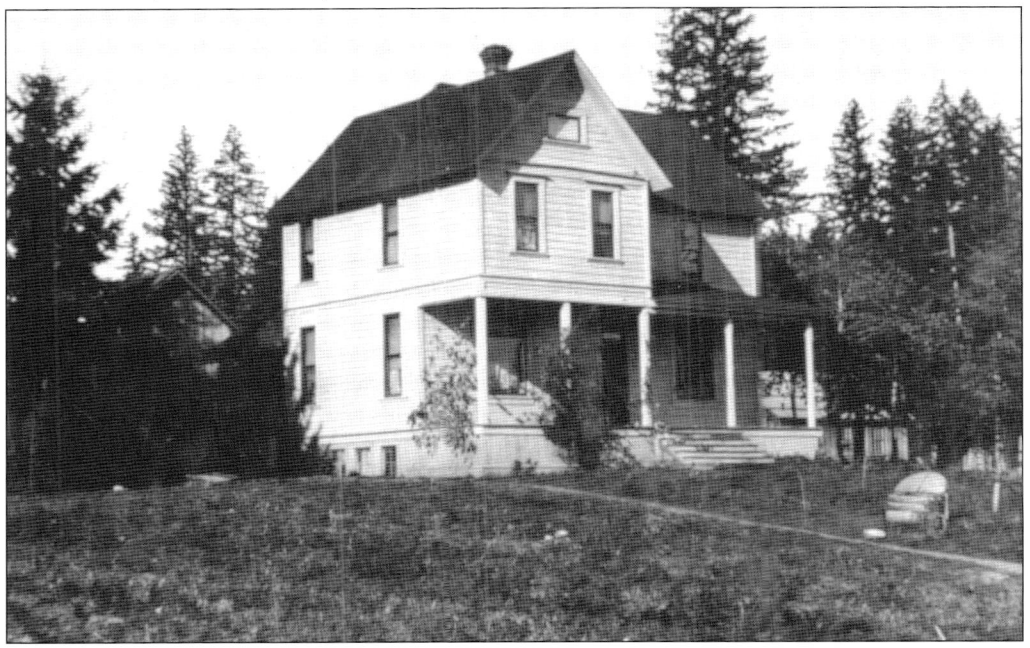

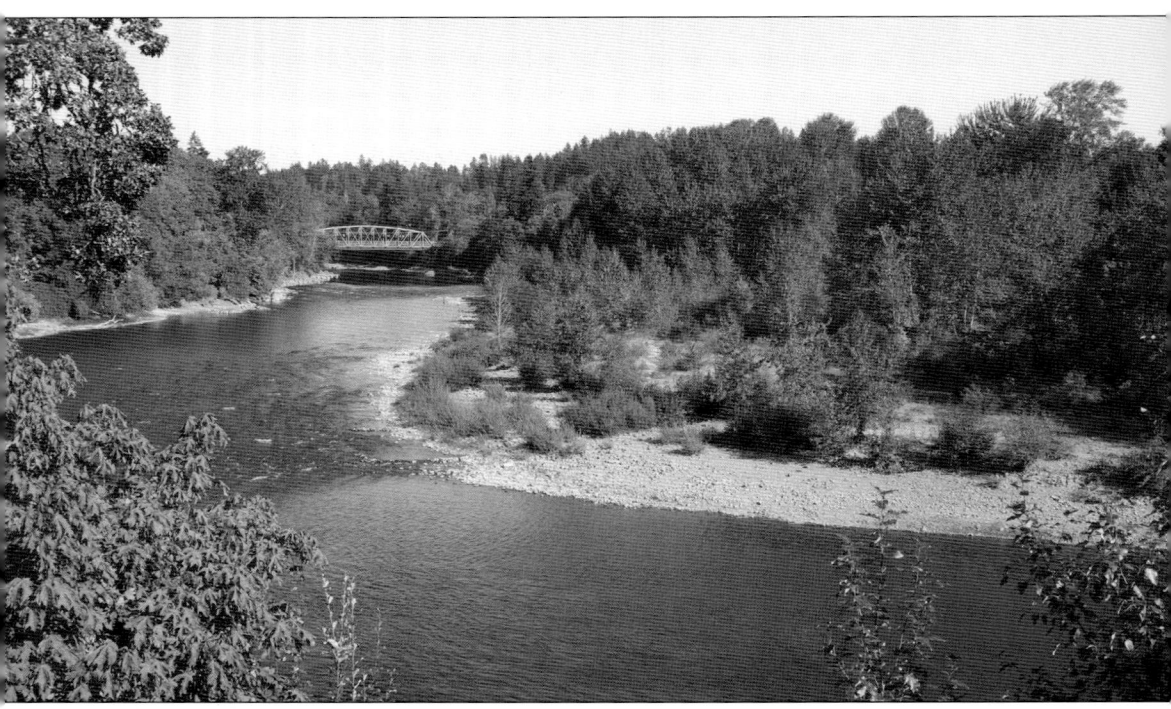

In 1844, while exploring the woods on his land, Pickett stumbled upon a distillery manufacturing "blue ruin," a potent whiskey made from blackstrap molasses brought from the Sandwich Islands. The still belonged to well-known professional bootleggers Richard McCrary and James Conner, along with newcomer Hiram Straight. The Methodists, organized by former wagon train leader and now sub–Indian Agent Elijah White, had become the self-appointed moral vigilantes for eradicating liquor in Oregon. With authority over the Indians' consumption of liquor only, White and cohorts swooped into Pickett's woods, surprised the whiskey-makers, and destroyed the still. McCrary ran, but an enraged Connor challenged White to a duel. Pickett, furious over White's commandeering of the law and trespassing on his property, set out to destroy White in the press. This photograph of the Clackamas River, taken facing east, shows the area of Pickett's Clackamas City to the right. In the background is the 1921 automobile bridge. (Courtesy of Devon Huey.)

In June 1845, while Connor and White took their fight to court, Pickett published the first newspaper west of the Rocky Mountains, called the *Flumgudgeon Gazette and Bumble Bee Budget.* Editorializing as "Curtail Coon," Pickett hand-wrote all eight editions and pegged copies to trees for the public to read. Pickett's tirades paid off. White was reassigned, and Clackamas City gained attention and new residents. No sooner had several houses, a sawmill, and a school been constructed, than newly appointed sub–Indian agent Pickett sprang off to California, leaving his empire behind. In 1849, a flood destroyed Clackamas City. At right is the August 1845 final edition of Pickett's newspaper. Below, in 1921, the Clackamas River is shown flooding the area of Clackamas City. (Right, OHS; below, GHS.)

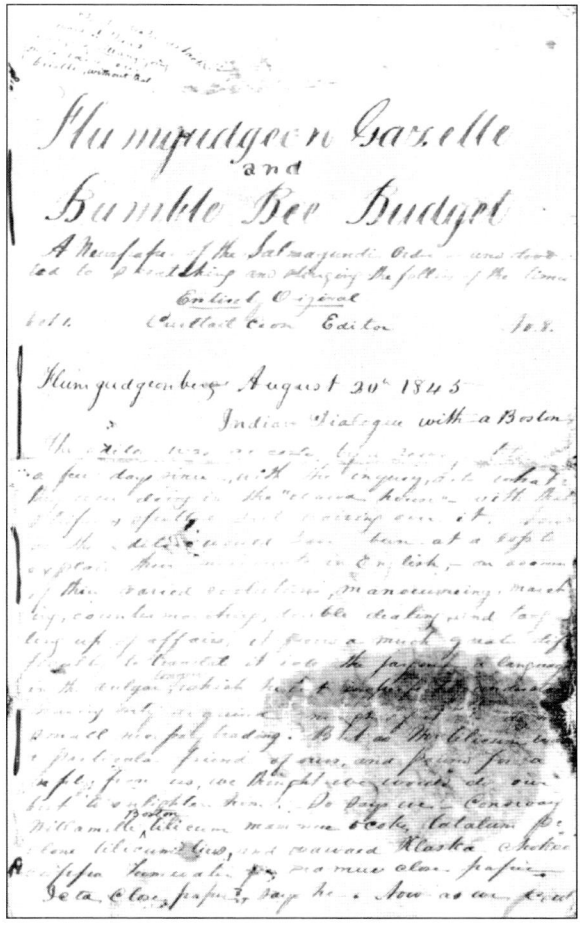

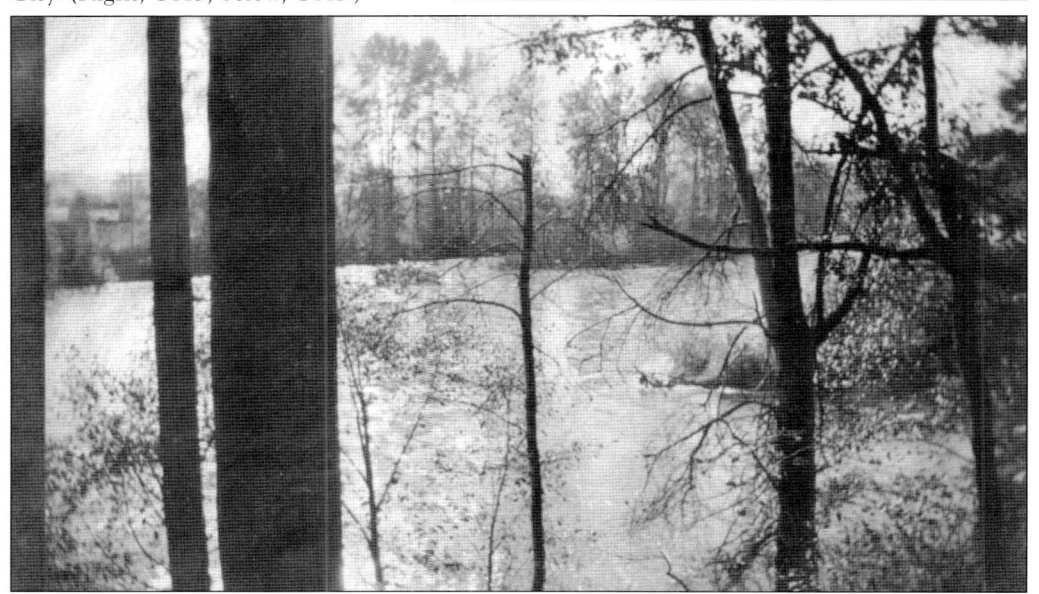

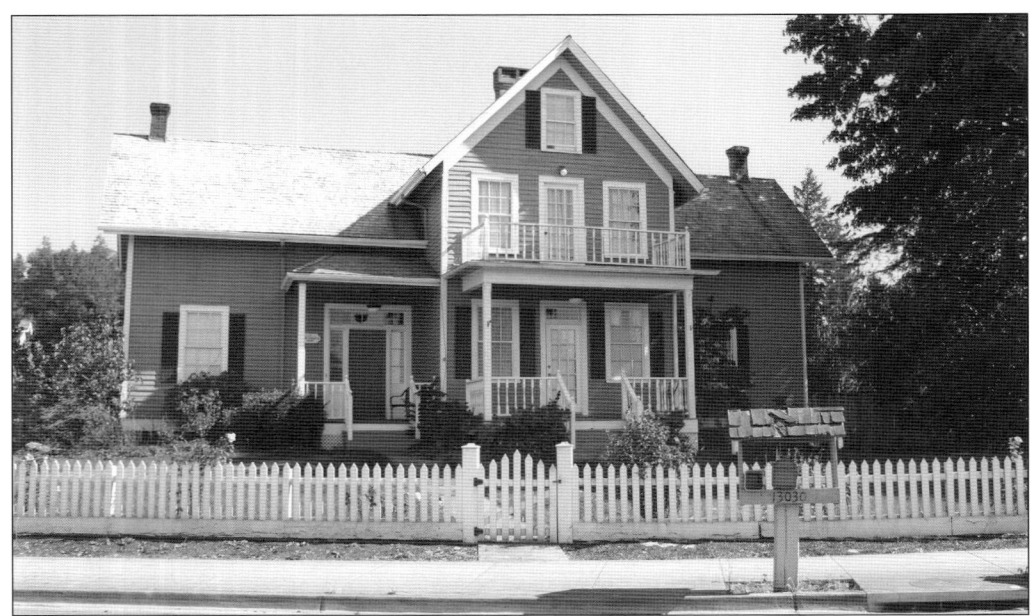

Before departing for California, Charles Pickett sold 399 acres of Clackamas City to Hiram Straight, who then sold 69 of those acres to Theophilus McGruder, who sold the same 69 acres to Jacob Hunsaker. Later, Straight purchased 572 more acres along the south bank of the Clackamas River, making him one of the largest landowners in the area. In 1856, Straight built a house at the south end of the wagon bridge and became Fendel Cason's new nearest neighbor. Jacob Hunsaker, Straight's neighbor to the east, inspired by the magnificent apple orchard growing alongside his new acreage, named his home "Fruit Hill Farm" and started his own successful orchard business. Above, Hiram Straight's house still stands in Park Place. The Hunsaker house, shown below in 1904, no longer stands.

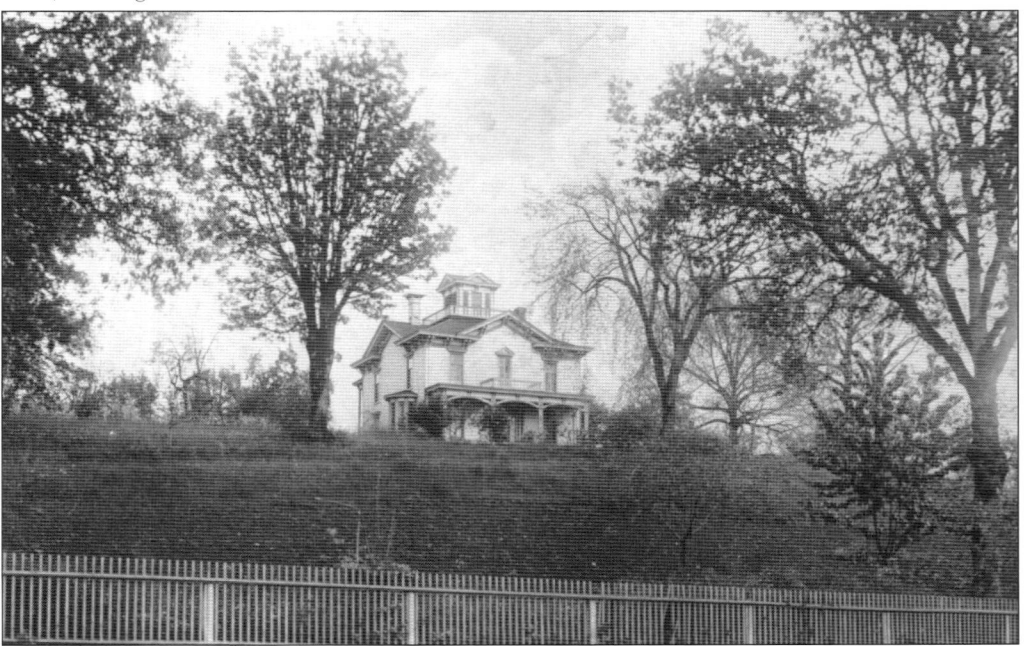

Three

First Ferries, Bridges, and Roads

In 1843, there were no bridges across the Clackamas or Willamette Rivers. The Clackamas Indians who navigated these waters traveled either by canoe or used ferries to transport their loads of furs and dried fish. The Indian ferry, a type of crude raft made from cedar or fir planks tied together by leather straps, was guided through the water by long poles. Approximately 1,000 feet west of High Rocks, the Clackamas Indians operated a raft-ferry, and the settlers took note.

In 1845, before his departure, Charles Pickett championed the cause of building a bridge across the Clackamas River. The settlers enthusiastically agreed, but the territorial government was unsupportive. Finally, due to Pickett's expertise in persuasion, the territorial government approved the incorporation of the Clackamas River Bridge Company. But then Pickett charged off to California, and enthusiasm for a bridge disappeared. Instead, everyone went into the toll ferry business, including the Casons and the Rinearsons.

In 1852, Jacob Hunsaker, who did not own a ferry business, began constructing bridge piers, only to be met by howls of protests from the ferry owners who insisted a toll bridge would undermine their businesses. The argument went to court. Much to the dismay of the ferry owners, the territorial government sided with Hunsaker.

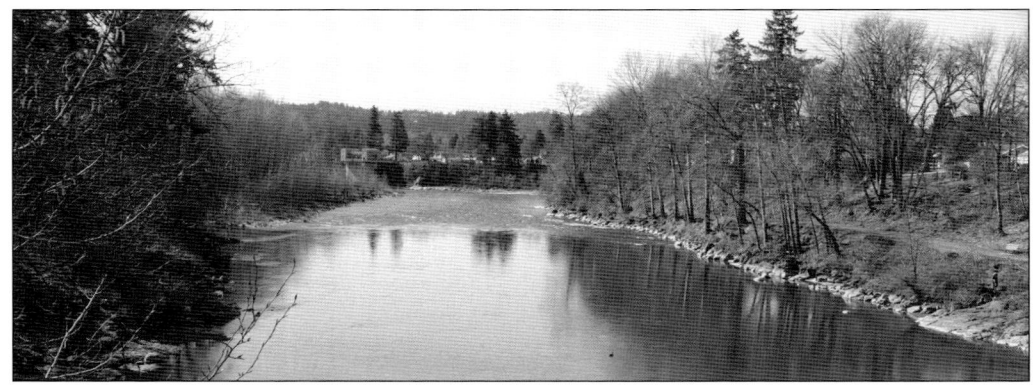

In 1850, three ferry businesses were started within a half mile of each other. Joseph Henderson, another of Hiram Straight's neighbors, received permission from the territorial government to operate a toll ferry west of High Rocks. Because Henderson's ferry docked on Fendel Cason's land, Henderson could not charge the Casons passage or portage tolls. Cason then decided to start his own toll ferry service 600 feet west of High Rocks at the former Indian ferry location, or about where the water ripples begin in the above photograph. At the same time, Jacob and Peter Rinearson started a high-water ferry approximately a quarter mile west of the Cason ferry, or about the location of the rowboat in the early 1900s photograph below facing east. Also shown below is the 1908 trolley bridge. (Above, courtesy of Devon Huey.)

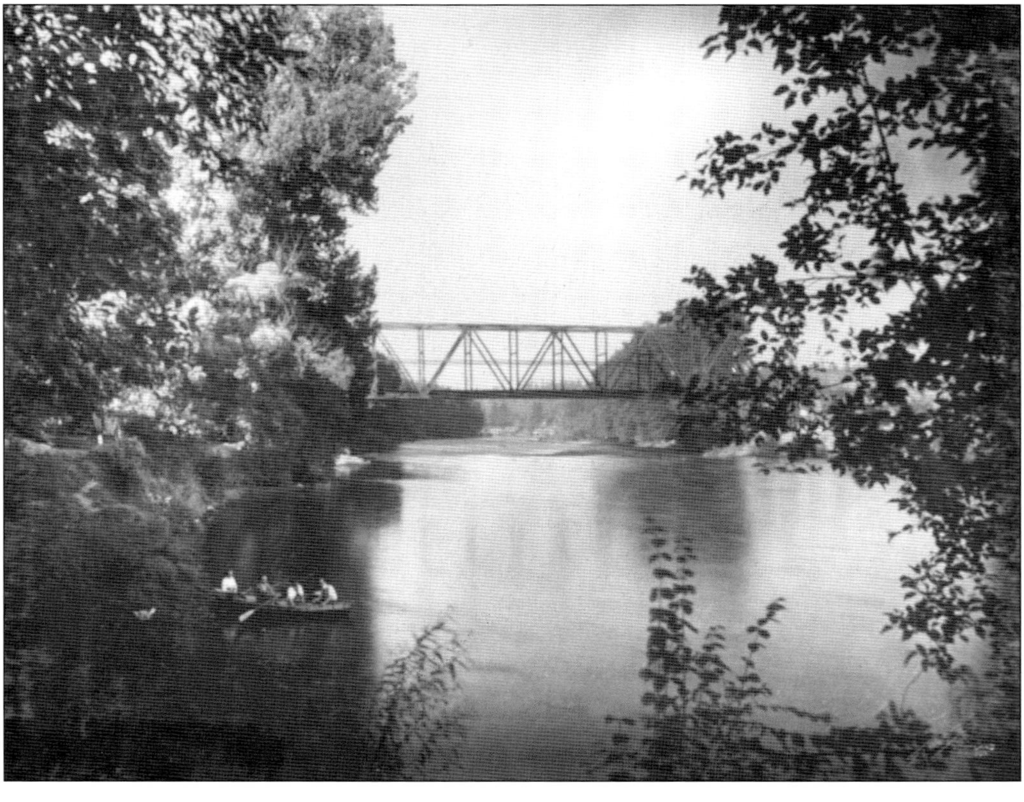

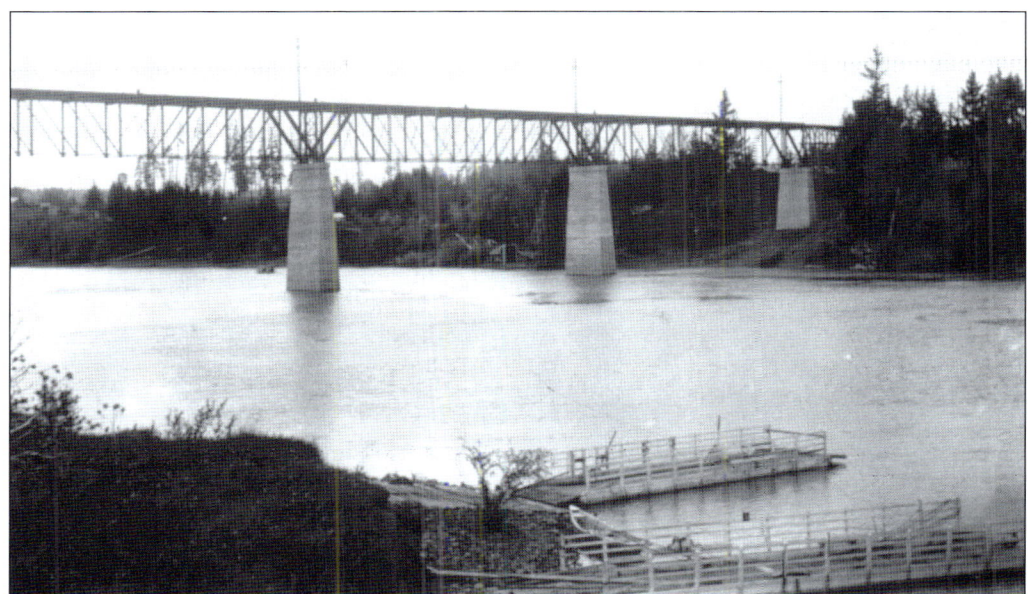

In 1853, Henderson departed Oregon City, and Cason assumed Henderson's ferry permit. Immediately, Cason moved his business to the more lucrative Henderson route, only to be challenged by other Henderson neighbors who also claimed the route. Everyone went to court, and Cason won. Toll ferry service officially ceased in 1874, but the ferry remained available for several decades. Above, in 1909, two ferries similar to those that operated on the Clackamas River at Gladstone are shown near the Oregon Electric Railway trestle across the Willamette River. Below, in 1900, a group fishes from the south bank of the Clackamas River where Henderson and Cason operated their ferries. Also shown is the 1892 railroad bridge, now covered. (Above, SLO.)

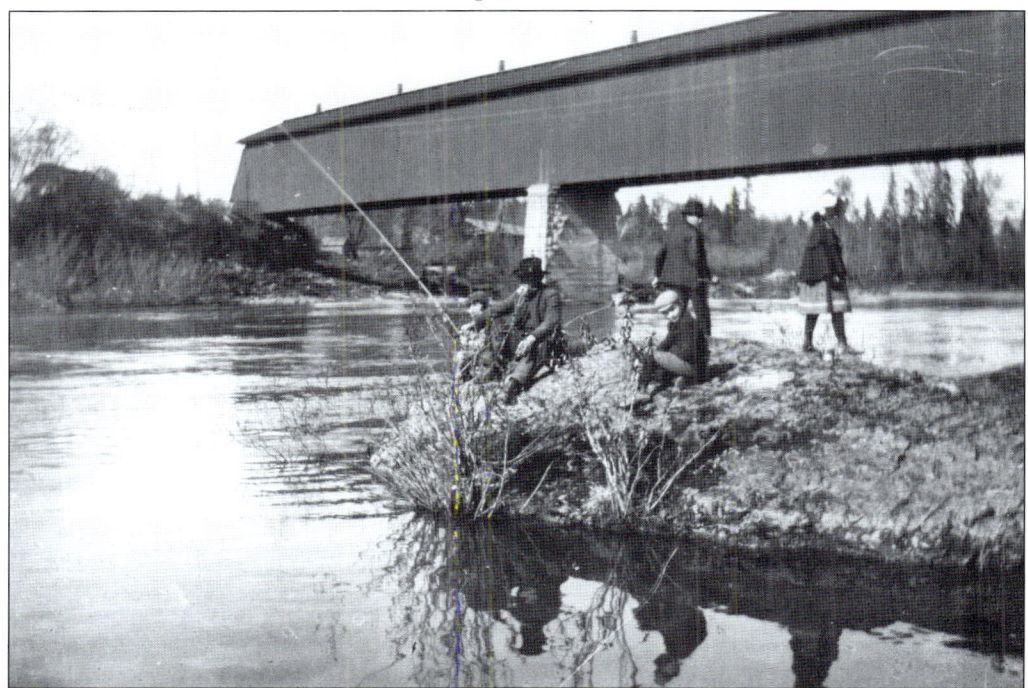

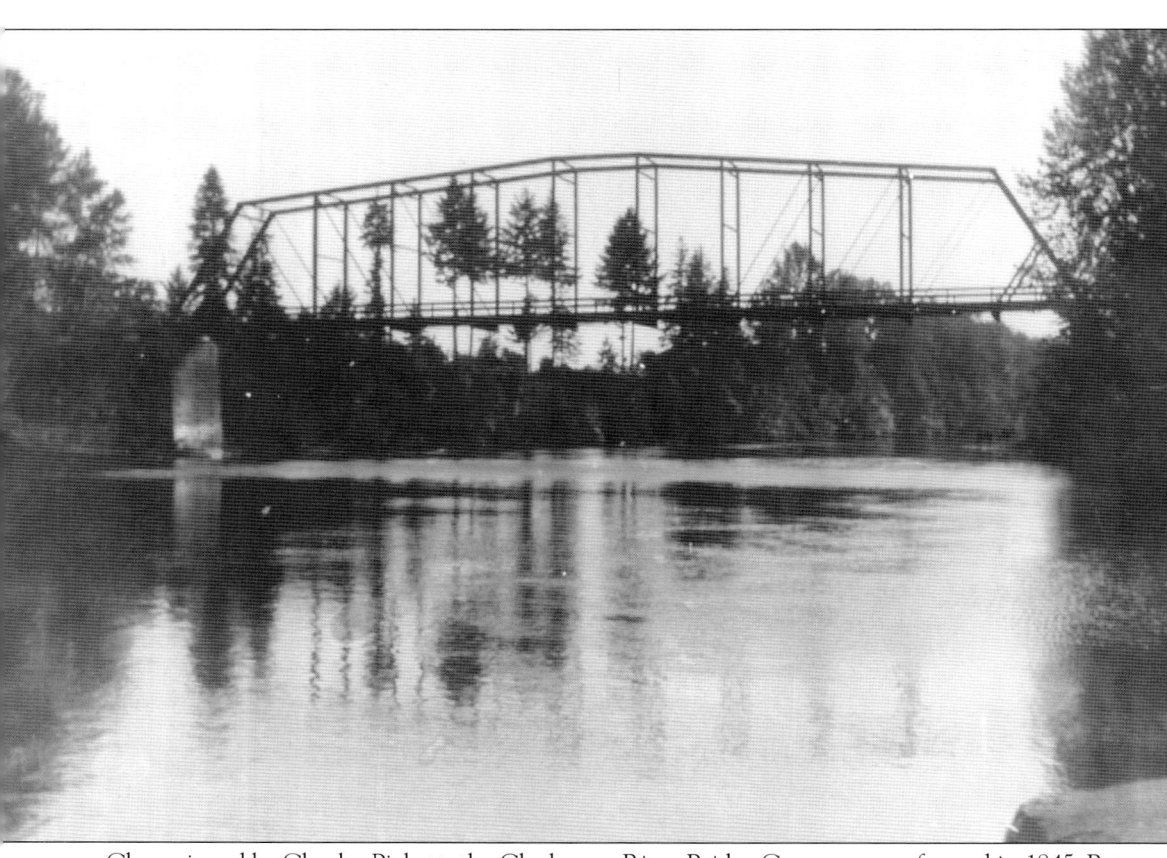

Championed by Charles Pickett, the Clackamas River Bridge Company was formed in 1845. But when Pickett left, so did the enthusiasm for building a bridge, especially from the Casons and the Rinearsons, since a toll bridge would threaten their ferry businesses. In August 1853, Jacob Hunsaker began construction on the first bridge to cross the Clackamas River. Locating it alongside Fendel Cason's ferry route, Hunsaker's bridge connected to Cason land on the north. An irate Cason promptly fenced off the bridge and filed a lawsuit against Hunsaker. Cason lost but was granted exemption from paying bridge tolls. The fence was removed and the bridge completed. Within a year, Cason's ferry business failed. Five wagon or automobile bridges, including Hunsaker's bridge, have spanned the Clackamas River at the same location. No photographs exist of the first three wagon bridges, but this 1895 photograph, taken facing west, shows the fourth, which was built in 1892. (GHS.)

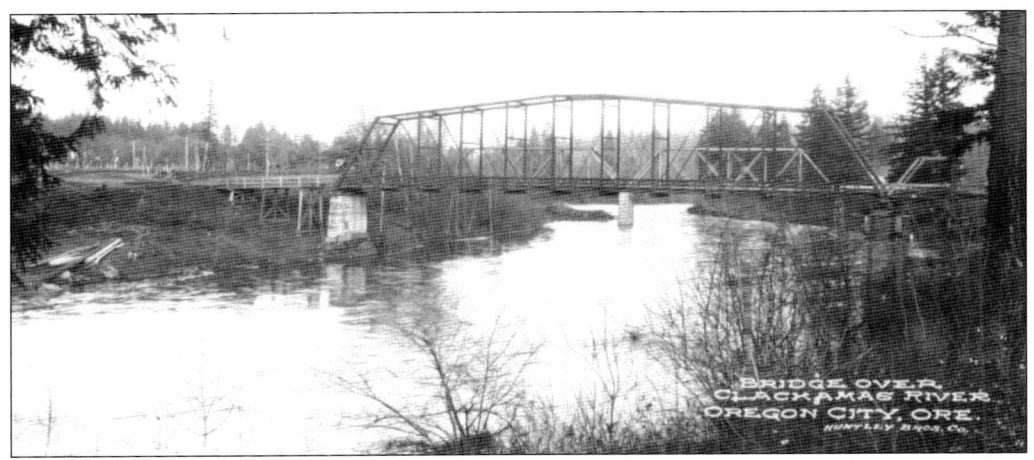

The battle over the bridge continued, with Hunsaker claiming that Cason's sons weakened the bridge's underpinnings. Nothing could be proved, and eventually Hunsaker sold his bridge to Cason. Within a year, a team of oxen broke through the bridge's roadbed. Cason barely finished repairs when the 1856 flood swept away the bridge. The second bridge built in 1856, was lost in the 1873 flood. The third bridge, the only covered wagon bridge, was built in 1873 and destroyed in the 1890 flood. Two years later, in 1892, a wood and steel fourth bridge was built, as shown above in 1903 facing east. The yet to be covered 1903 railroad bridge in the background. In the winter of 1919, both bridges withstood flooding, ice, and snow, as seen below. (Above, SLO.)

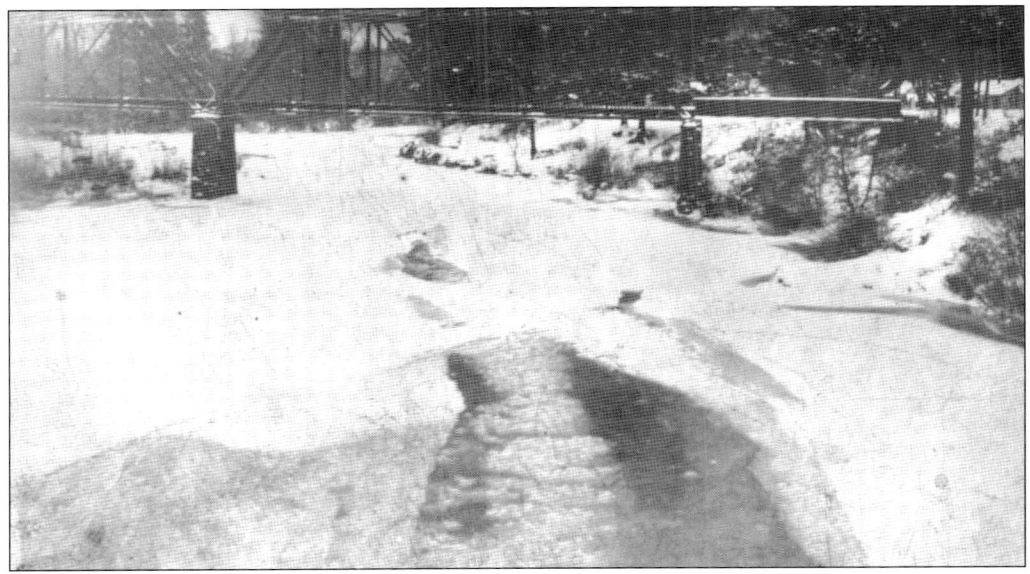

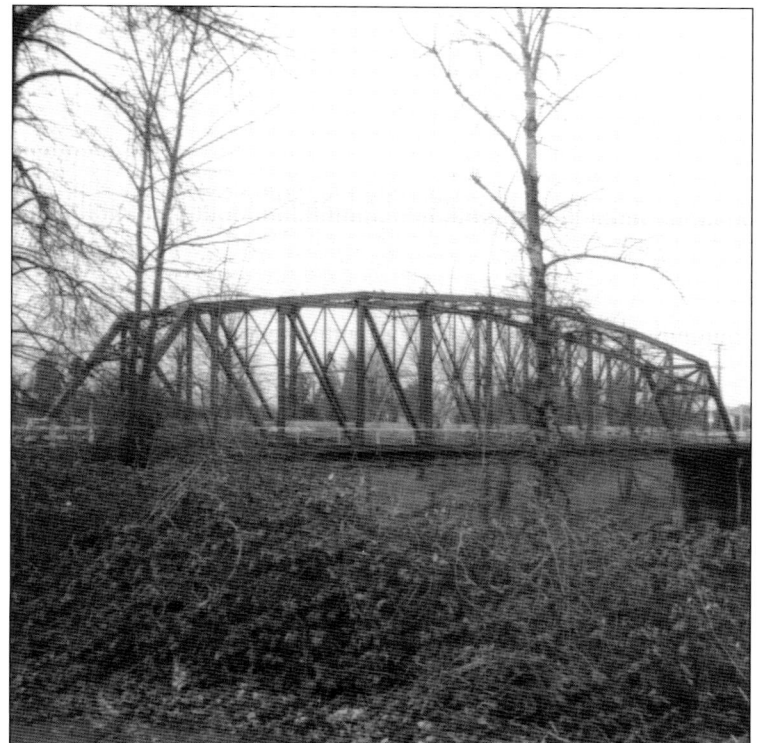

The fourth bridge did not succumb to floods, but instead became unable to bear the weight of the ever-increasing load of automobile traffic. In 1921, the fifth bridge, an all-steel bridge seen here in the early 1940s, was built to replace the fourth bridge.

In December 1964, a severe cold spell froze the ground and produced record snow, followed by heavy warm rains. The melting snow could not be absorbed into the frozen ground, causing one of the worst floods ever recorded in the Willamette Valley. The fifth bridge barely stayed above water.

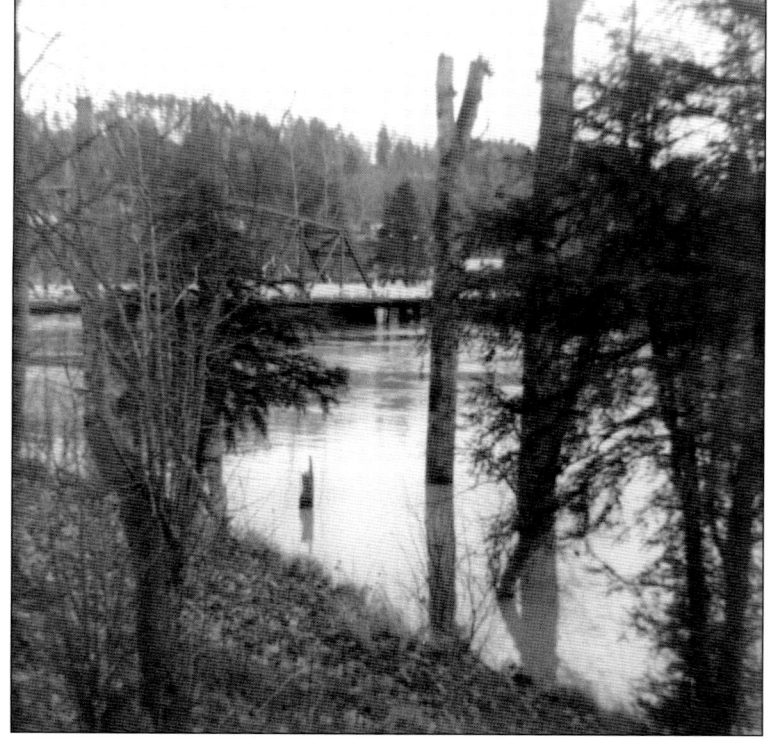

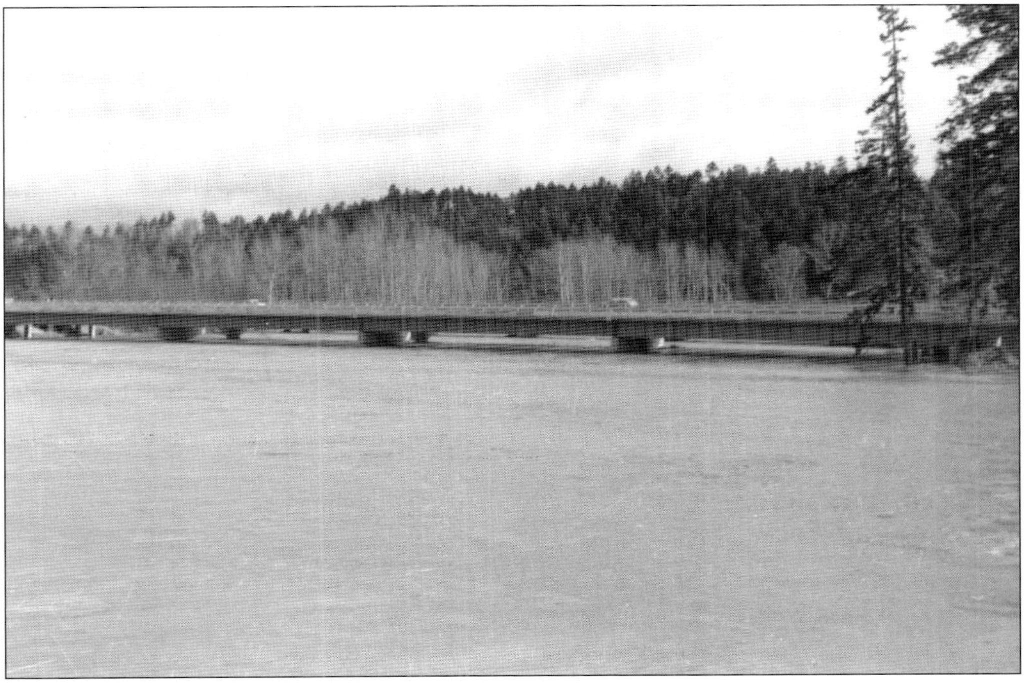

In 1962, the new Interstate 205 freeway was constructed along the eastern border of Cason land, approximately 1,200 feet east of the 1921 automobile bridge. The two new freeway bridges had only recently opened to traffic when the December 1964 flood hit. This photograph shows the southbound freeway bridge during the worst of the Clackamas River's flooding.

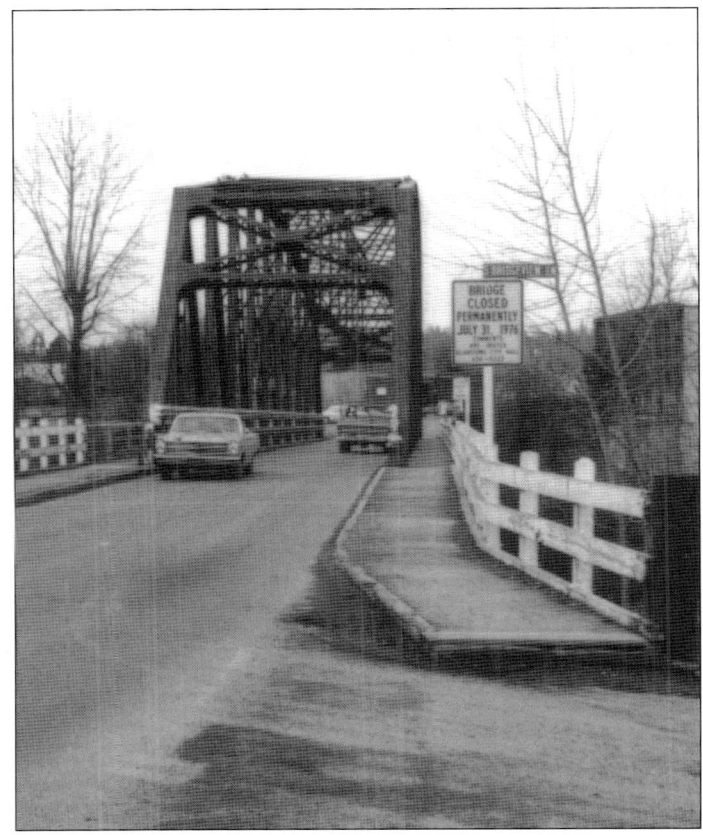

Even though the freeway bridges were available, many still preferred to use the 1921 bridge. In 1975, when the 1921 bridge could no longer handle daily traffic, it was closed to motor vehicles, as stated on this sign at the south end of the bridge. In 1986, after some refurbishing, the 1921 bridge reopened for bicycle and pedestrian use only.

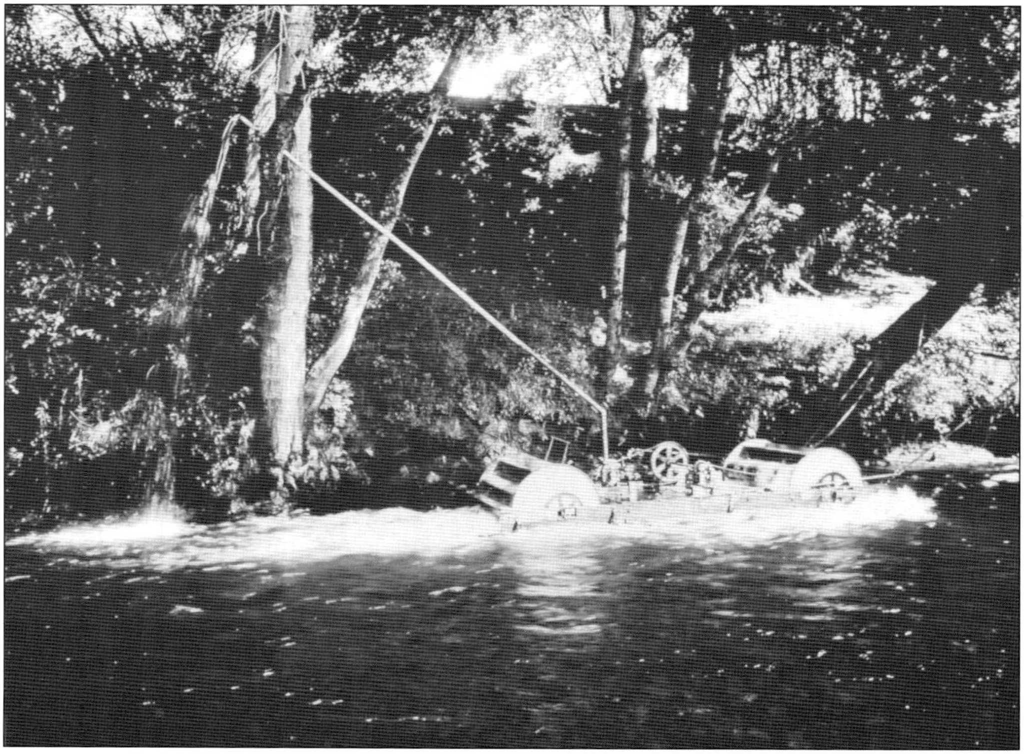

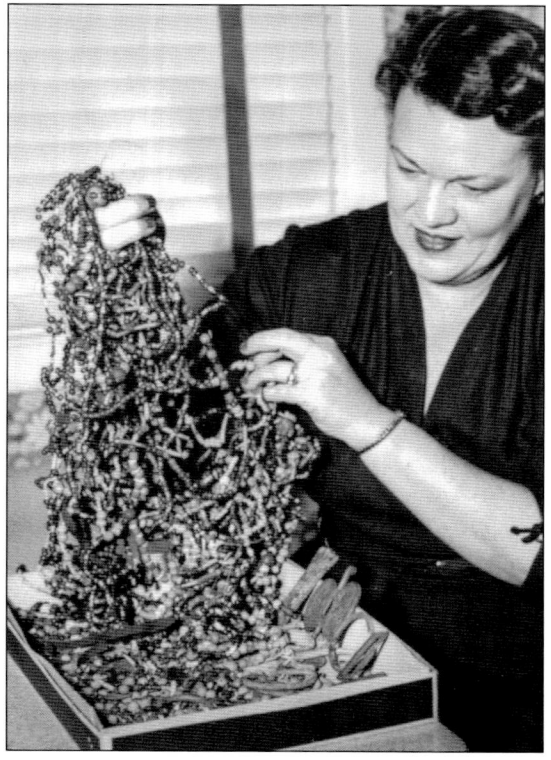

Clackamas River floods were never good, yet they left surprising treasure. In 1860, a Molalla prospector found gold in a tributary of the Clackamas River and started a small intermittent gold fever that lasted 40 years. Little if any gold was found in Gladstone, but receding floodwater often revealed prized Indian beads. Above, in 1900, a small dredge mines the Clackamas River for gold and brings up buckets of Indian beads. At left, in 1956, Donna Forsberg displays a box of Clackamas Indian beads she found in her parents' attic. Once belonging to Indian Dave, some of these bead strings were likely ones he wore to the Indian wedding. (Both, courtesy of the *Portland Oregonian*.)

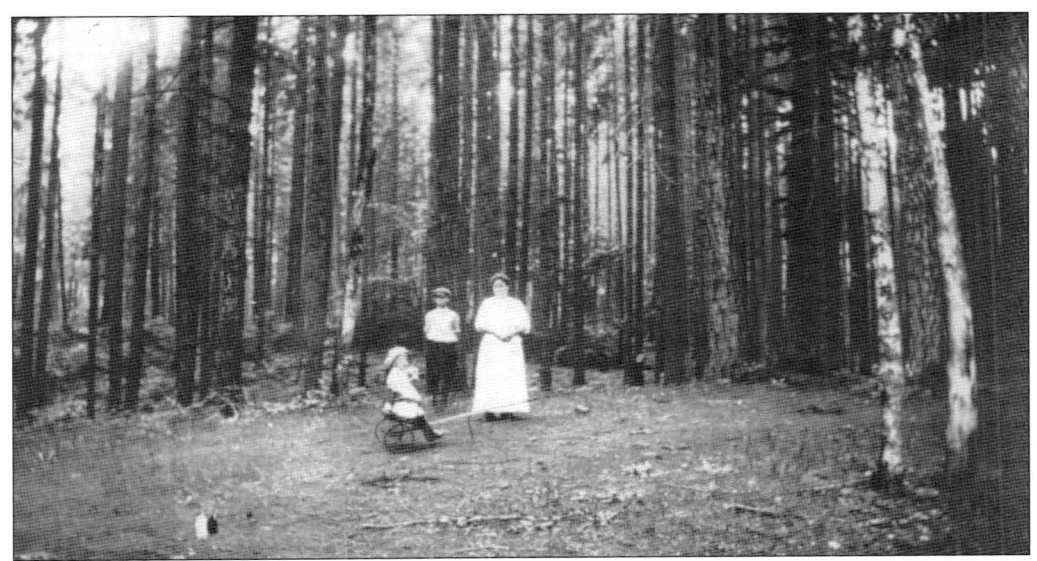

Trees grew in abundance along the banks of the Clackamas River. Even though lumber could be bought from sawmills in Oregon City, many settlers produced their own boards. In 1856, William Buck, coleader of the 1845 wagon train that brought the Rinearsons, built the first sawmill on the south bank of the Clackamas River near High Rocks. Buck powered his mill with a dam that he built a short distance upriver. Above, from left to right, Ted, Lloyd, and Sarah Nickerson stand among Gladstone's tall trees in 1910. Below, looking west in the early 1900s, a small logging camp can be seen on the south bank of the Clackamas River. Also shown is the 1892 wagon bridge with the 1893 trolley bridge in the background. (Above, courtesy of Diane Nickerson Timmons.)

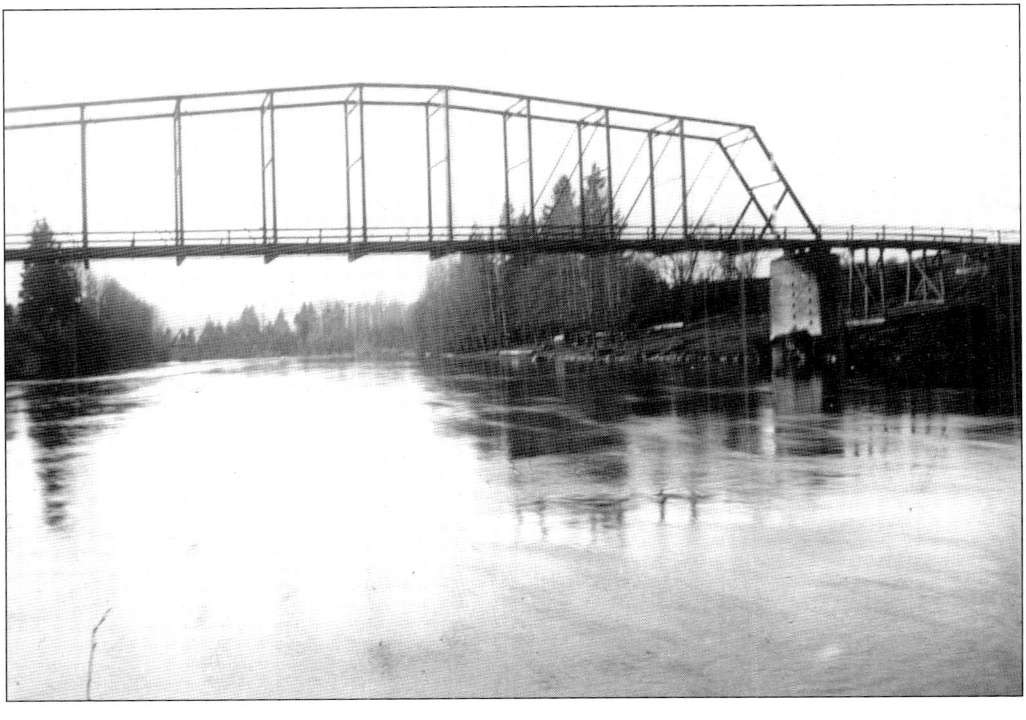

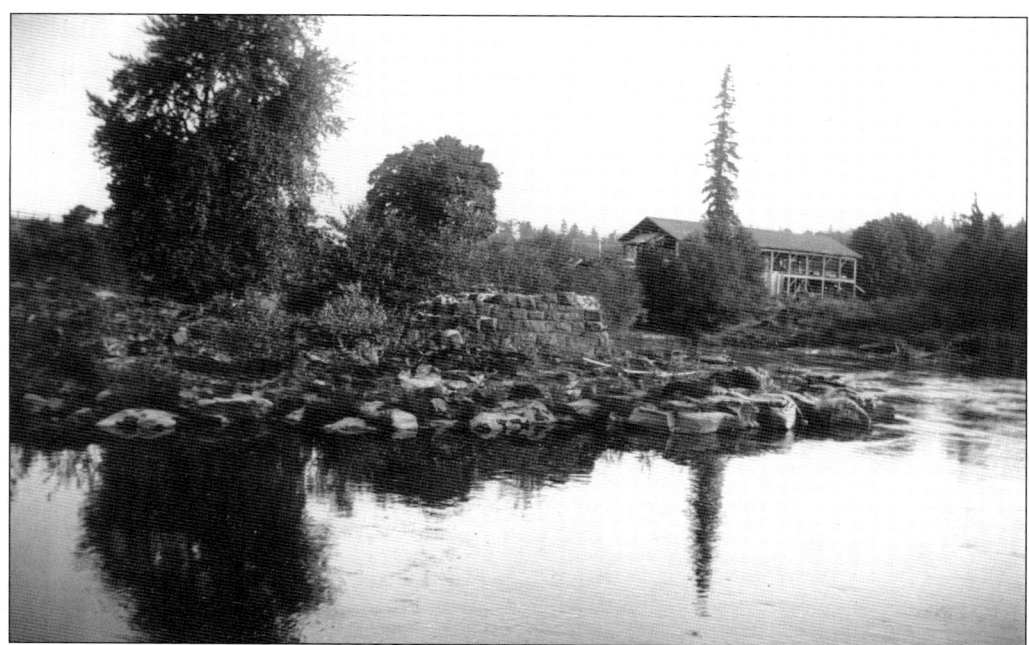

In 1867, William Buck cofounded Oregon's first paper mill at Oregon City. When that mill went broke during its first year, Buck converted his sawmill into a new paper-making mill. For 17 years, Buck and his partner, Henry Pittock, supplied all the newsprint for the *Portland Oregonian*. As seen above in 1890, Harvey Cross, Gladstone's founder, built a sawmill across the river from Buck's old paper mill. Employing 40 men, Cross's sawmill cut up to 30,000 feet of lumber daily and supplied all the wood used by the Gladstone Furniture Factory next door. In 1896, high water washed away both the Gladstone Sawmill and the Gladstone Furniture Factory. Cross did not rebuild his sawmill, but the furniture factory relocated to Buck's empty paper mill building, seen below.

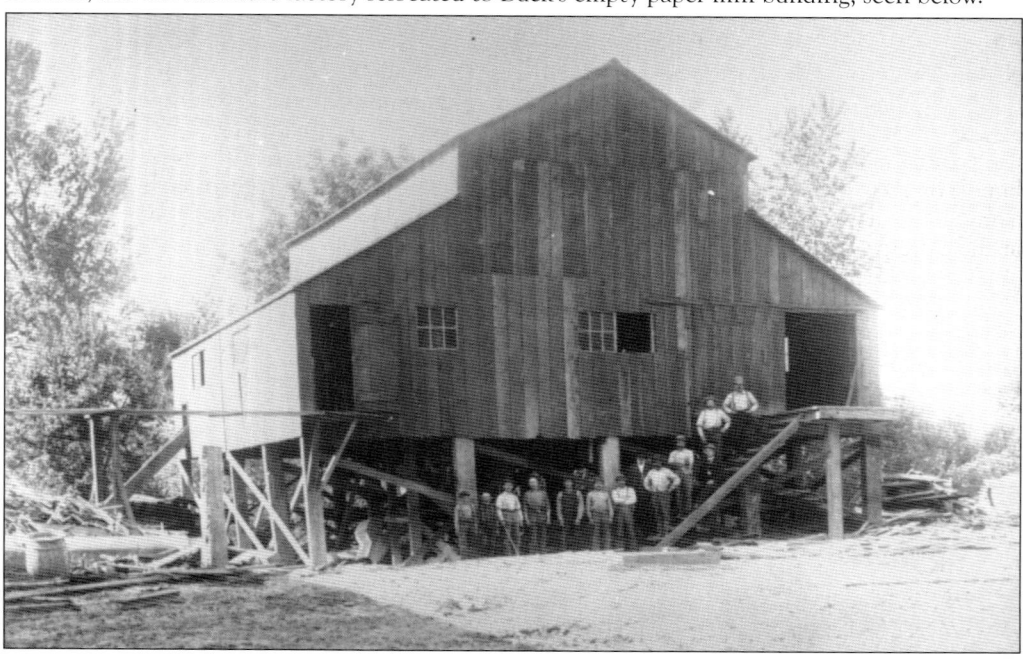

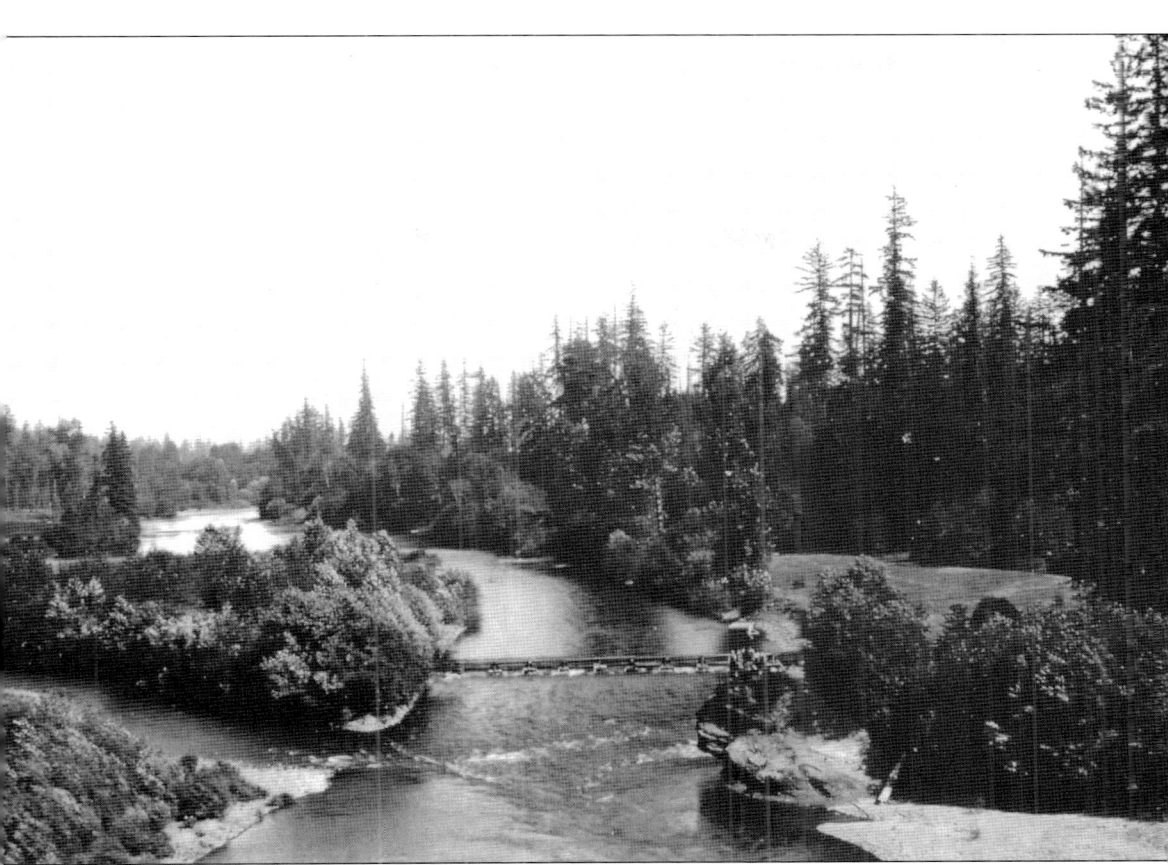

William Buck constructed his dam out of brush and rocks. Only three feet high, floods and logging debris continually swept parts of it away. In 1890, Harvey Cross took over Buck's old dam and rebuilt it to 12 feet high, adding pilings. Cross's dam was sturdy enough to withstand most of the abuse from the Clackamas River and generated enough power to run both his sawmill and the furniture factory. In 1907, the Gladstone dam was no longer needed. H.K. McFarland of Portland was given permission to test a new explosive called "Trojan powder." Filling a gunny sack with the volatile substance, McFarland rowed out to the middle of the river, lit the fuse, dropped the bundle on the dam, and rowed away just before the powder exploded. As shown here in the 1890s, a group stands on the south bank of the Clackamas River beside a dam (possibly the Cross Dam) at the eastern edge of Gladstone. (OHS.)

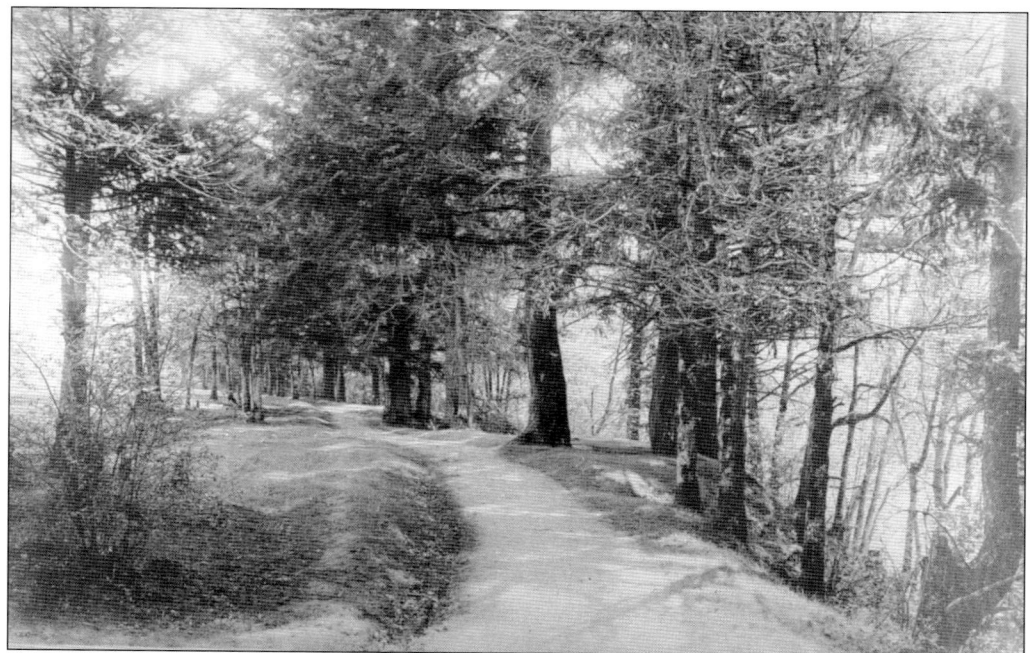

When the settlers arrived, the only roads in existence were trails made by Indians or fur trappers. Later, some of these paths evolved into roads that accommodated stagecoach and wagon traffic. A path along the north bank of the Clackamas River, as shown above in 1909, became so popular with courting couples it was nicknamed "Lover's Lane." Below, in the early 1900s, Clackamas Boulevard, also located along the Clackamas River's north bank, was one of the first Indian paths to be transitioned into a main thoroughfare. Various accounts describe the Clackamas River road as both beautiful and frightening to travel. The thick, overhanging trees provided shade, but also made for a dark trip.

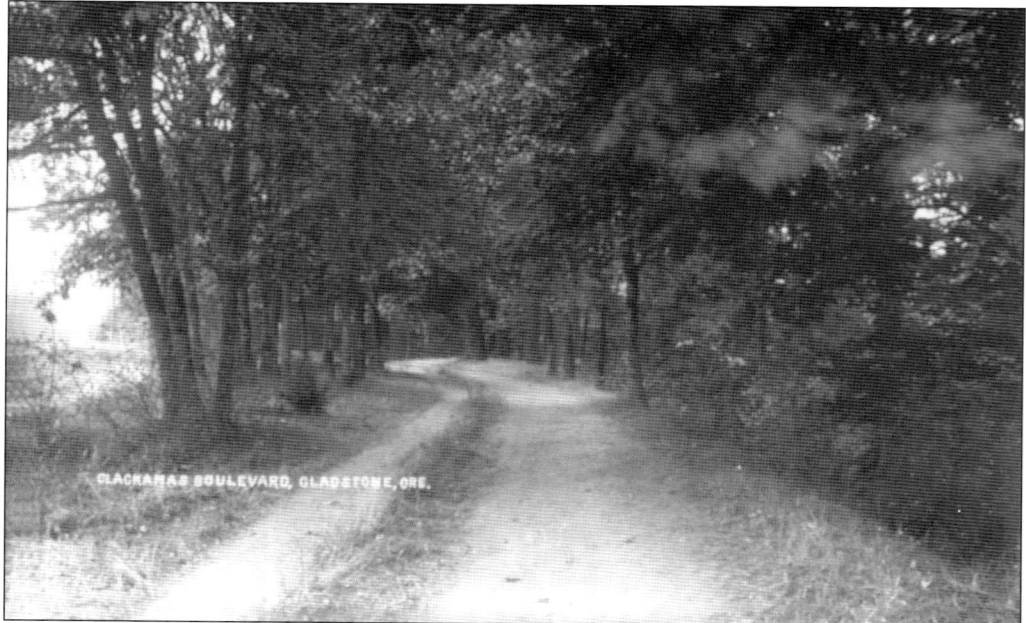

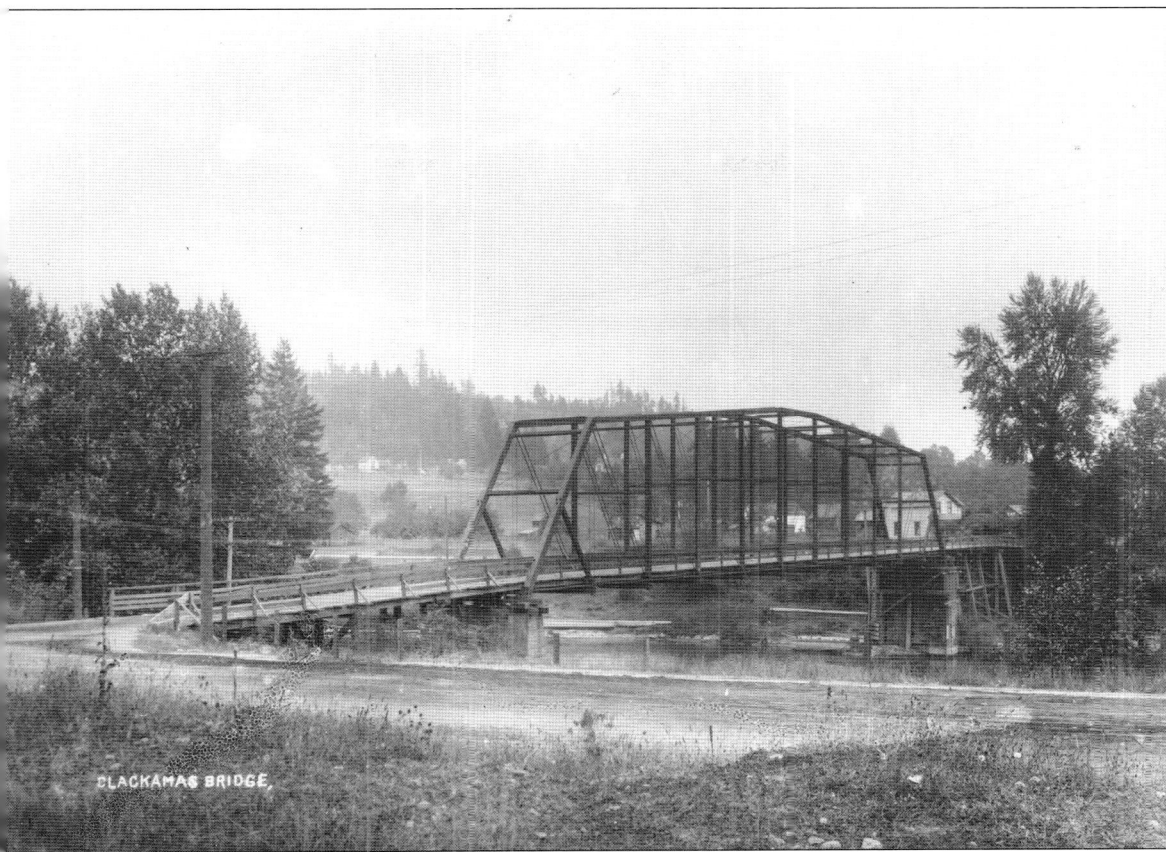

Many Gladstone area roads have similar names. This 1909 photograph featuring the north end of the 1892 wagon bridge also shows Clackamas Boulevard, which was first called River Road because of its connection to the road by the same name that still runs north to south along the east bank of the Willamette River. River Road was once the main route between Oregon City and Portland. Also, the Cason land was divided midpoint, north to south, by an Indian trail that transitioned into a stagecoach route, then a county road, and finally, Oatfield Road, the main thoroughfare between Oregon City and Milwaukie. Oatfield Road once joined River Road at the wagon bridge. Later, as topography changed, the south end of Oatfield Road became present-day Eighty-Second Drive, which was originally called the Damascus Road and sometimes referred to as Clackamas River Road. Across the bridge, the strip of road to the left is Bakers Ferry Road, later called Market Road, and finally, Clackamas River Drive.

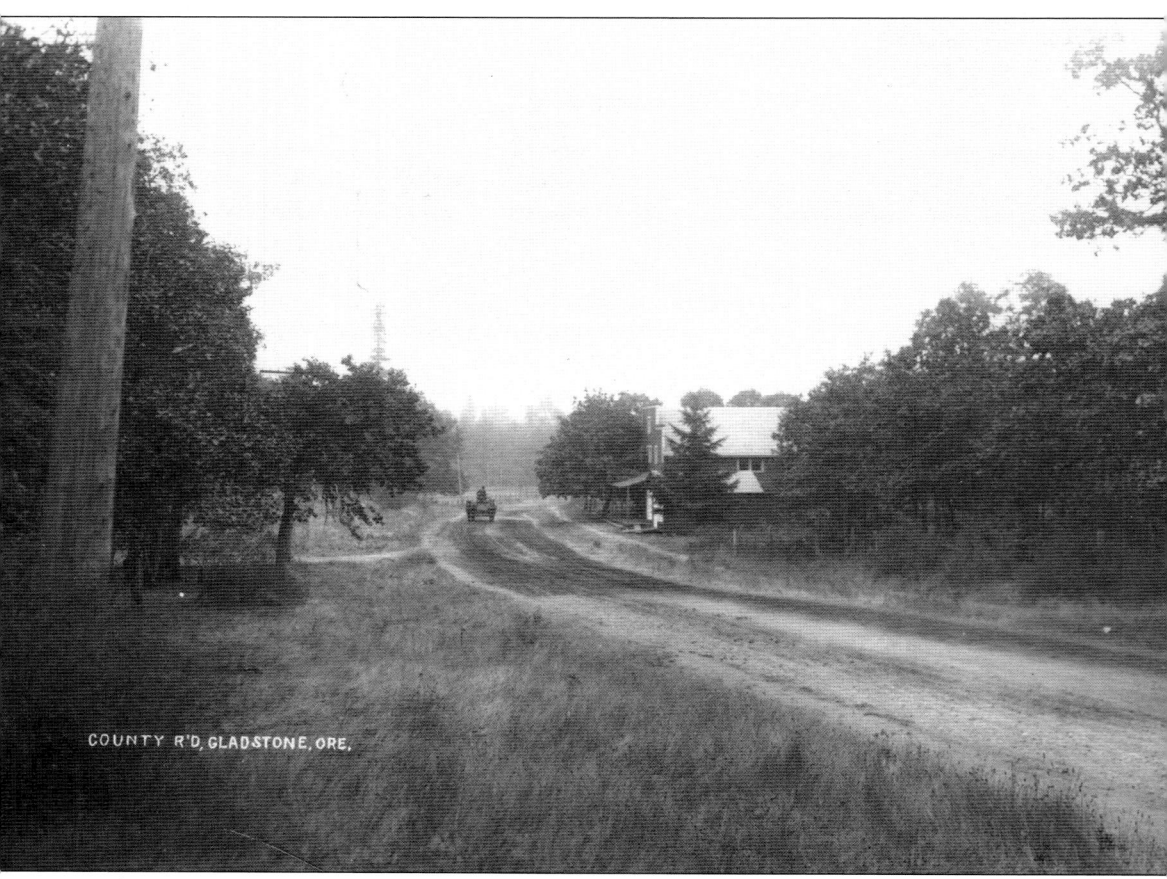

The south end of Oatfield Road is shown in 1910 between the present-day streets of Dartmouth (foreground) and Berkley (the location of the wagon). At this time, roads in Gladstone were still hard packed dirt. Depending on the season, some heavily traveled roads like Clackamas Boulevard were dragged, rolled, oiled, or graveled to keep them passable. The Damascus Road had sections that were planked. A quarter mile beyond the wagon is the wagon bridge. To the right of the wagon and hidden behind the large tree is the Cason house. Also on the right is the Turel House, halfway between the Southern Pacific's Gladstone Chautauqua Station and Gladstone Park's main gate. Built around 1900 and no longer standing, the Turel House is believed to have briefly operated as a stagecoach stop. On the left is a dirt path leading into the athletic field of Gladstone Park, the site of the summer Chautauqua.

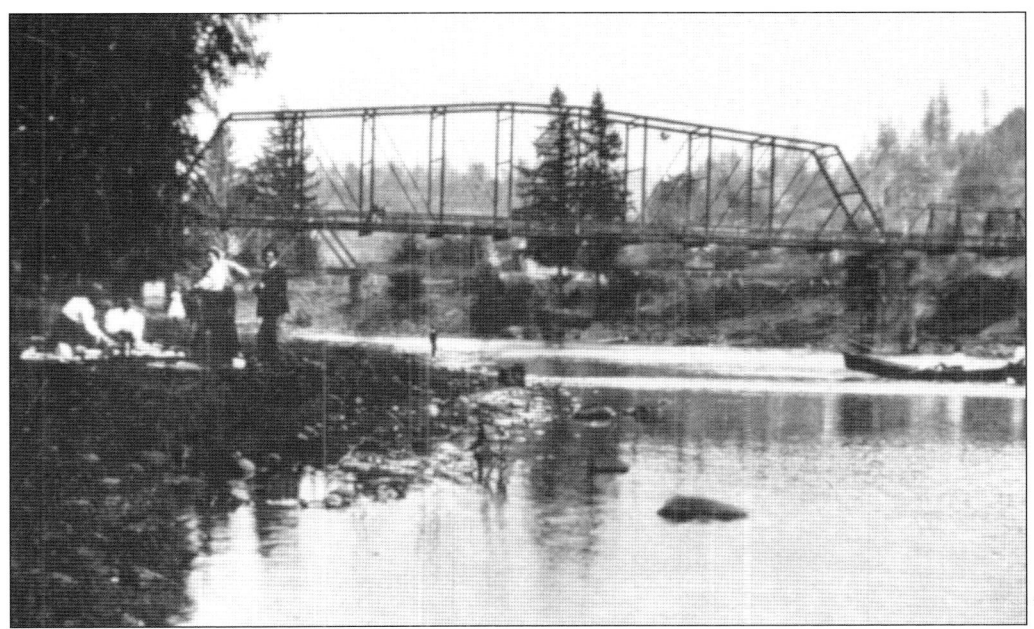

When word got out that the River Road (meaning Clackamas Boulevard) promised a pleasant afternoon drive, crowds flocked to early Gladstone. A group picnic is seen above in 1892 on the north bank of the river. In the background is the 1892 railroad bridge. The Clackamas River became famous for its spectacular fishing and high-quality salmon. In June 1889, Rudyard Kipling detoured on his way to British Columbia to tromp through the underbrush several miles east of Gladstone and fish for salmon in the Clackamas River. Thrilled with his catch, Kipling published his adventures beginning with the words, "I have lived!" Below, a woman and children prepare to fish at the 1892 wagon bridge in 1902.

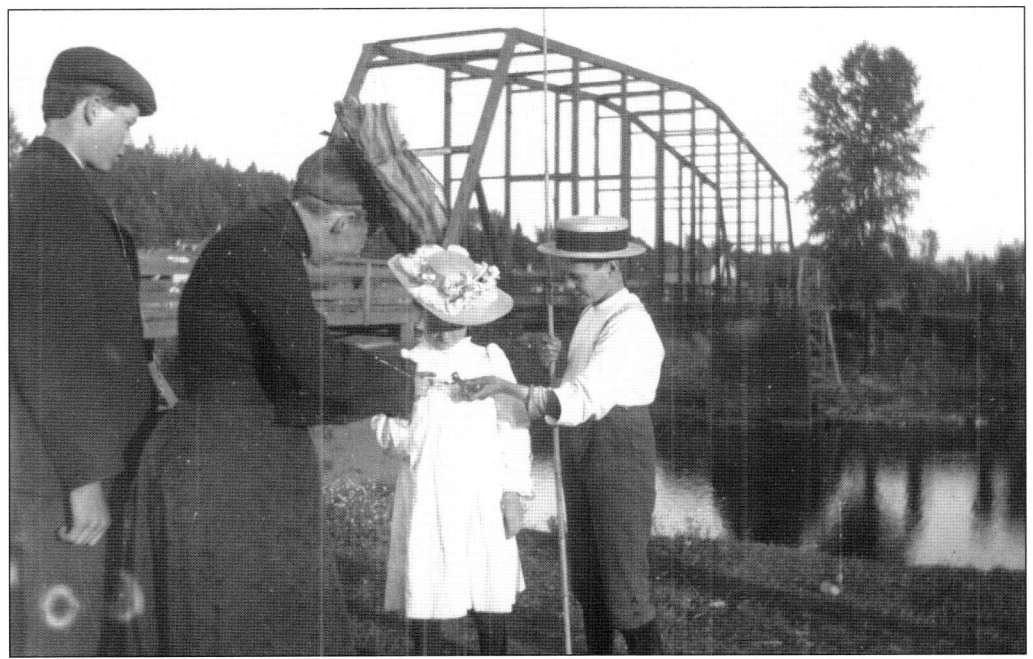

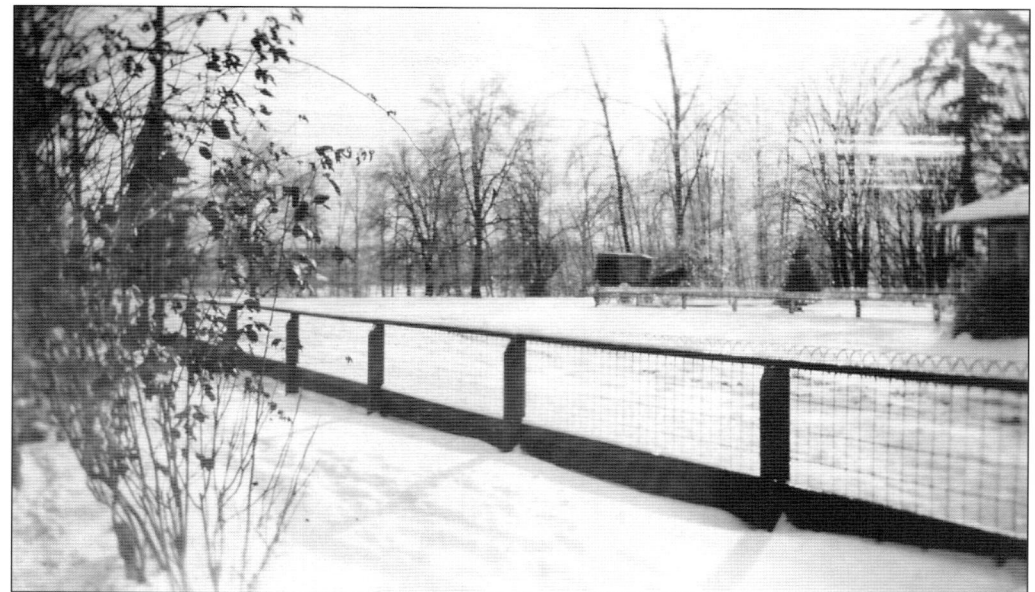

In 1903, C.G. Miller opened the first automobile dealership in Oregon City; soon, automobiles outnumbered horse-drawn conveyances. On July 2, 1912, the Oregon City government posted its new traffic ordinance in local newspapers and vowed to enforce the rules, with citizens encouraged to report speeders. Punishment for the first speeding offense was a $50 fine or 25 days in jail. Gladstone did not enact traffic laws for another two years. Above, in 1915, a horse-drawn delivery wagon makes its way down Clackamas Boulevard in winter. Although motorized delivery vehicles were steadily coming into use, until tire chains were available starting in 1904, nothing maneuvered in snow quite as reliably as a horse. Below, in 1921, an automobile races along Clackamas Boulevard unmindful of speed limits or high water. (Both, GHS.)

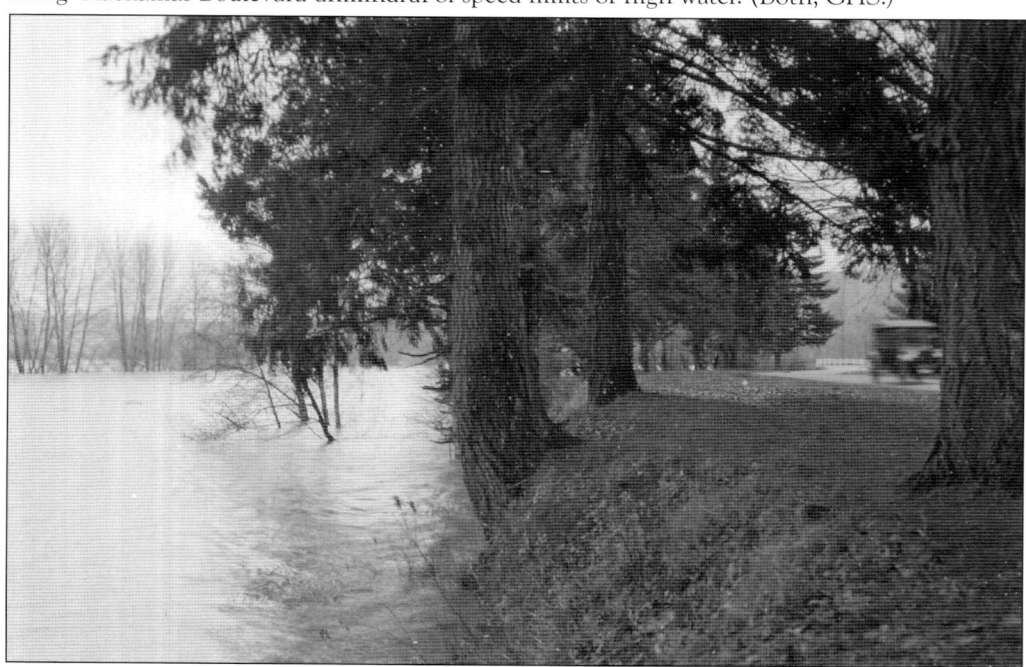

By 1910, roads in Clackamas County were being macadamized. In 1918 (right), the Pow-Wow tree stands on the north side of a newly paved Clackamas Boulevard, now better able to accommodate the ever-increasing automobile traffic. Residents along Clackamas Boulevard, hoping to profit from the increased traffic, soon opened small home businesses that included summer concession stands, a gift shop, and gas station, all of which further increased traffic. In 1927, Fred and Katie Winningham opened the Pow-Wow Inn, a small home café that became a popular place to eat. Below, in 1930, Clackamas Boulevard looks worn. The car across the street from the Pow-Wow tree sits in the driveway of the Pow-Wow Inn.

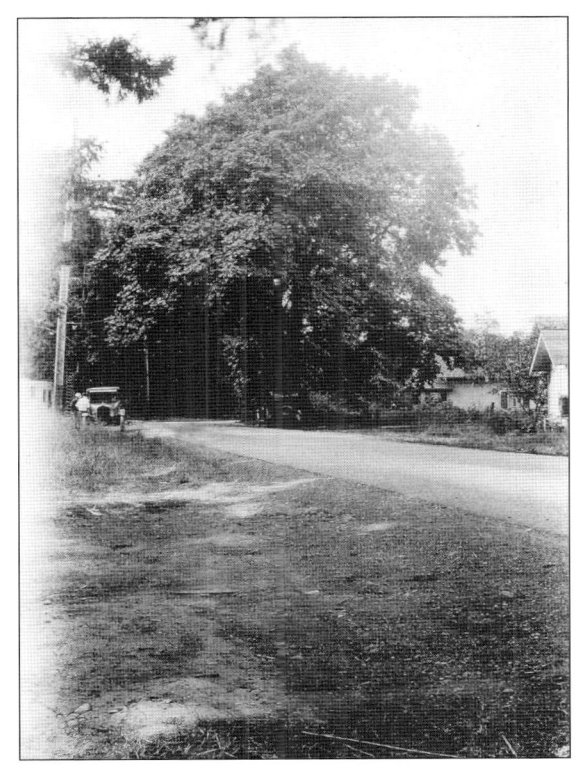

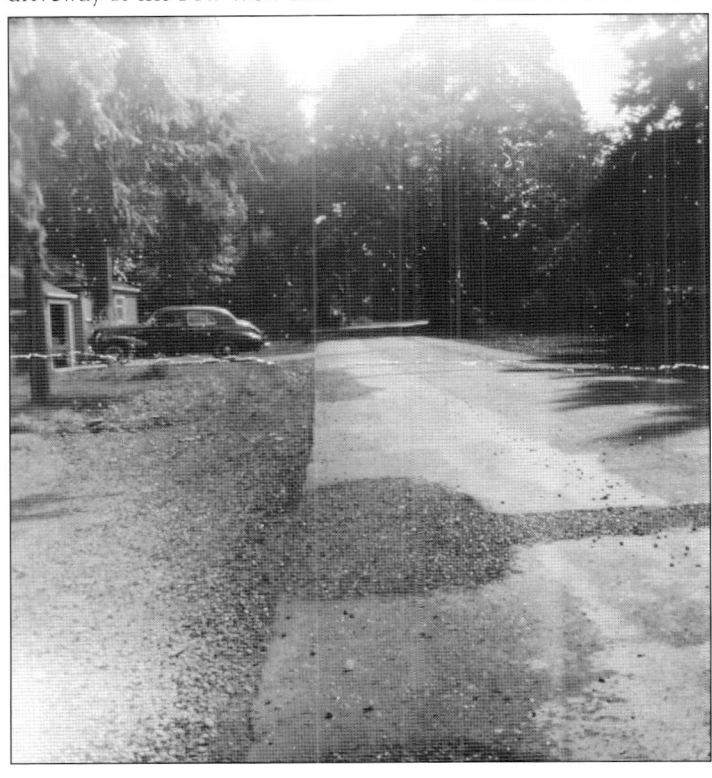

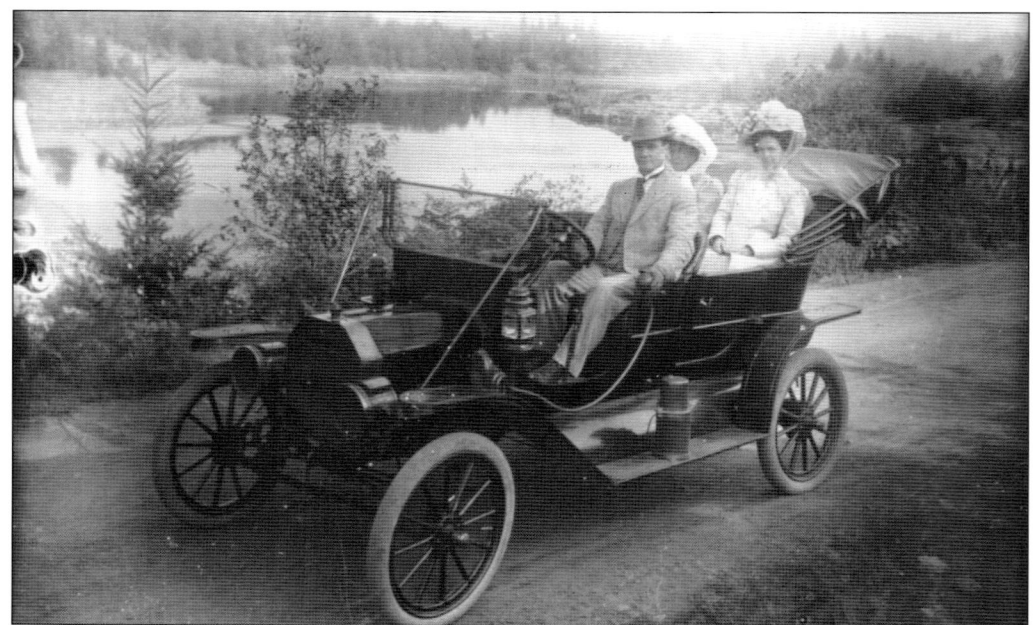

In 1926, US Highway 99, also called the Super Highway, was completed from Canada to Mexico. In Oregon, Highway 99 was divided into an east and west route, with each following the Willamette River on their respective sides. The east route, from Portland's Ross Island Bridge to the Clackamas River, was named McLoughlin Boulevard and replaced River Road as the main road to Portland. Above, in 1908, T. Chambers Howell and family drive south along River Road in Gladstone. Below, in 1933, the John McLoughlin Memorial Bridge, which connected McLoughlin Boulevard to Oregon City, became the first "new" Clackamas River crossing between Gladstone and Oregon City in 80 years. Upon completion, the American Institute of Steel Construction honored the McLoughlin Bridge as the "Most Beautiful Steel Bridge" ever built.

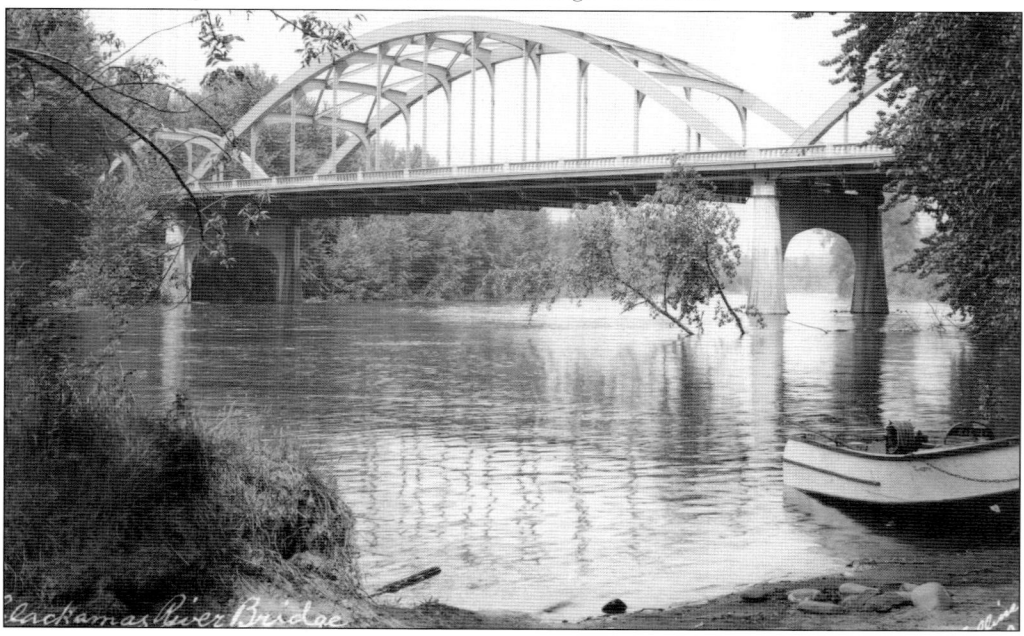

Four

First Fairs and a War

The focus of Gladstone's early settlers was to make a living and survive, not to be the center of attention. While Fendel Cason farmed, his son Ad operated a gunsmith shop next door to their toll ferry. Hiram Straight acquired land, farmed, and served in the Oregon government. No mention is made of his ever brewing blue ruin again. However, in 1850, he and Jacob Hunsaker gained some notoriety for being members of the jury that convicted five members of the Cayuse Indian tribe for their role in the Whitman Massacre.

Jacob and Peter Rinearsons' plan was to raise horses, but Peter found farming to be a more lucrative occupation. In an 1880s agricultural report, Peter Rinearson is listed as having produced in one year "824 bushes of onions per acre, 1,133 bushels of carrots per acre, and 82,260 pounds of turnips per acre, along with disease and pestilence-free potatoes."

Surprisingly, in 1860, Jacob Rinearson, who had discovered that being a career soldier suited him best, decided to join the Clackamas County Agricultural Society as a founding member and became instrumental in bringing both the first Clackamas County Fair and the first Oregon State Fair to the Rinearson farm, along with hundreds of attendees. Then, he brought the entire First Oregon Volunteer Cavalry to the Rinearson farm to train for Indian hostilities. All of this set into motion the coming of the newly formed Oregon National Guard to future Gladstone and the use of the entire town to stage a mock battle, much to the amazement of an audience of thousands.

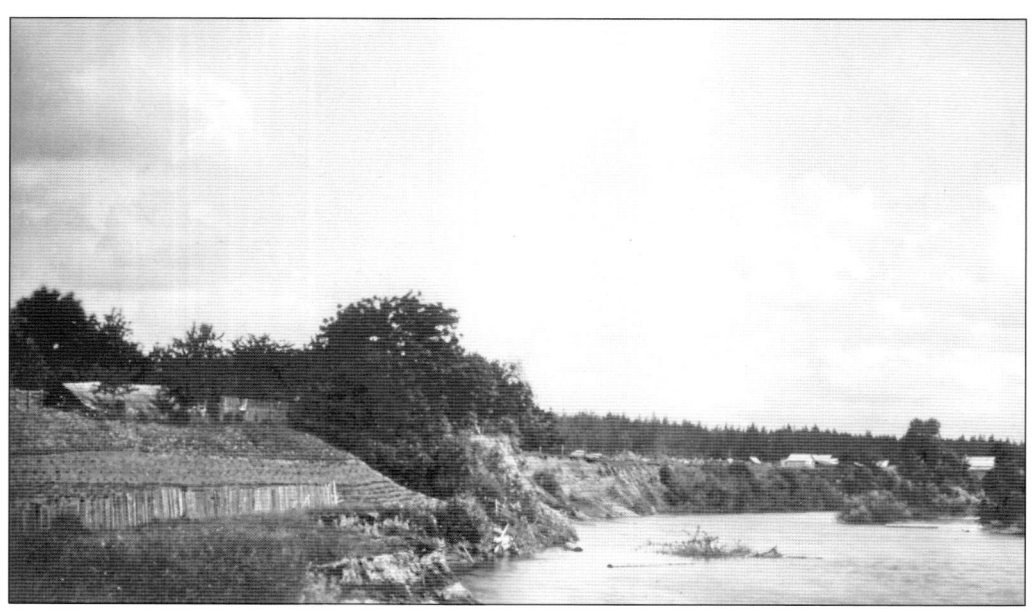

On February 14, 1859, Oregon became the 33rd state. The following year, the Clackamas County Agricultural Society held the first Clackamas County Fair, September 27–28, 1860, on four acres of Rinearson land bounded by present-day Clarendon Street to the north, Bellevue Avenue to the east, the Clackamas River to the south, and Beatrice Avenue to the west. The 1908 view of the mouth of the Clackamas River above shows the Rinearson land (left) where the fair was held. On October 1–4, 1861, the Oregon State Agricultural Society also held the first state fair on the Rinearson acreage. Rough buildings that were erected for use by both fairs can be seen behind the men in the wagon below. (Above, OHS; below, SLO.)

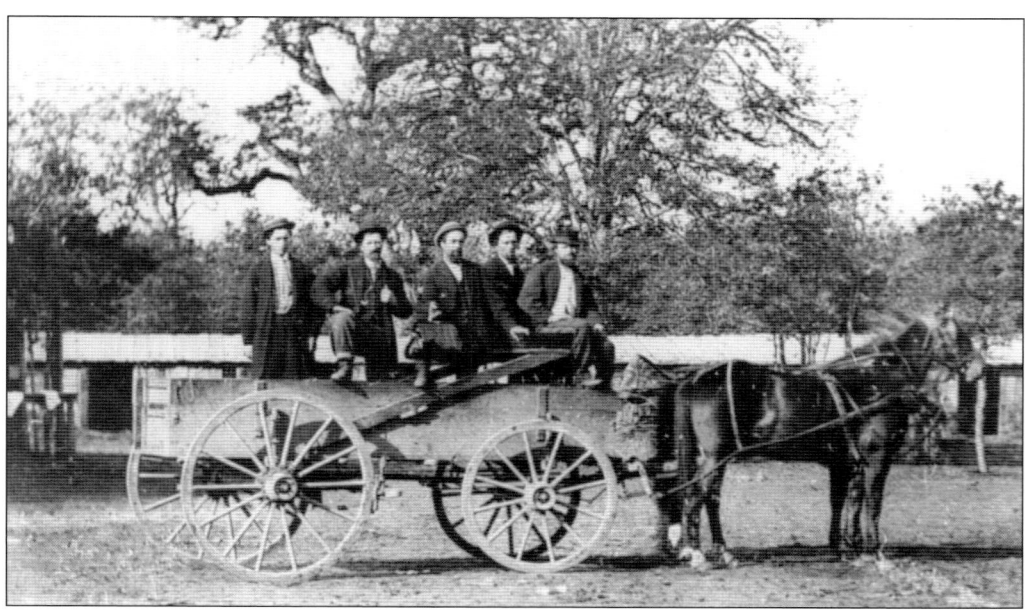

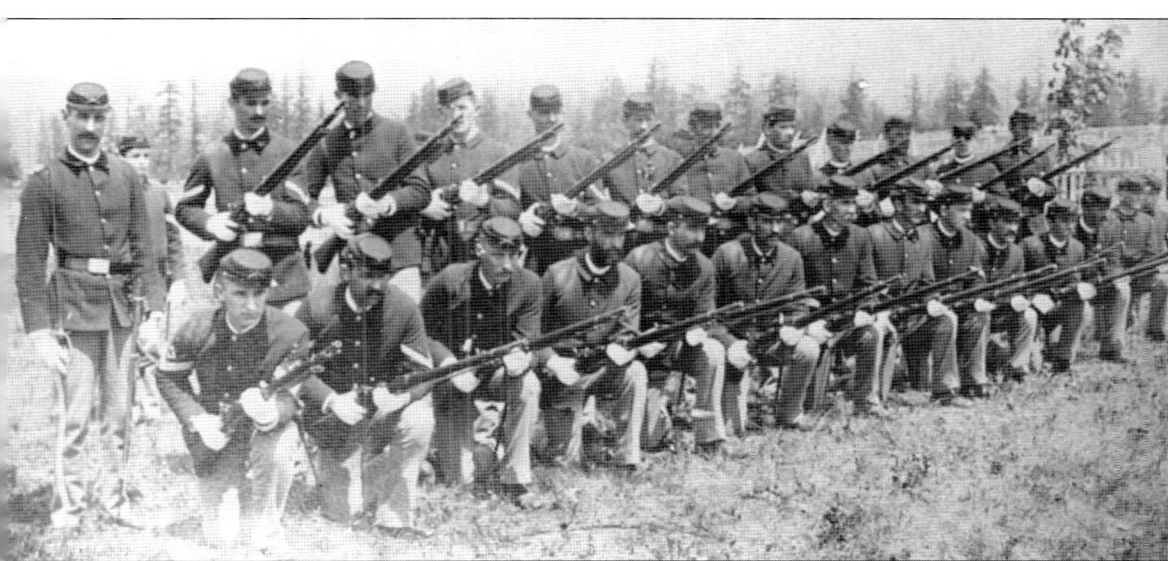

When the Civil War erupted, Oregon was expected to send soldiers for the Union army. In 1861, all of Oregon's military officers and their men departed for the East, leaving Oregon without a way to control Indian uprisings. To rectify the problem, the First Oregon Volunteer Cavalry was organized, with Jacob Rinearson, newly promoted to major, assigned to train the volunteers. Most of the men could ride well and were accurate shots, but few had any military experience. Using the four-acre Rinearson fairground, Indian racetrack, and the abandoned fair buildings, Major Rinearson set up a military camp and trained his men for active duty, as shown here in 1861. Shortly after this photograph was taken, Rinearson and Volunteer Cavalry Company F were ordered to western Idaho, where they engaged in hostilities with the Nez Perce Indians. (SLO.)

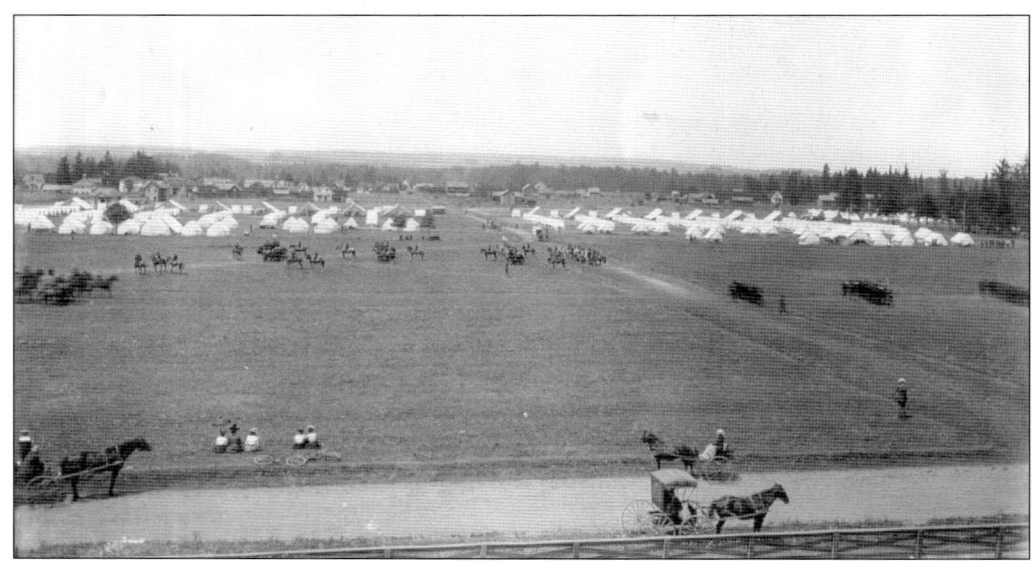

In 1887, the Oregon National Guard was formed with approximately 1,700 volunteers. Because few recruits had enough military experience to engage in civil duty or combat, field training camps were held throughout Oregon. The above photograph, taken between 1890 and 1905, shows an unidentified Oregon National Guard training camp. On August 12–22, 1893, Gladstone Park became Camp Compson, a National Guard training camp for 500 men plus officers. In the park's athletic field, 150 soldier tents were pitched along with a field hospital tent housing two doctors, two kitchens, a battery containing two Gatling guns, and a rifle range. Below, in 1955, the covered tents of a church camp line the rear of the athletic field on the site of the former Camp Compson's rifle range. (Above, SLO; below, KAH.)

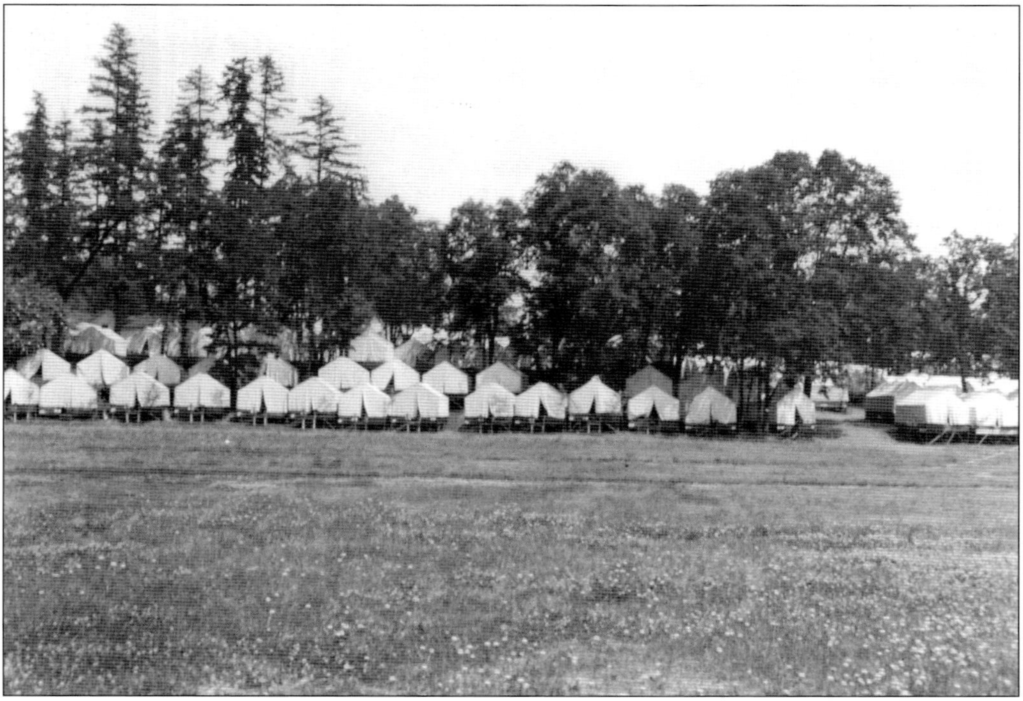

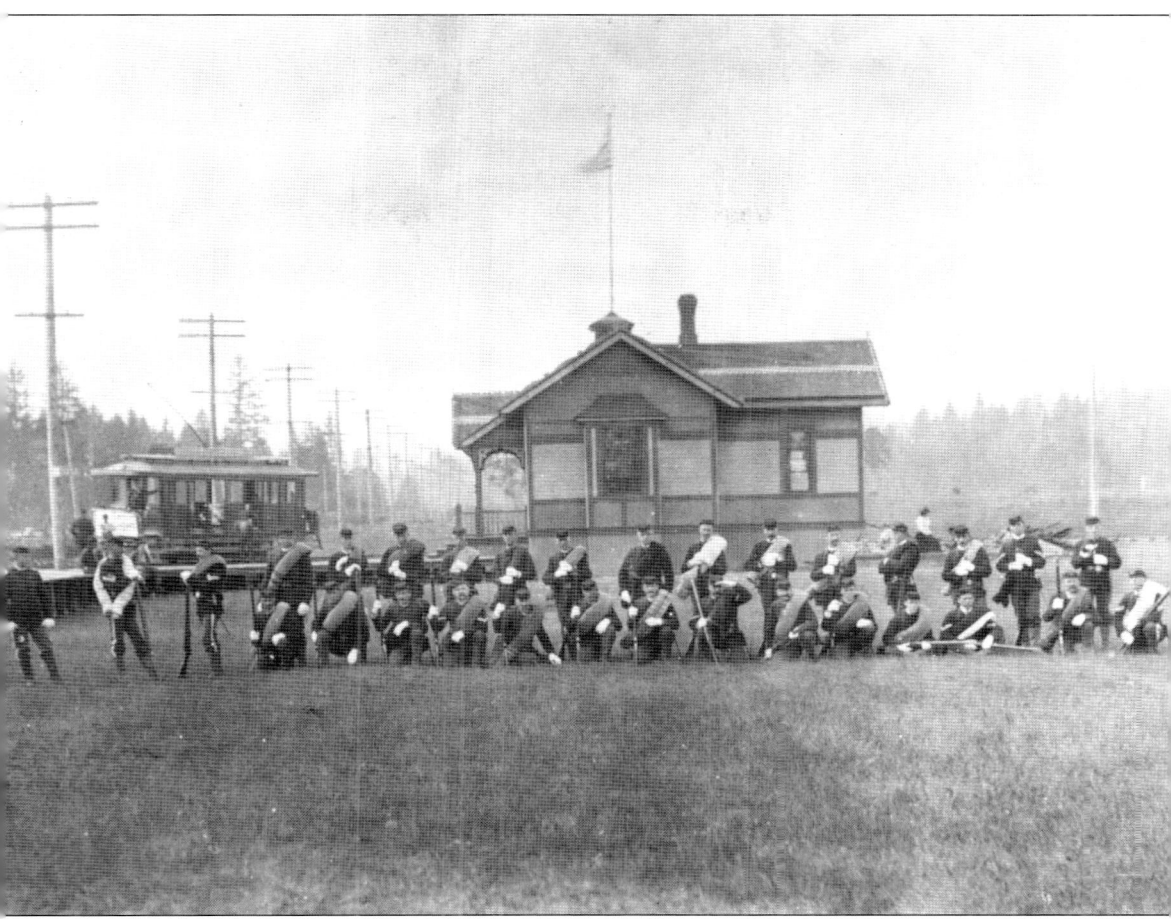

Attending Camp Compson was voluntary. New recruits were encouraged to train, but were not required to do so. The men who did attend came by train or trolley. For 10 days, the volunteers drilled, learned discipline, practiced maneuvers, and bathed in the cold Clackamas River, much to the shock of unsuspecting female Gladstone residents out for a morning stroll. On the final day of camp, a mock battle was enacted, precipitated by the simulated seizure of the camp's supply train. The battle raged over several hundred acres of future Gladstone and was watched by a crowd of thousands. Even though blank rounds were fired, one soldier was seriously wounded. A call for an ambulance brought an open trolley car that transported Lt. C.E. Nelson to the Portland Good Samaritan Hospital, where he later died. In this 1893 photograph, National Guard soldiers leaving Fort Compson line up at the first Gladstone Trolley Depot, on the northeast corner of present-day Dartmouth Street and Portland Avenue. The depot burned in 1906.

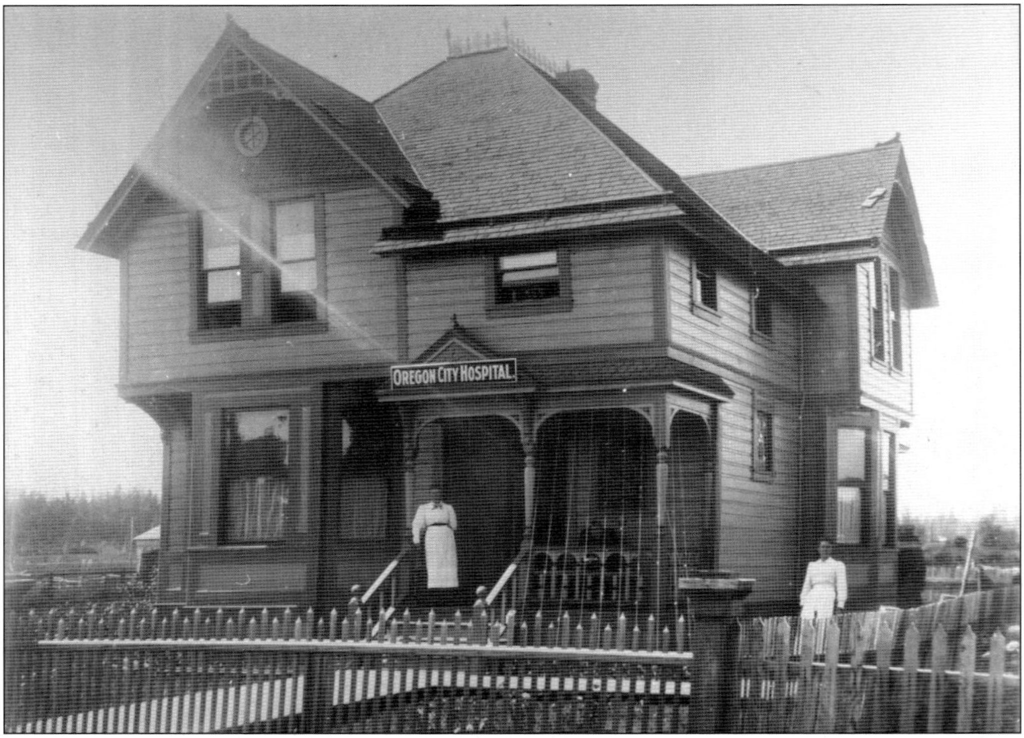

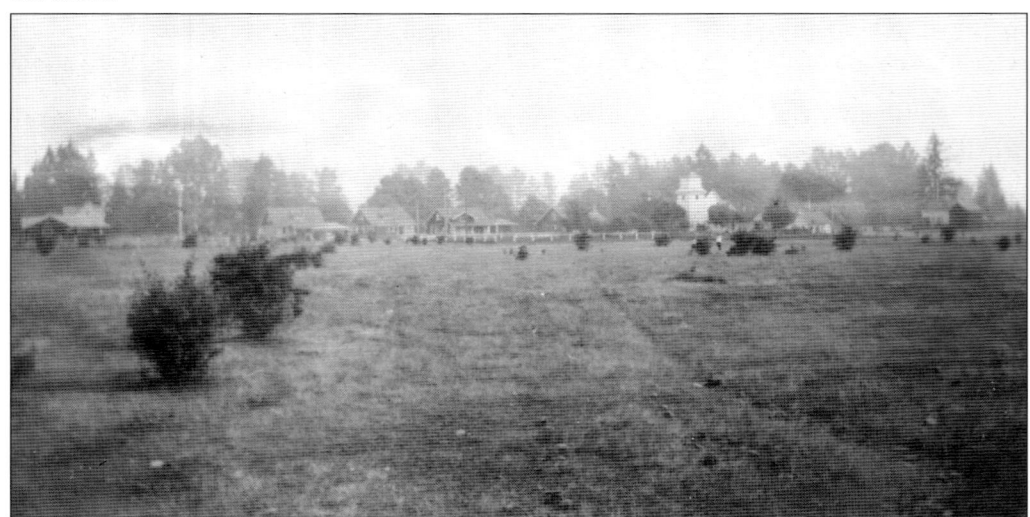

In 1894, the first Oregon City Hospital, shown here in 1895, was opened in Gladstone under the direction of Mary Liibker and Miss Utter. By 1905, the hospital had expanded into two buildings: one for general medicine and surgery and one for tuberculosis patients along with typhoid fever and smallpox quarantine. The hospital relocated several times and continued operating into the 1930s.

As early as 1908, sanitarium and health homes began appearing in private houses along Clackamas Boulevard, as seen here in 1911. One health home, operated by Dr. and Mrs. A.O. Alexander, was considered the finest sanitarium west of Salt Lake City. The home offered steam baths, massage, violet ray treatments, and magnetic treatments. The Clackamas River is behind the trees.

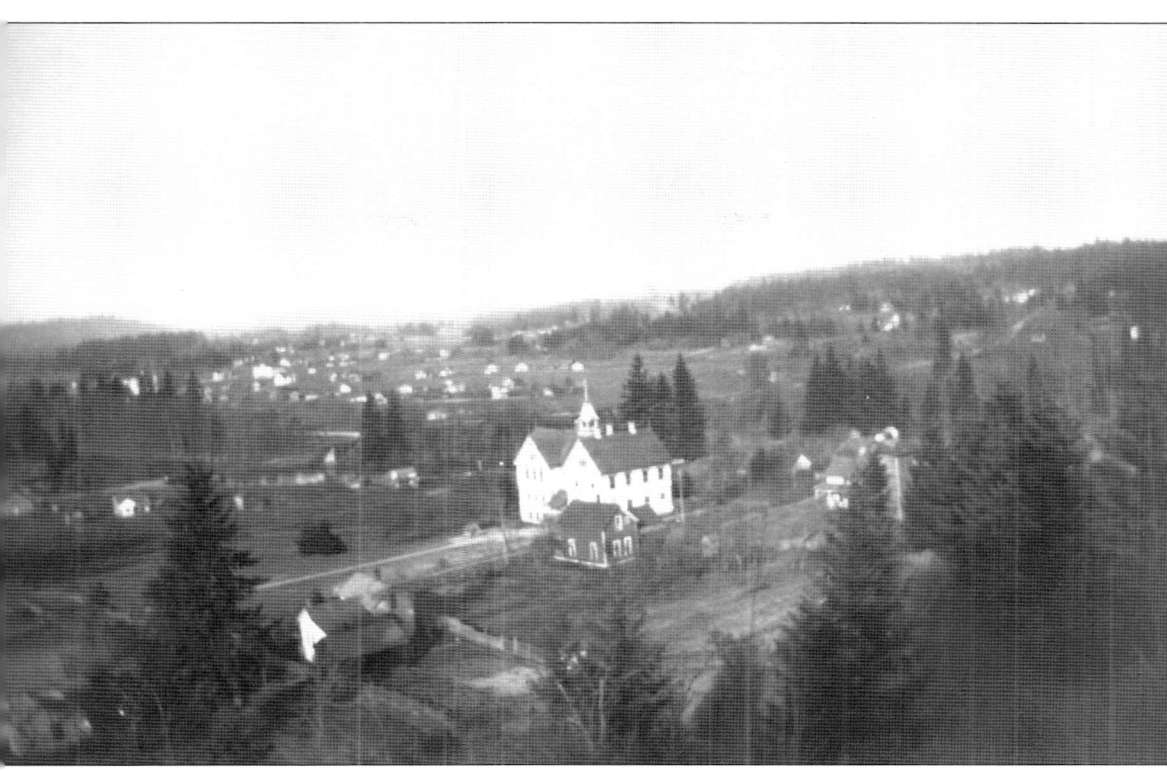

In 1860, Fendel Cason died. Ad Cason, Fendel's oldest remaining son, became head of the Cason family. In 1869, Ad built the first school in Gladstone in what would become Gladstone Park. The one-room "Little Red Schoolhouse" measured 25 feet by 40 feet and cost $400 to build. It opened with five students. Teachers included 13-year-old Clara Greaves (Peter Rinearson's step-daughter), E.A. Hackett, a Mr. Randall, John Tuttle, Mary E. Post, Lena McCowan, George Dedman, and Kate Dolan. In 1895, the overcrowded Little Red Schoolhouse closed and the approximately 50 students were transferred to the larger 12-grade school in Park Place, built in 1892 and shown here in the early 1900s. In the background is the tree-lined Clackamas River and Gladstone. In the far right background, Oatfield Road ascends the hill. To the right of the base of the hill is a building that is possibly the Little Red Schoolhouse. The cleared area around that building is Gladstone Park.

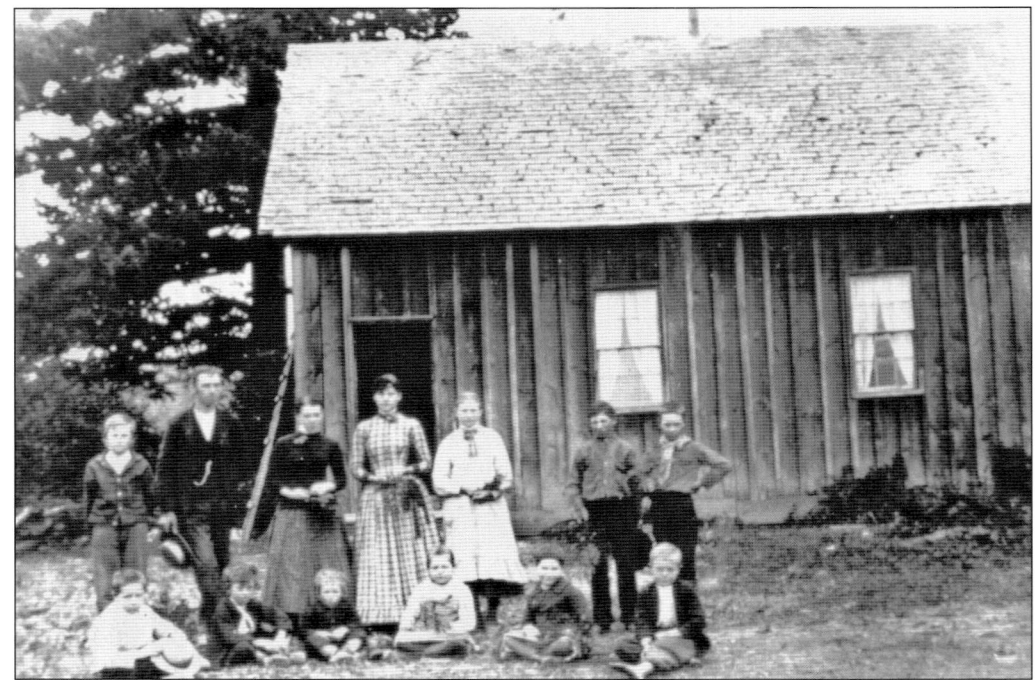

In the 1880s, a teacher and his students stand in front of their schoolhouse on River Road in the west Jennings Lodge area north of Gladstone. This wooden schoolhouse was constructed similarly to the Little Red Schoolhouse. Students from the east side of Jennings Lodge walked down Oatfield Road to attend classes in Ad Cason's school.

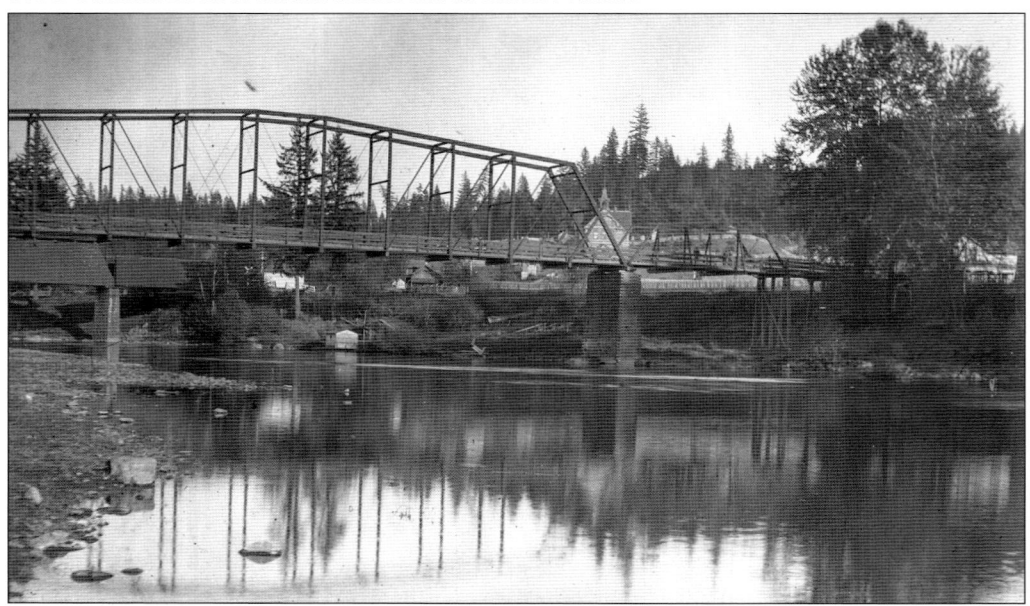

Parents fearing for their children's safety demanded a new school be built in Gladstone because attending the Park Place school, as shown behind the 1892 wagon bridge in the late 1890s, meant crossing the temperamental Clackamas River by bridge and sometimes by ferry. Also shown is the 1892 railroad bridge. Hiram Straight's house is nestled in the trees to the right.

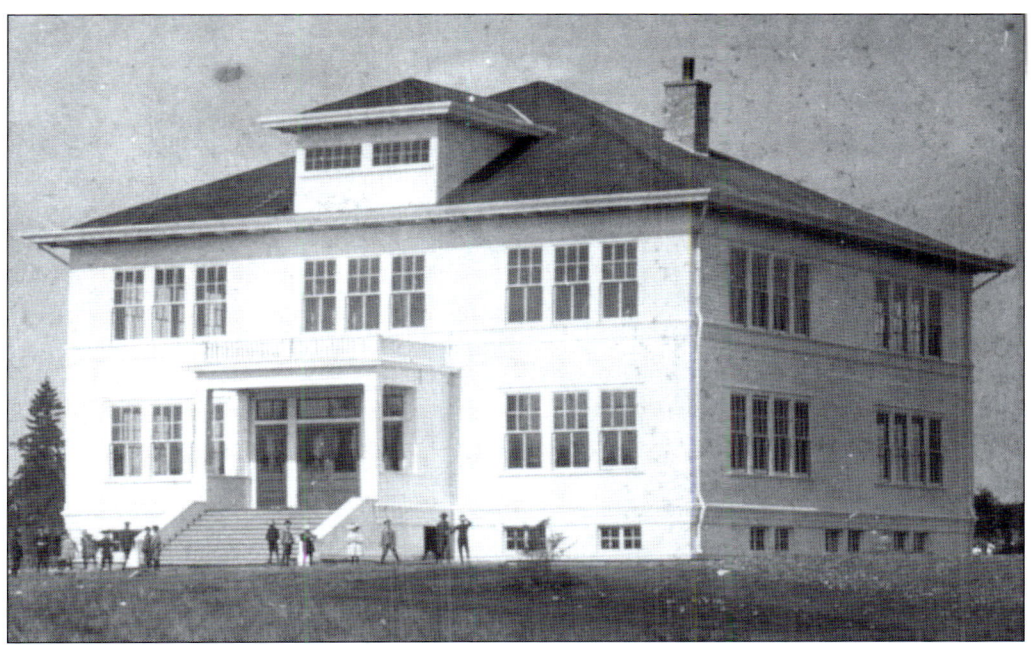

In 1908, Harvey Cross donated two blocks of future Gladstone for a new eighth-grade school. Comprised of two floors, eight classrooms, an attic, basement, and 16-foot-long hallways, the new building was described as the most artistically pleasant of environments for learning. The first teaching staff included principal Brenton Vedder, May Munson, Edna Caufield, and Pearl Sievers. The new Gladstone Grade School is shown above on the first day of school in September 1908. This building, located at present-day Gloucester Street (north), Harvard Avenue (east), Exeter Street (south) and Chicago Avenue (west), later burned. Below, students of grades five through seven pose for a class photograph in 1908.

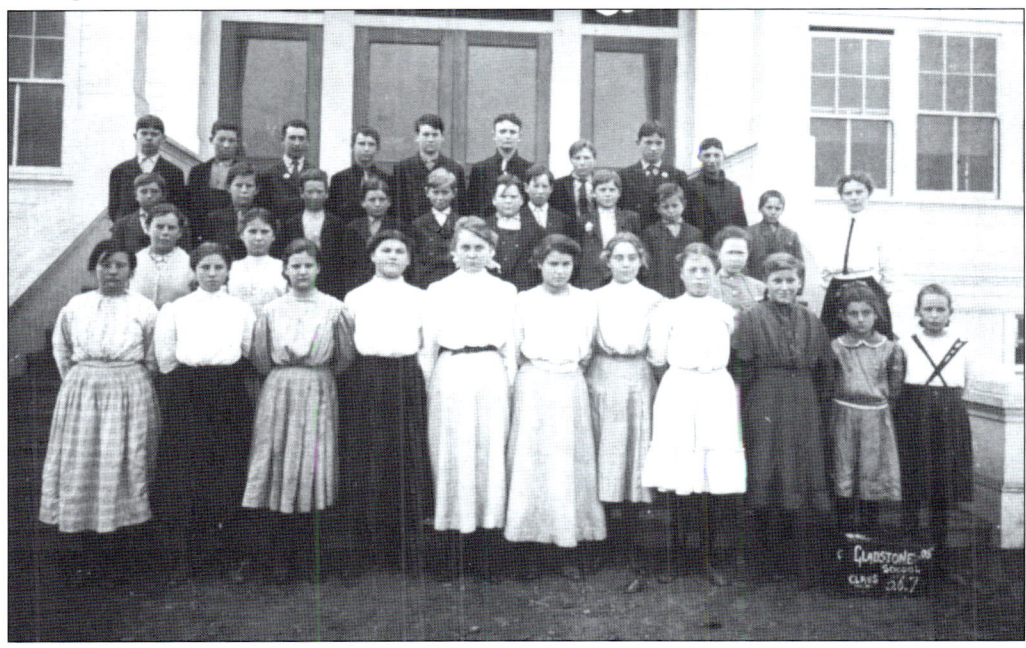

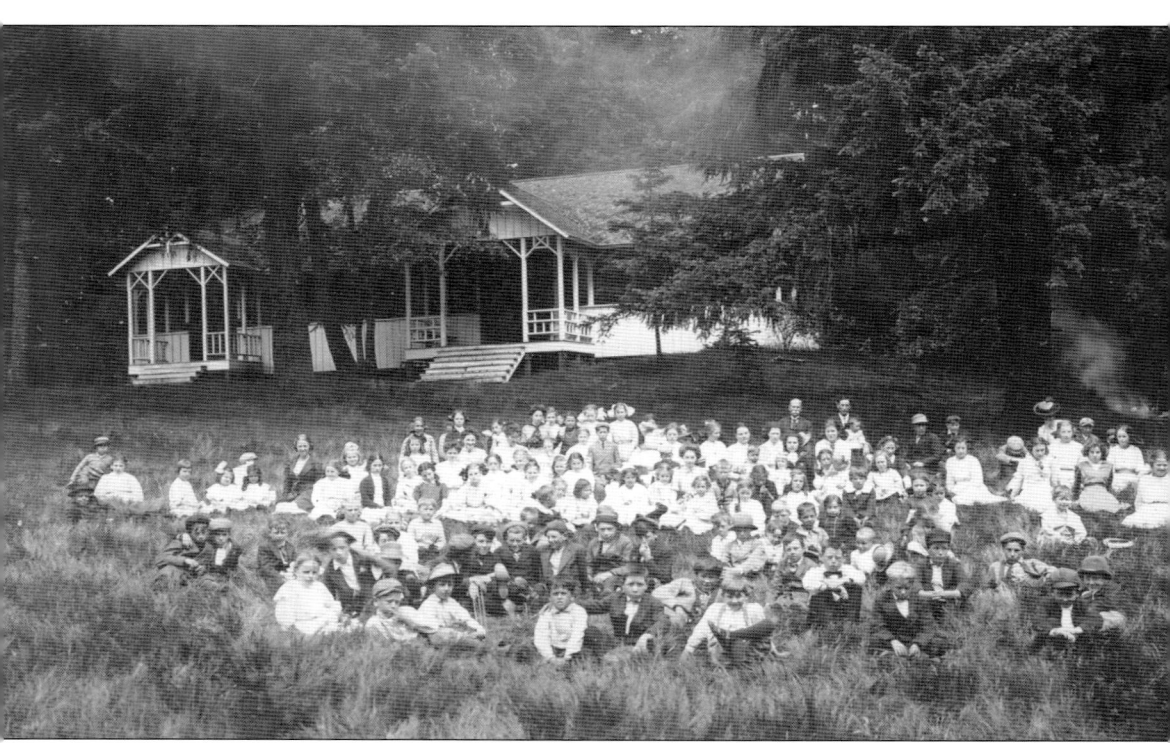

What happened to the Little Red Schoolhouse is one of the historical mysteries of Gladstone. In September 1895, the building was renovated into a house for Mr. and Mrs. Bray, who were relocating to Gladstone Park for Mr. Bray to become the park watchman. In 1903, Harvey Cross, Gladstone's founder and owner of Gladstone Park, placed an advertisement in the *Oregon City Courier* announcing, "Home lots for sale in Gladstone" and noting that "the Little Red Schoolhouse yet stands in the Chautauqua grounds." Why Cross thought home buyers would want to know this information is uncertain, unless the school was a beloved landmark. Shown here in 1910 are the students from the Gladstone public school picnicking in front of the Chautauqua restaurant building in Gladstone Park. For many years, it was believed this restaurant building was the remodeled Little Red Schoolhouse, but that has been disproved. Ironically, in 1932, the Chautauqua restaurant was enclosed and used as a two-room private school until 1966.

Five

The First Railroad

In July 1866, after work had begun on the Transcontinental Railroad, the US government decided to build a north-south railroad that would link Portland to San Francisco, as well as connect with the Transcontinental Railroad at Sacramento. To ensure that this north-south line could be financed, and construction could be completed in the difficult Western terrain, the government offered the huge incentive of 3.7 million acres of free land in California and Oregon. Doled out at the rate of 12,800 acres for each mile of track completed, the railroad company could then sell the land to recoup its investment while building and also earn a profit.

Competition was fierce. Rich Oregon businessmen who had never built a railroad suddenly saw an opportunity to increase their fortunes. Choosing sides, the businessmen formed two opposing corporations and gave their companies the same exact name: Oregon Central Railroad. Both companies applied for the government contract.

The inexperienced Oregon legislature was assigned the task of choosing a company to build the railroad and ended up not knowing who to pick. Both Oregon Central Railroads guaranteed they would complete the work, but both were found to have incorporated with illegalities. The matter exploded in court. To keep the land grant from being stolen by an unscrupulous railroad company, a race was declared. The first Oregon Central Railroad to complete 20 miles of track from Portland going south would be awarded the initial allotment of land and the contract to build the entire rail line. The race was to begin in April 1868 and end December 25, 1869.

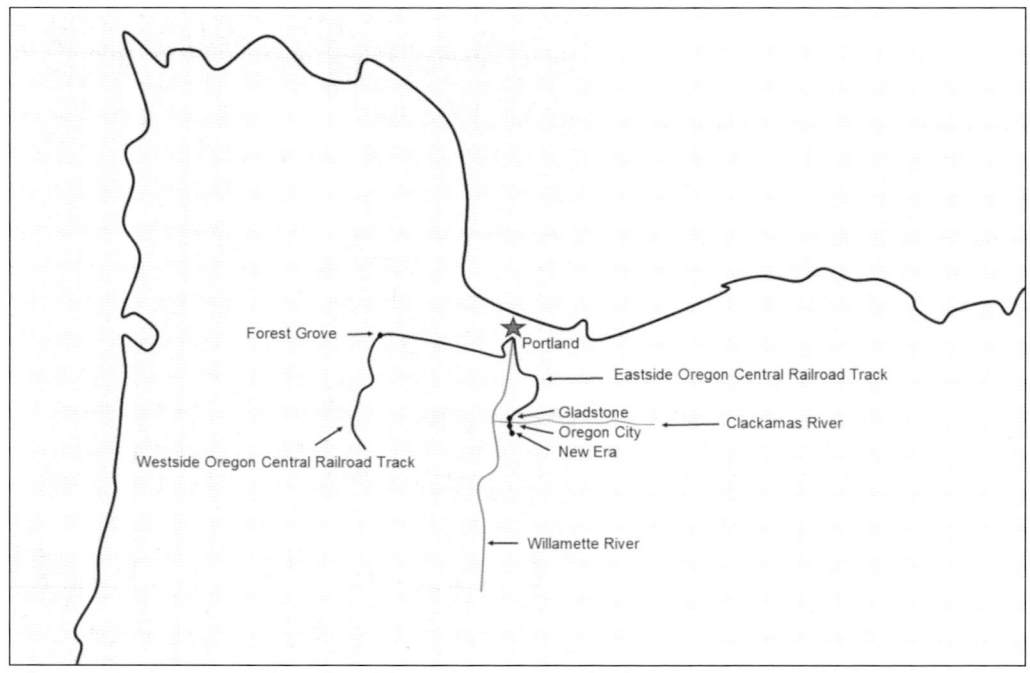

The two Oregon Central Railroad (OCR) companies built on opposite sides of the Willamette River. The "Westside" OCR was backed by John Ainsworth, William Ladd, and Simon Reed, three of the most wealthy and powerful merchants in Portland. The "Eastside" OCR was backed by California promoter Simon G. Elliot, Oregon governor George Woods, and the wheat farmers of southern and eastern Oregon who wanted to ship grain some other way than by steamships owned by wealthy Portland merchants. The map above shows the route of each OCR. Below, a crowd watches the Westside OCR drive its first spike at Washington Street and First Avenue in Portland. Immediately, the Westside OCR took the lead by laying five miles of track over hilly terrain. (Above, GHS; below, OHS.)

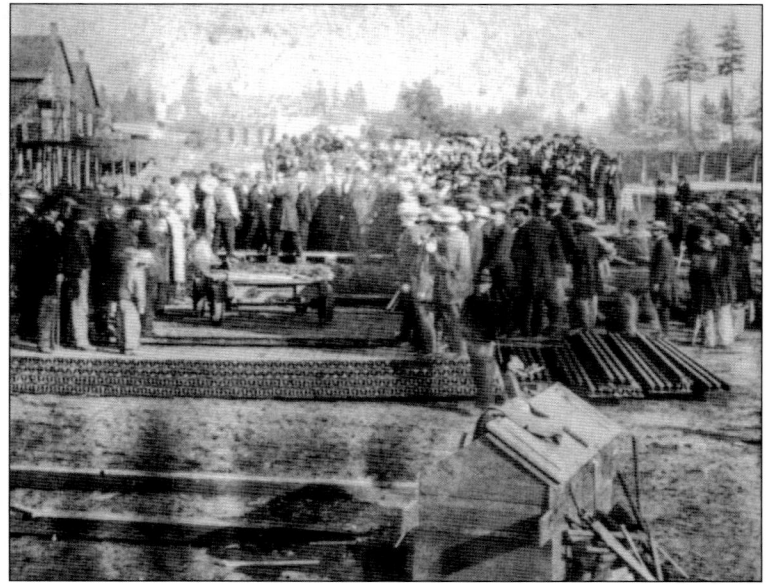

In the fall of 1869, Ben Holladay, the undisputed transportation king of Pony Express–Overland Stage fame, arrived in Portland from San Francisco. At 50 years old, he stood a commanding six feet tall, was worth millions of dollars and had an urge to build a railroad. With the Christmas deadline looming, the nearly bankrupt Eastside OCR had yet to lay any track. Holladay stepped in, and using his own money, hired hundreds of workers, including 600 Chinese laborers, and began building track. By November, he had outpaced the Westside OCR by completing 14 miles. With eight weeks remaining, Holladay had only six more miles and one bridge to construct. The 1908 photograph below shows the farmland of New Era that was the finish line for the Eastside OCR. The tracks shown were built by Holladay. The Willamette River is to the right. (Right, OHS.)

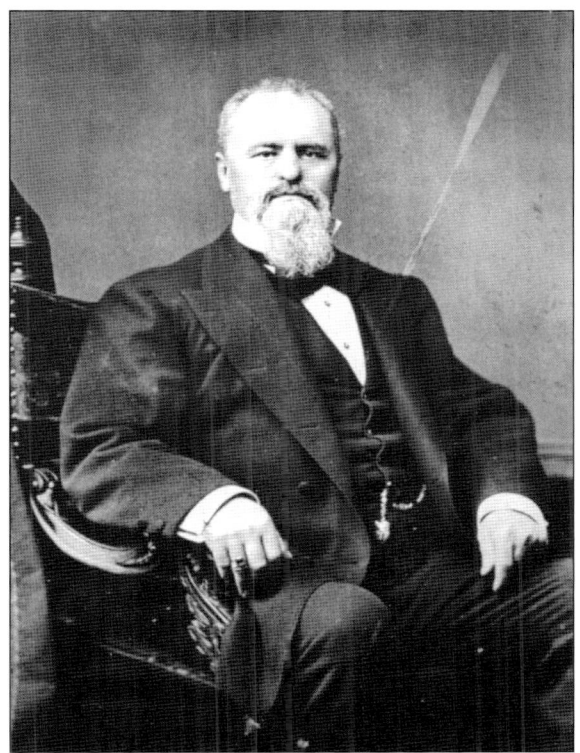

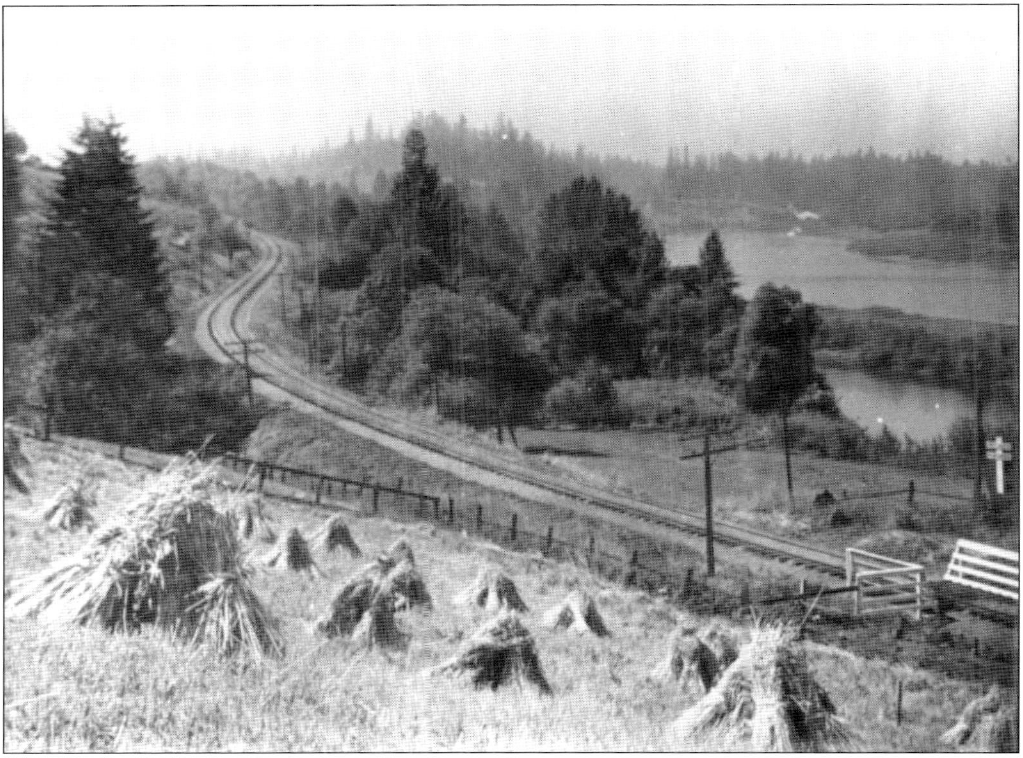

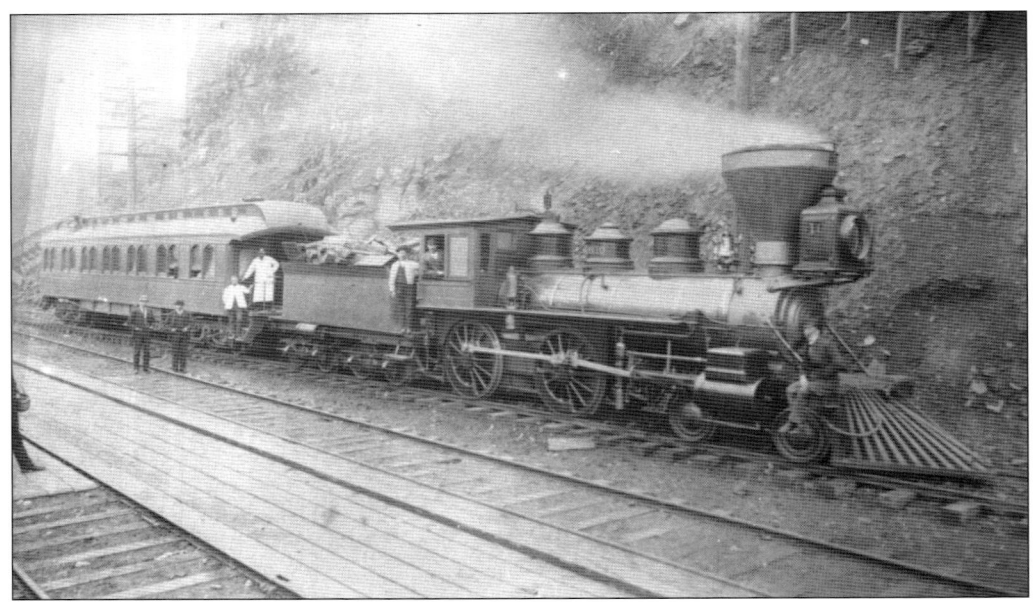

The last six miles were the most difficult of the entire course. Ahead lay the high-running Clackamas River and the rock of Oregon City. In 1895, a Southern Pacific payroll train stands on track that Ben Holladay laid. Behind the train is Oregon City's rock bluff where Holladay's men blasted.

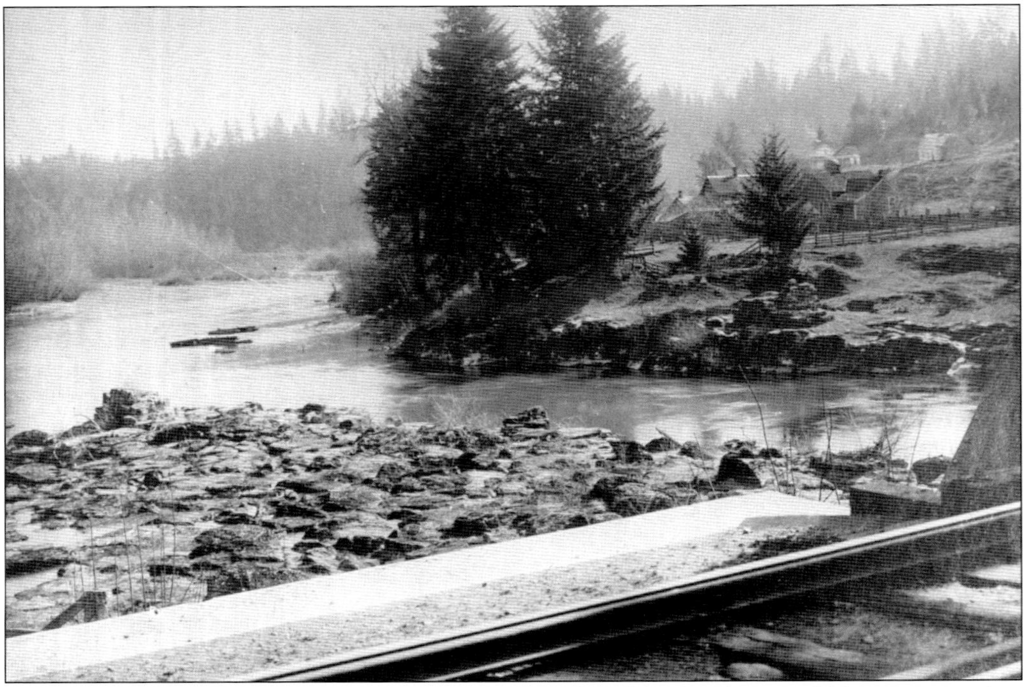

At High Rocks, Holladay constructed a 380-foot railroad bridge that would become the first railroad bridge built in the Pacific Northwest. The night following the bridge's completion, the Clackamas River unleashed a flood that destroyed Holladay's bridge. In this 1904 photograph, taken facing east, high water covers High Rocks, sending logs toward the 1903 railroad bridge.

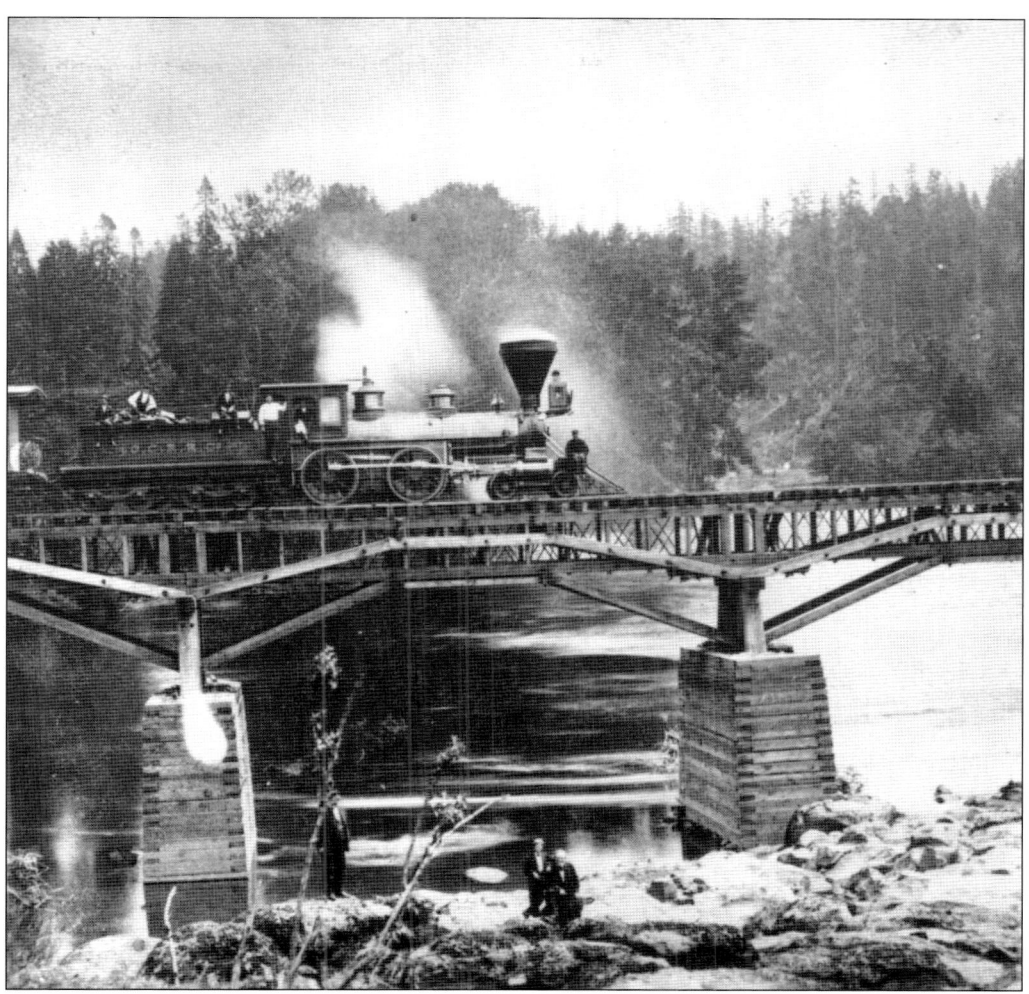

Public consensus was that the Clackamas River had beaten Ben Holladay. The lagging and somewhat directionless Westside OCR now built track with new confidence. But Holladay had a plan. Dividing his men into two groups, he ferried one crew and a locomotive across the Clackamas River to continue building track to Oregon City and beyond, while the other crew and locomotive remained behind to construct a new bridge. Working nonstop, a second railroad bridge was built on the same piers that had held the first bridge and was completed on Christmas Eve 1869. On Christmas Day, at 6:00 a.m., Holladay climbed aboard his locomotive, the *J.B. Stephens*, and triumphantly drove across the Clackamas River, pausing only long enough to have the event memorialized in this photograph. He then drove on to New Era and the victory celebration that awaited him. Holladay is believed to be the man standing in the engineer's window.

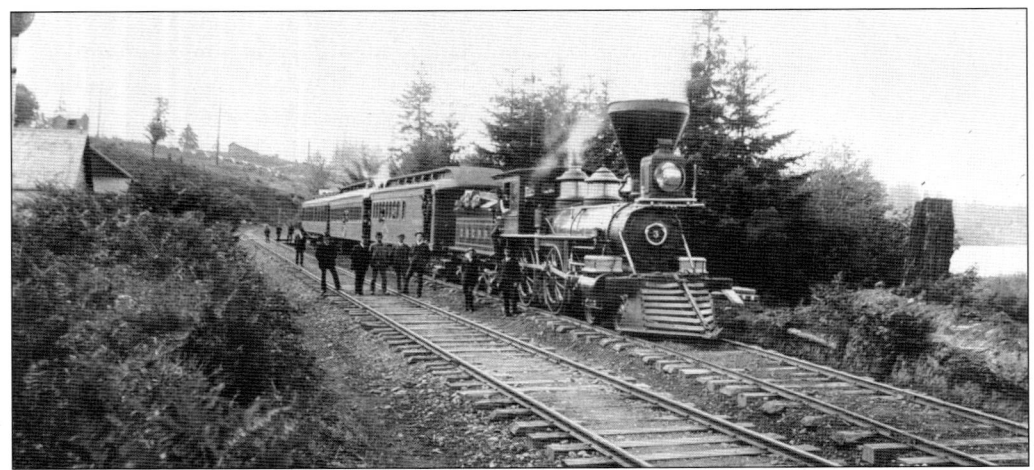

Once Ben Holladay was awarded the first allotment of land and the contract to build track to Sacramento, he bought the Westside OCR and merged it with the Eastside OCR to form the Oregon & California Railroad. In the early 1880s, an Oregon & California Railroad train sits on the track at New Era.

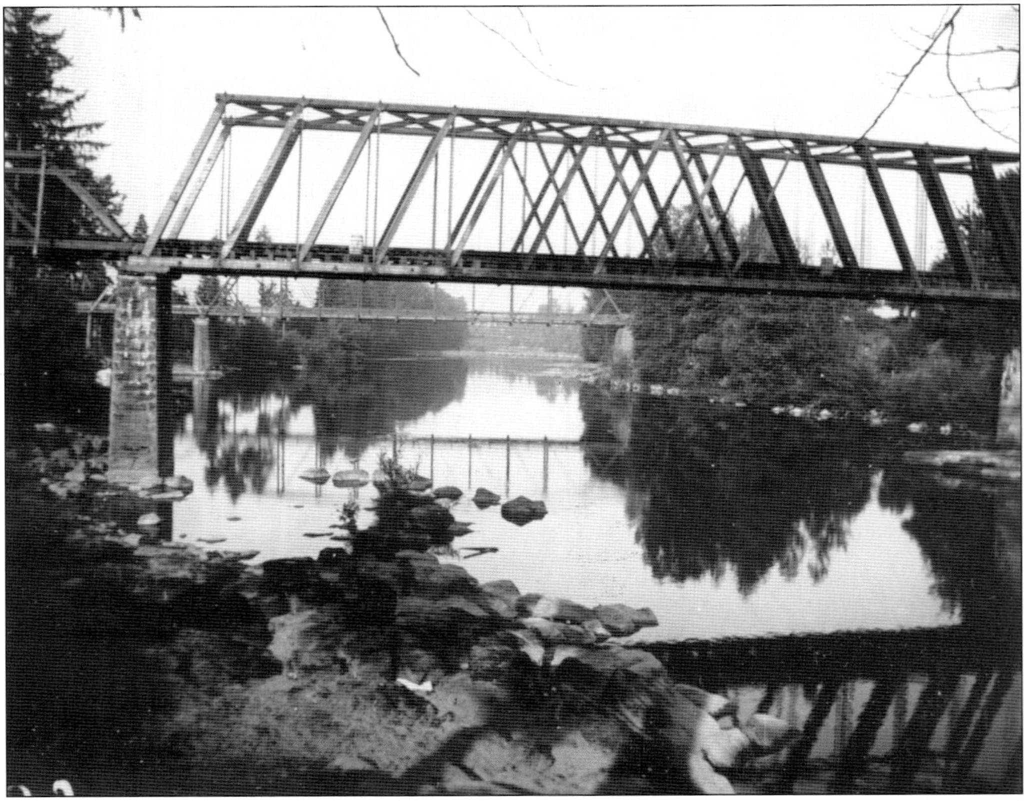

Ben Holladay's second railroad bridge nearly succumbed to an arsonist before being destroyed by the 1872 flood. Construction was then begun on a third railroad bridge at the same location. Shown here in 1895 facing west is railroad bridge No. 5. Because fires could start from wheel or smokestack sparks, water barrels were attached to the side of the bridge.

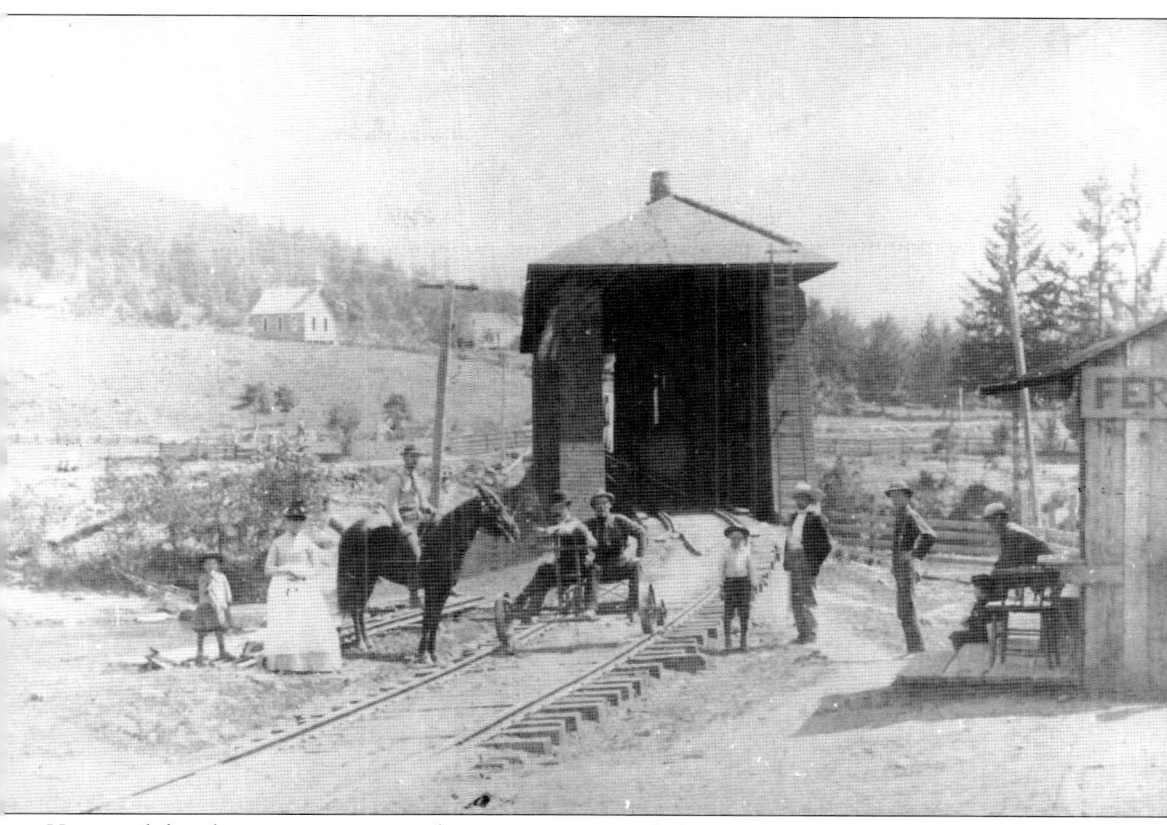

Historical details are sometimes confusing concerning Gladstone's railroad bridges. Photograph dates and records do not always match. In 1873, local newspapers announced, "work finally beginning on new wood railroad bridge. Completion expected next October." By 1874, the bridge was completed and paid in full. Then, in July 1876, newspapers again announced, "work is to be commenced immediately on the new railroad bridge across the Clackamas." What happened to railroad bridge No. 3 is unknown. Most likely, a flood led to its early demise. Shown here in the late 1880s is railroad bridge No. 4, the first of two covered bridges across the Clackamas River at Gladstone. Also shown are members and friends of Judge Harvey Cross, Gladstone's founder. From left to right are Freddie Cross, Margaret Cross, Truman Cross (on the horse), Frank Cross, Elmer Cross, Davy Cross, Del Cross, Louie Himler, and Johnny Griner. The ferry, now owned by Harvey Cross, was kept for use when bridges were lost or under repair. In the left background is the First Congregational Church of Park Place. (GHS.)

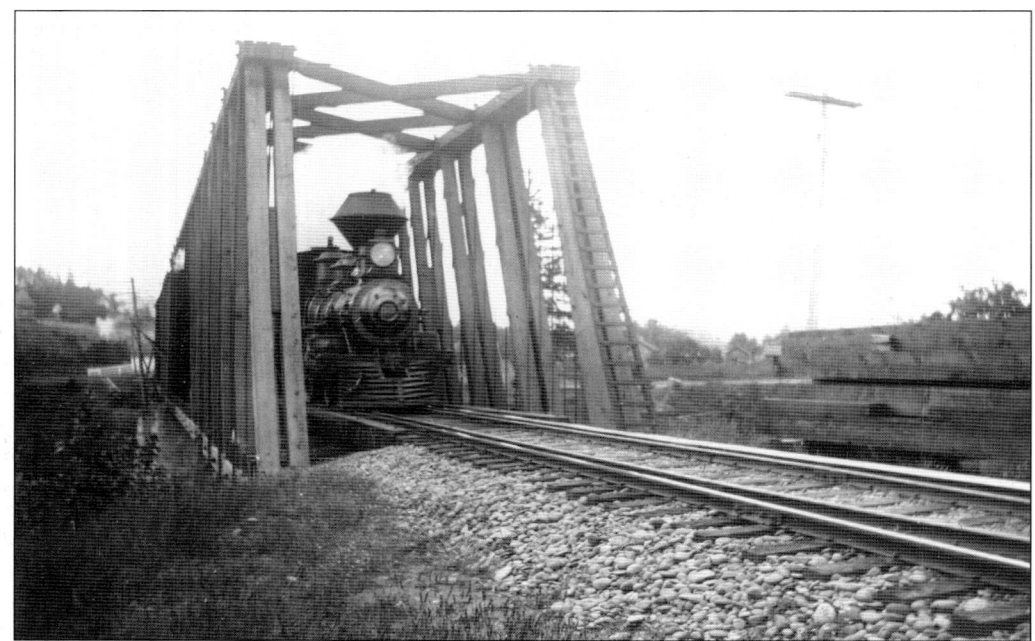

Covered railroad bridge No. 4 survived high water, assaults by river debris, two floods (one of which swept away the wagon bridge), and a windstorm that sent a tree crashing across one end. In 1892, railroad bridge No. 4 was replaced by railroad bridge No. 5, shown here in 1900 with a locomotive crossing it from Park Place into Gladstone.

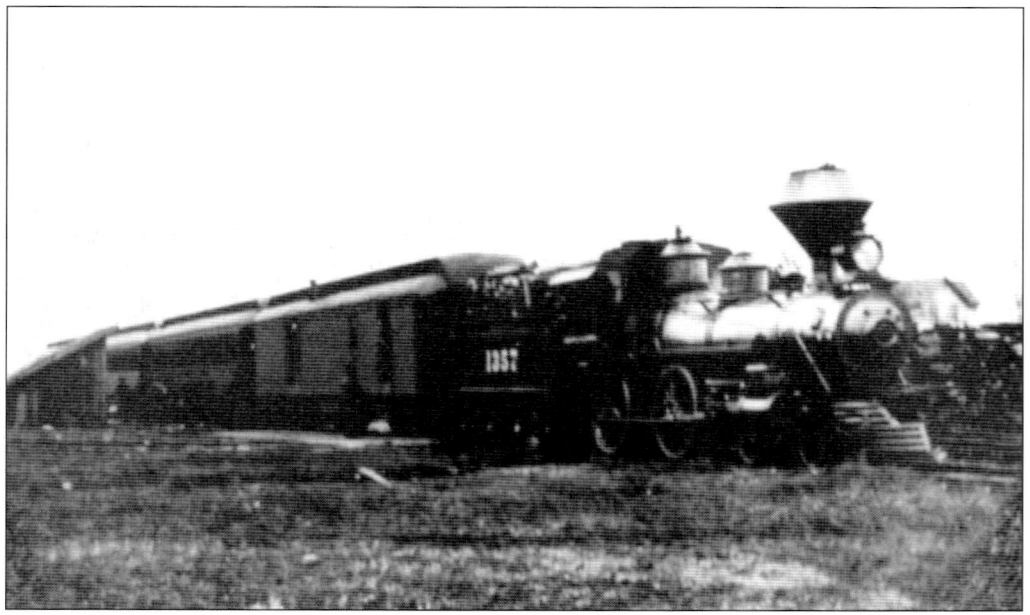

To accommodate Gladstone passengers, the Southern Pacific Railroad built a depot at the south end of Gladstone Park, near the present-day intersection of Arlington Street and Eighty-Second Drive. Seen here in 1895, a Southern Pacific train has stopped at the Gladstone (Chautauqua) Depot. To the left, passengers are buying tickets. To the right, the Cason house can be seen behind the engine.

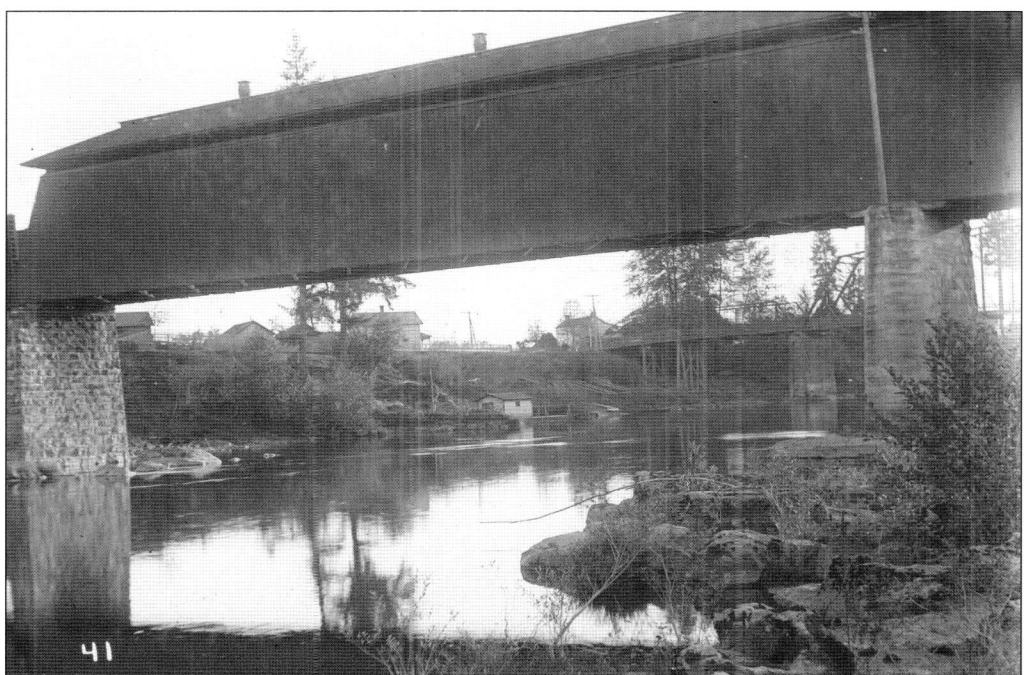

Railroad bridge No. 5 was covered sometime between 1893 and 1894, as shown here in 1895. The water barrels have been moved to the roof. In the background is Park Place, with an occupied houseboat floating along the Clackamas River's south bank. To the right is the 1892 wagon bridge.

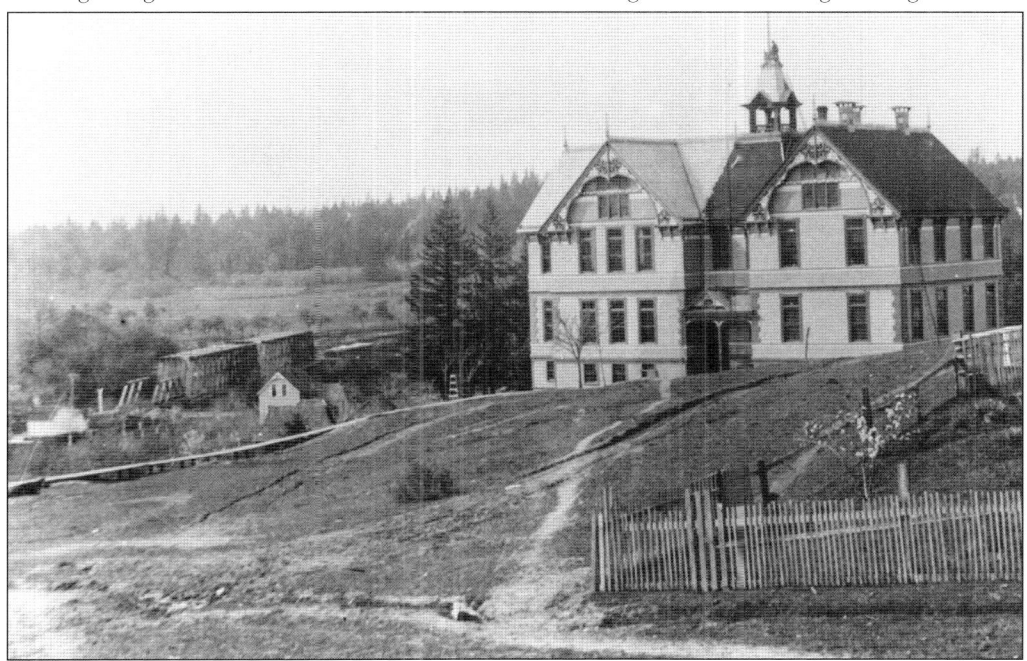

During the summer of 1903, railroad bridge No. 5 was removed and construction began on the all-new steel railroad bridge No. 6. To the left of the Park Place School displaying its newly added second wing is the new railroad bridge under construction. Gladstone is in the background.

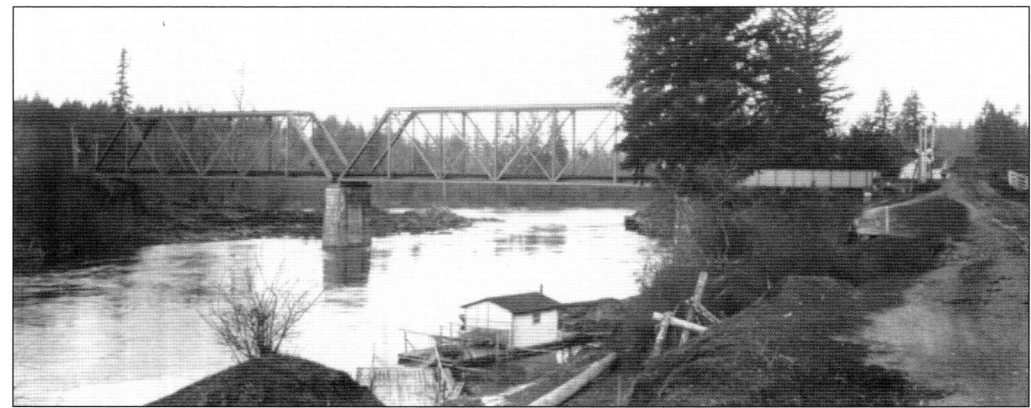

In 1907, the now-finished railroad bridge No. 6 was photographed from the south bank of the Clackamas River in Park Place. The pile of stones to the right of the bridge's central pier is one of two rubble piles that are the remains of the piers of Ben Holladay's first two railroad bridges.

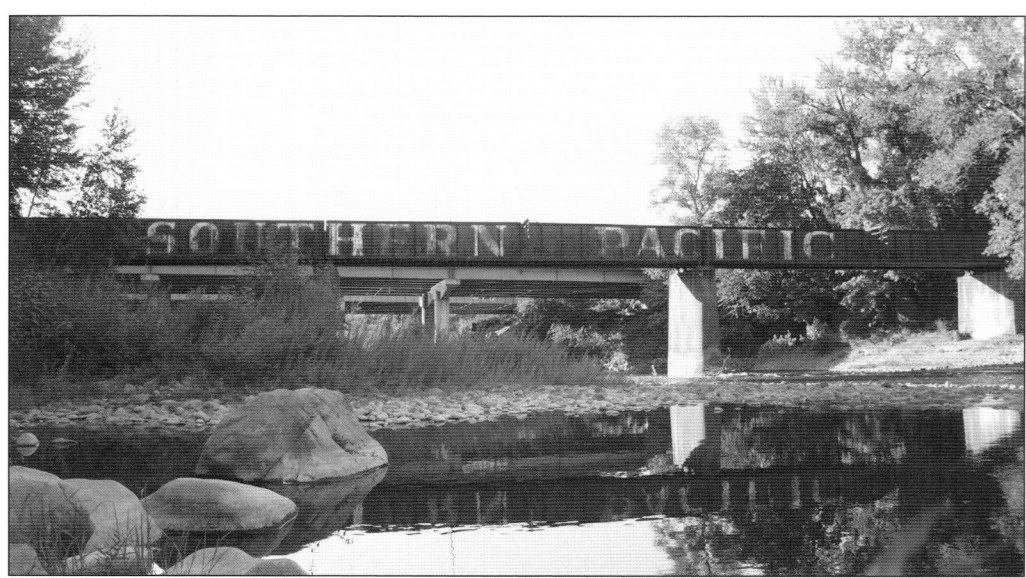

In 1955, during construction of Interstate 205 at the eastern edge of Gladstone, railroad bridge No. 6, after 22 years of use, was removed to make room for the two new automobile bridges. Railroad bridge No. 7 was then constructed 500 feet upstream from the previous location. The extra piers visible in the background belong to the two highway bridges. (Courtesy of Devon Huey.)

Six

Judge Harvey Cross, Gladstone's Founder

By the 1880s, the pioneer era was ending, and a modern age was arriving. Fendel Cason died in 1860, with Rebecca following in 1870. Jacob Hunsaker became a widower and moved to Woodburn, Oregon. Hiram Straight no longer acquired land and instead collected grandchildren—34 in all. Peter Rinearson mostly retired from farming, and Jacob Rinearson, after 20 years in the military, mustered out and settled near Rainier, Washington.

In 1883, Ad Cason was 54 years old and served as a Clackamas County commissioner in charge of supervising bridges. When his father died, as the oldest of the two remaining Cason children, he took control of the Cason land and resided in the family home for some time. What prompted him to start selling parcels of the family's acreage and move to Oregon City is unknown, but by 1888, Harvey Cross owned 400 acres of Cason land, the Cason house, and 60 acres of adjoining Rinearson land.

On June 3, 1889, the Willamette Falls Electric Company (WFEC) made history by producing the first long-distance transmission of electricity in the United States. Using old sawmill generators powered by the force of the Willamette Falls, the WFEC lit streetlights in Portland 14 miles away. The following November, Richmond, Virginia, also made history when electric trolley cars circulated through its neighborhoods. One year later, Portland also began operating a neighborhood street railway.

In 1893, history again was made when the East Side Electric Railway Company of Portland announced it would build the first interurban electric street railway in the United States and connect Portland to Oregon City.

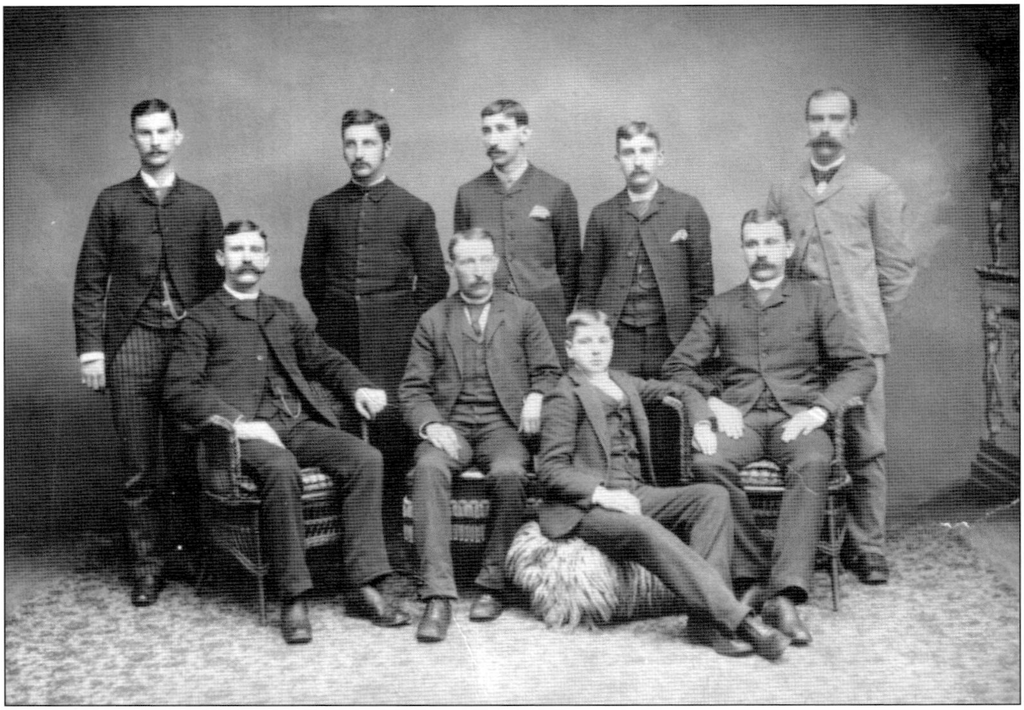

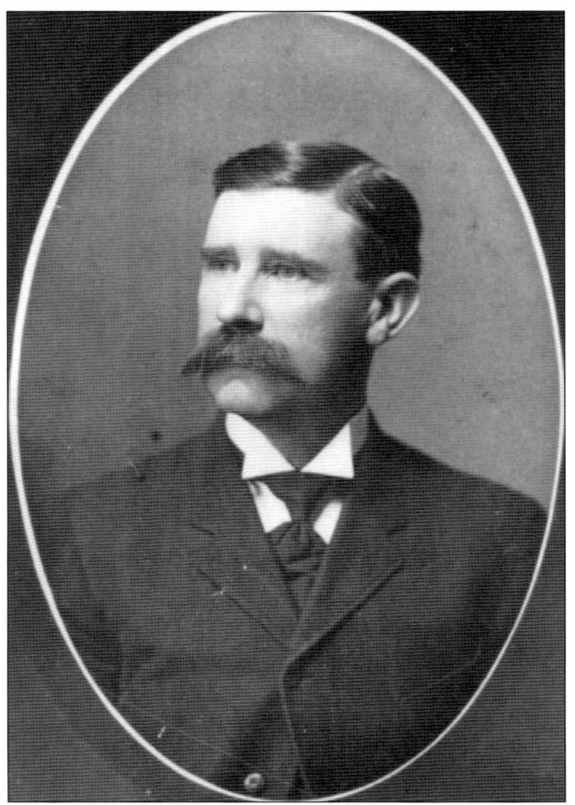

Born in 1856, in Canby, Oregon, Harvey E. Cross was the second oldest of 10 children. In 1862, the Cross family relocated to Oregon City, where Harvey's father, Lorenzo, died when Harvey was 16. A year later, Harvey's mother, Dorcas, married Charles Bolds, an adventurer with grown children. Together, Charles and Dorcas produced one son. At 18, Harvey graduated from school as a schoolteacher and began teaching in a one-room log cabin in the rural area of Sandy, Oregon. The mid-1880s photograph above shows the Cross-Bolds brothers. From left to right are (first row) Harvey, Caleb, Ed Bolds, and Mitt; (second row) Frank, Charles, Truman, Del, and Elmer. At left is Harvey Cross in about 1900. (Above, courtesy of Diane Nickerson Timmons.)

Harvey Cross taught school for two years before exploring other careers, which included recording mortgages in the Clackamas County clerk's office, serving as a deputy sheriff, collecting tolls on the Barlow Road, and studying law. In 1879, Cross passed the bar, opened a law office in Oregon City, and met 18-year-old Orpha Tingle. They were married five months later. At right, Orpha Tingle is shown at about the time she married Harvey Cross. In 1883, Cross began acquiring parcels of Cason land and soon afterward moved his family into the Cason house. Shown below are the members of the Cross family. From left to right are (first row) Frances, Harvey, Stella, and Orpha; (second row, standing) Georgiana, Marceline, Percy, Mable, and Juliette. (Both, courtesy of Diane Nickerson Timmons.)

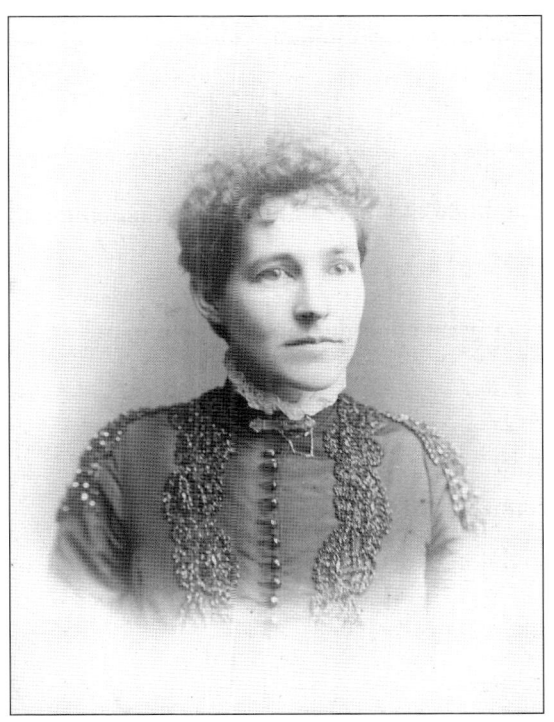

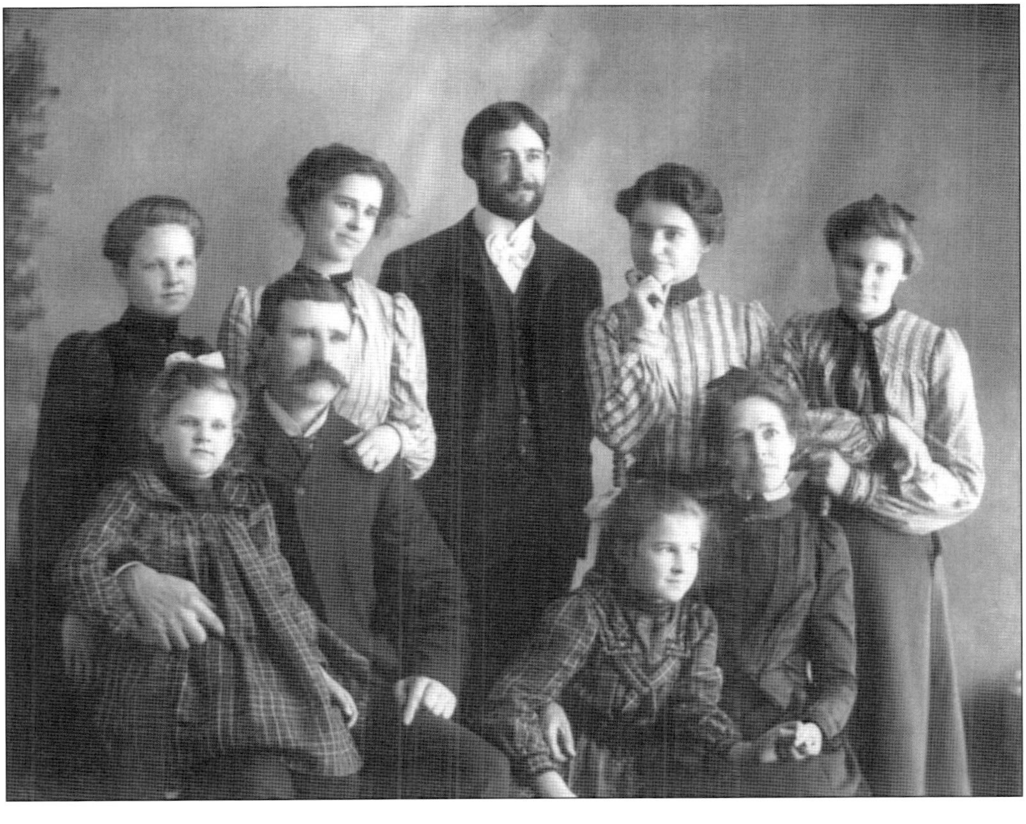

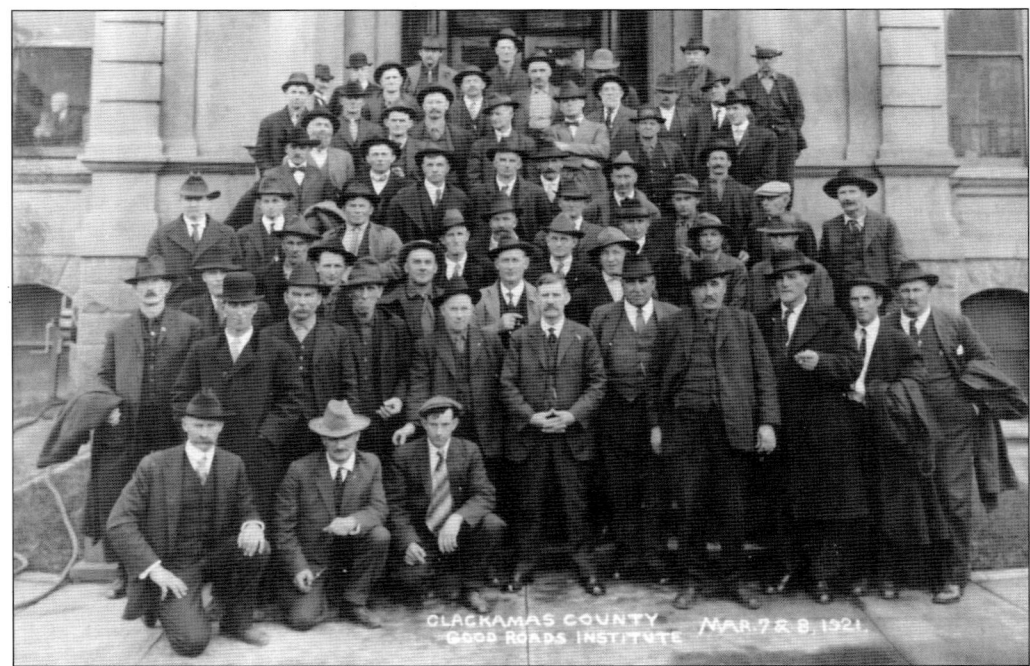

Harvey Cross's professional life was varied and eventful. Besides practicing law, he served as city attorney for Oregon City, treasurer for Clackamas County, and a term in both the state senate and state legislature. While in state congress, he crusaded to create the position of state attorney general, and in 1886, helped found the Clackamas County Board of Trade. In 1920, Cross became a prominent member of the Good Roads Program, which resulted in paving 250 miles of Clackamas County roadway. He is seen above standing in the front row, sixth from the left. In 1920, Cross was elected Clackamas County judge. Seen below in 1890 is the Clackamas County Court House in Oregon City, where Cross heard cases. (Below, SLO.)

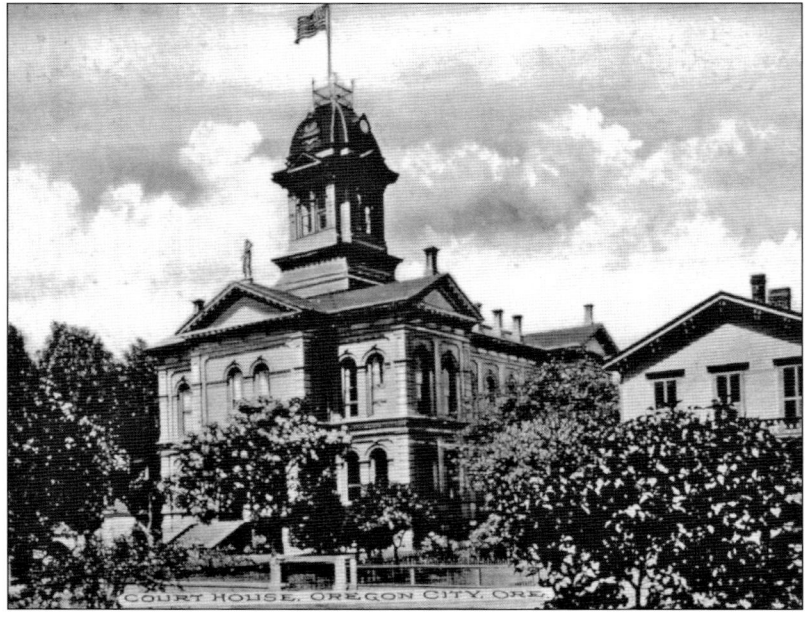

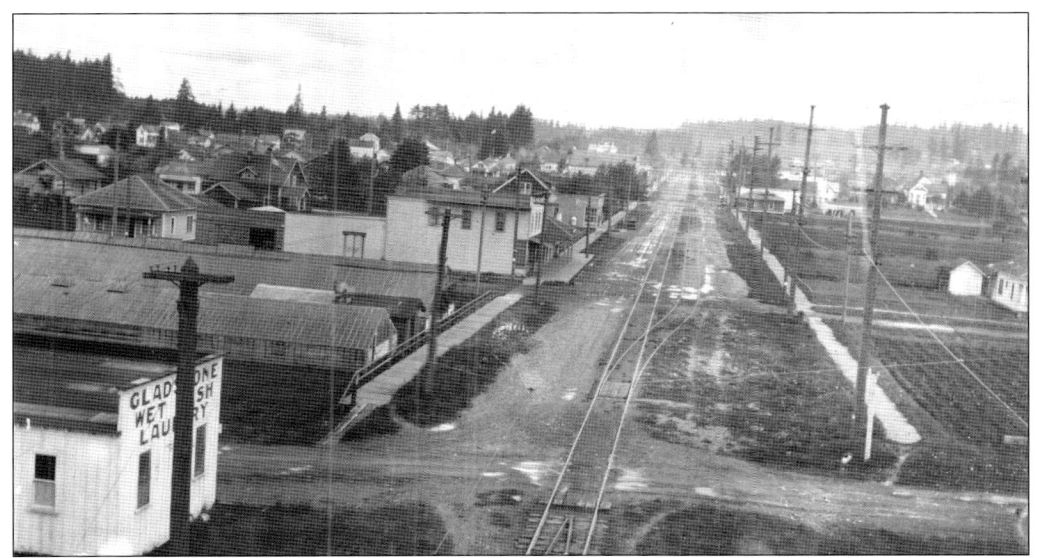

When the Eastside Electric Railway Company (EERC) announced plans to construct the first electric railway between Portland and Eugene, Harvey Cross worked tirelessly to convince the EERC to build the line through Gladstone. Above, in the early 1920s, trolley tracks can be seen running north on Portland Avenue, Gladstone's main street. On the right side of Portland Avenue, at Dartmouth Street, the small dark building is the 1907 Gladstone trolley depot that replaced the original 1893 depot. On February 16, 1893, the interurban trolley made its first round trip from Portland to Oregon City. Met by a cheering crowd when it entered Gladstone, the trolley then proceeded on to Oregon City, as shown below, pulling its passenger car filled with dignitaries across the new Clackamas River trolley bridge.

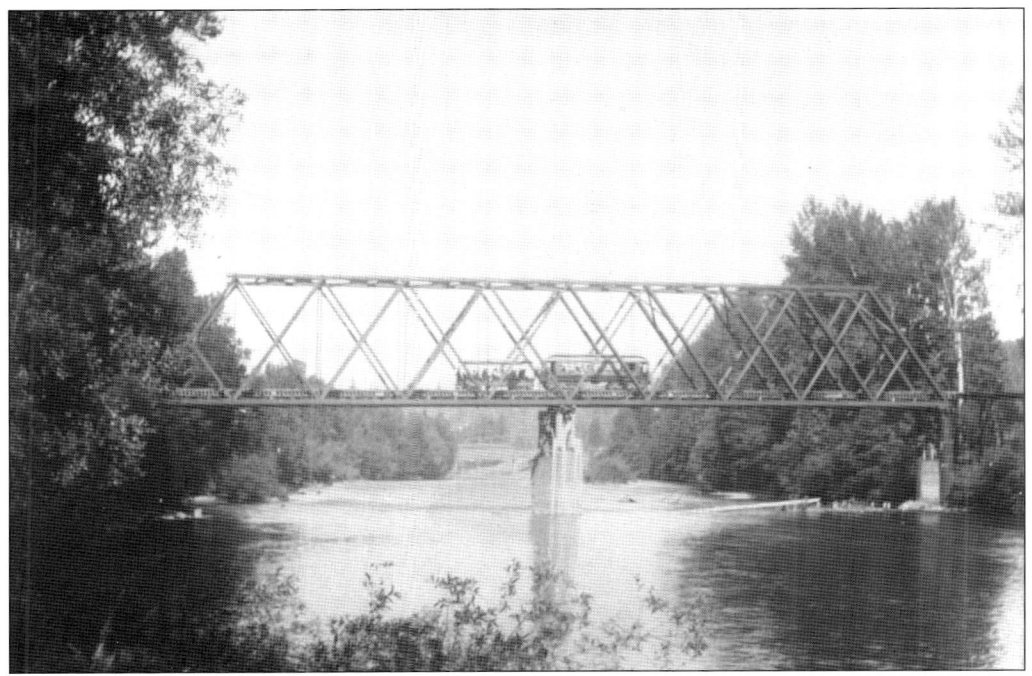

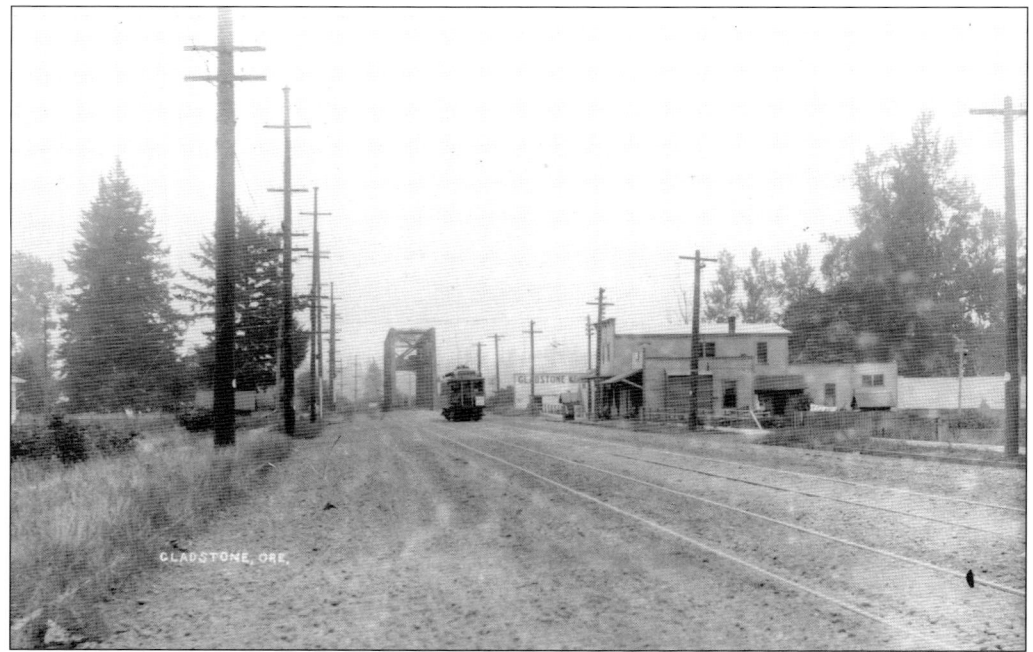

The ESRC made history again when it built its interurban tracks to railroad standards. Now, both trolleys and steam locomotives could use the same tracks. In 1894, shipping goods between towns by trolley became so popular that to accommodate all the loads, the ESRC built 20-ton freight cars that resembled boxcars. The new freight cars made deliveries along the trolley tracks, leaving packages at depots, along the roadway, and even on nearby doorsteps. Above, in 1910, a trolley hurries down Portland Avenue on its way to Oregon City. Notice the passenger waiting on the bridge. Below, in 1910, this trolley is either a freight car stopping for a delivery or a service car checking the tracks. Both sights were common.

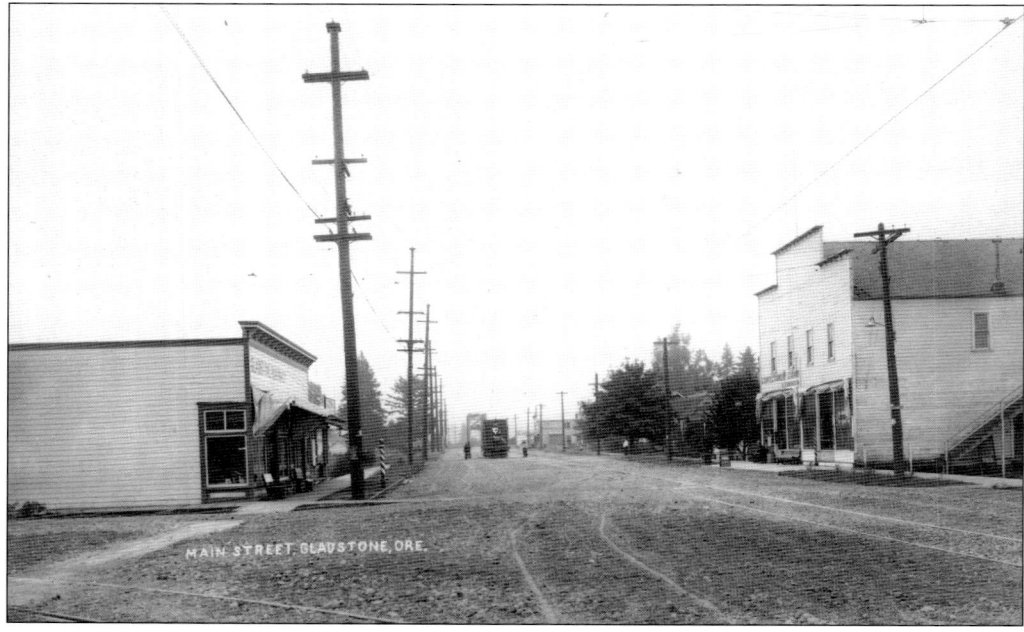

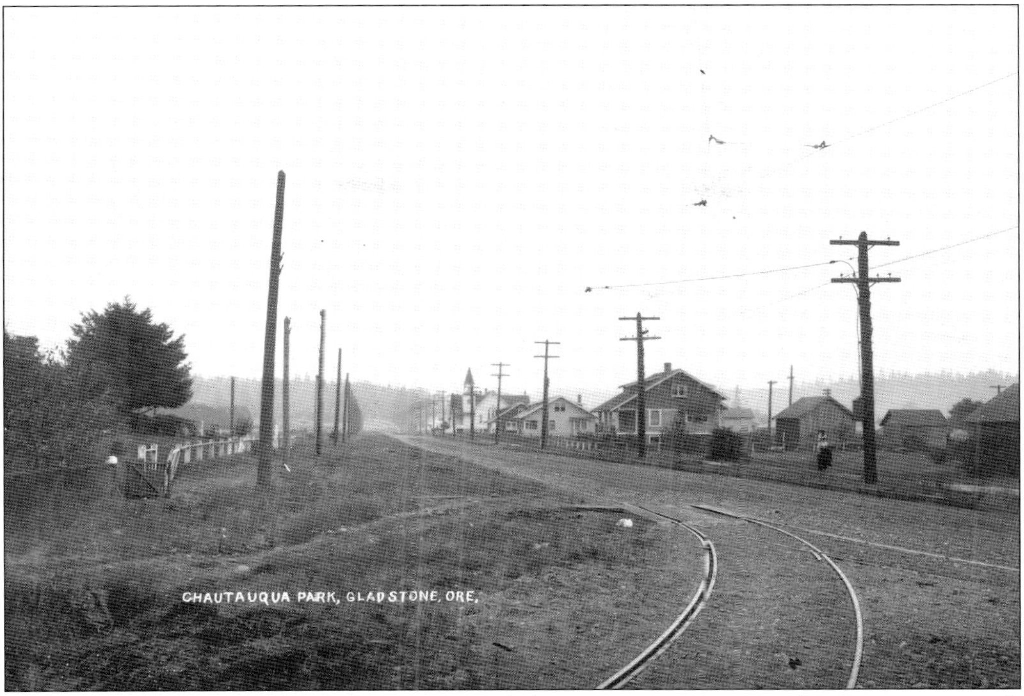

CHAUTAUQUA PARK, GLADSTONE, ORE.

Two weeks after the start of trolley service in Gladstone, Harvey Cross made an agreement with the ESRC to run a trolley car into Gladstone Park. Grading East Dartmouth Street 80 feet wide, so it could accommodate both wagon traffic and a trolley, Cross laid three quarters of a mile of track from Portland Avenue up the length of East Dartmouth Street, across Oatfield Road, and inside the main entrance of Gladstone Park. The track ended at a 300-foot-long platform above the Chautauqua athletic field. Above, in 1911, the trolley track turns east from Portland Avenue onto Dartmouth Street. In the background is the 1912 Gladstone Christian Church. Below, in 1915, the trolley tracks disappear under the closed gates of Gladstone Park.

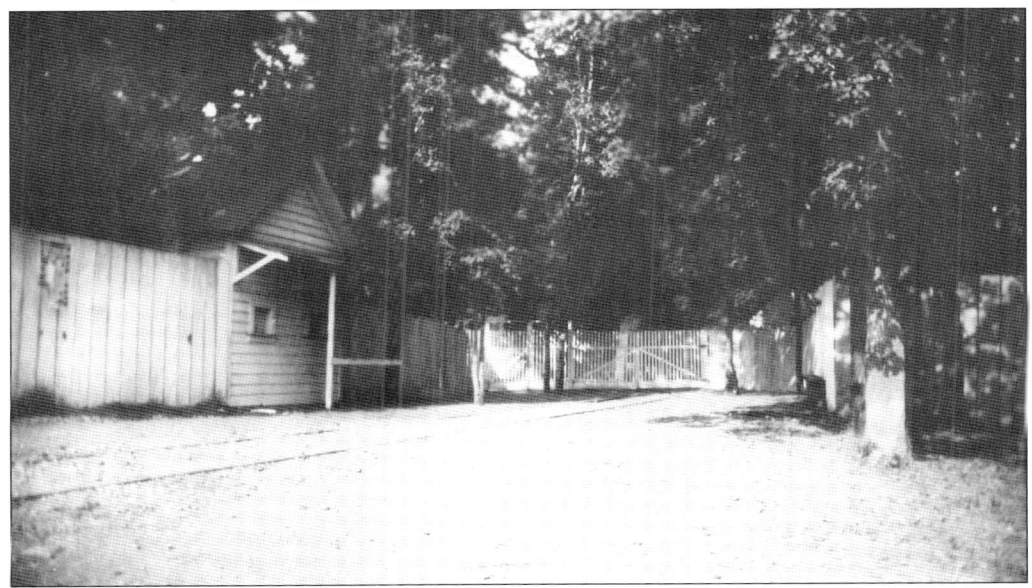

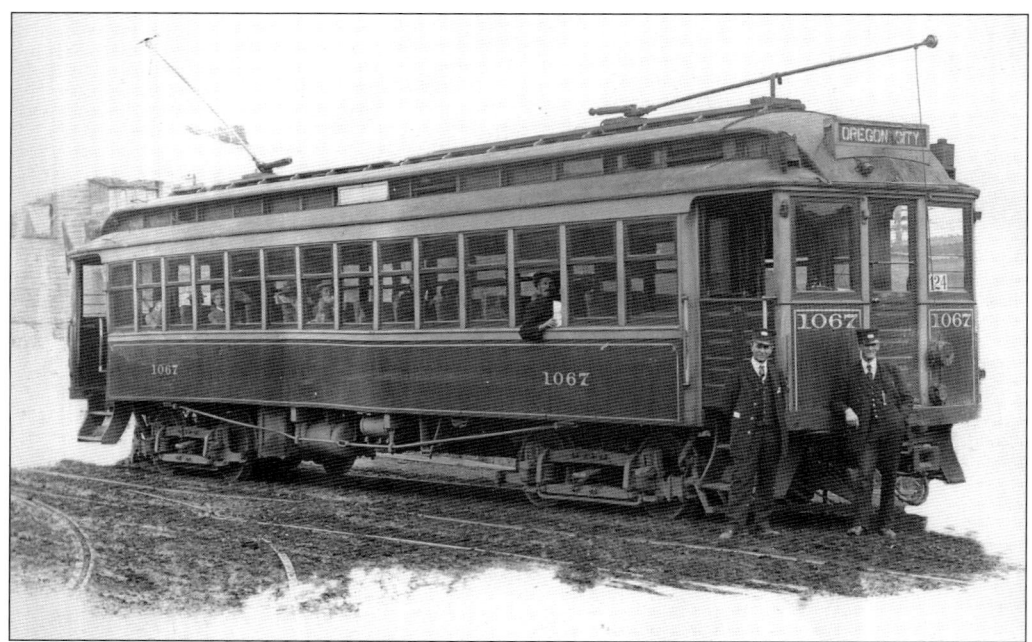

The park trolley ran seasonally and as required for events taking place in Gladstone Park. When in service, the trolley made hourly trips between the park and Oregon City, charging 2.5¢ for a one-way trip. A usual trolley ride lasted six to ten minutes. However, because events at Gladstone Park created excessive passenger loads for the regular trolley service, the park trolley also picked up and delivered regular passengers along its way. Above, in 1897, a trolley stops in Gladstone on its way from Portland to Oregon City. When not in service, the park trolley was kept in a car barn inside Gladstone Park, as shown below in 1895.

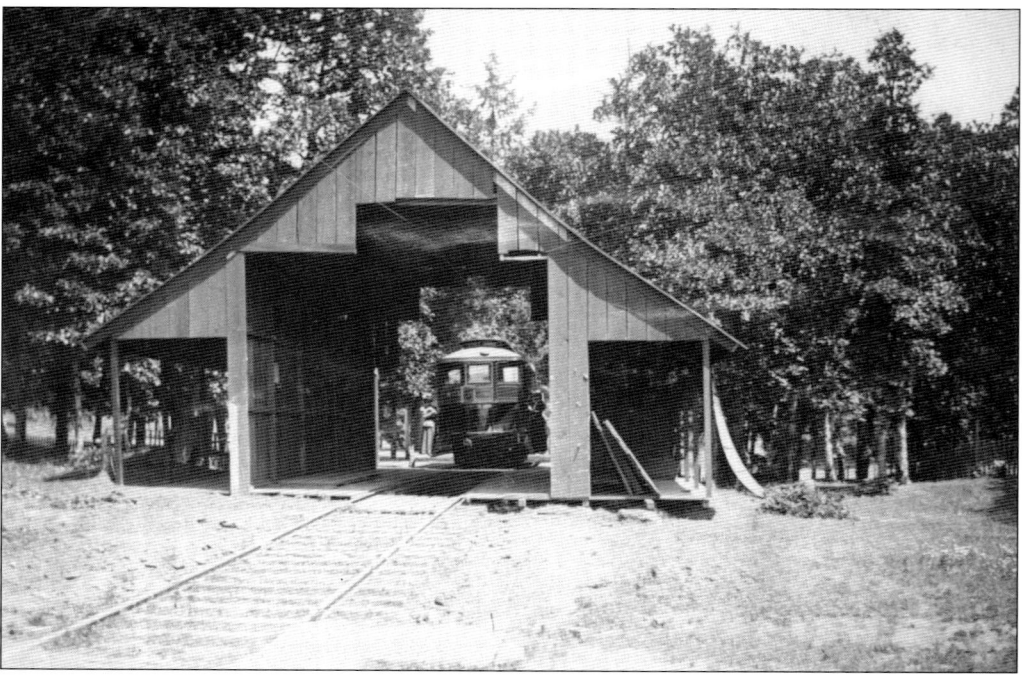

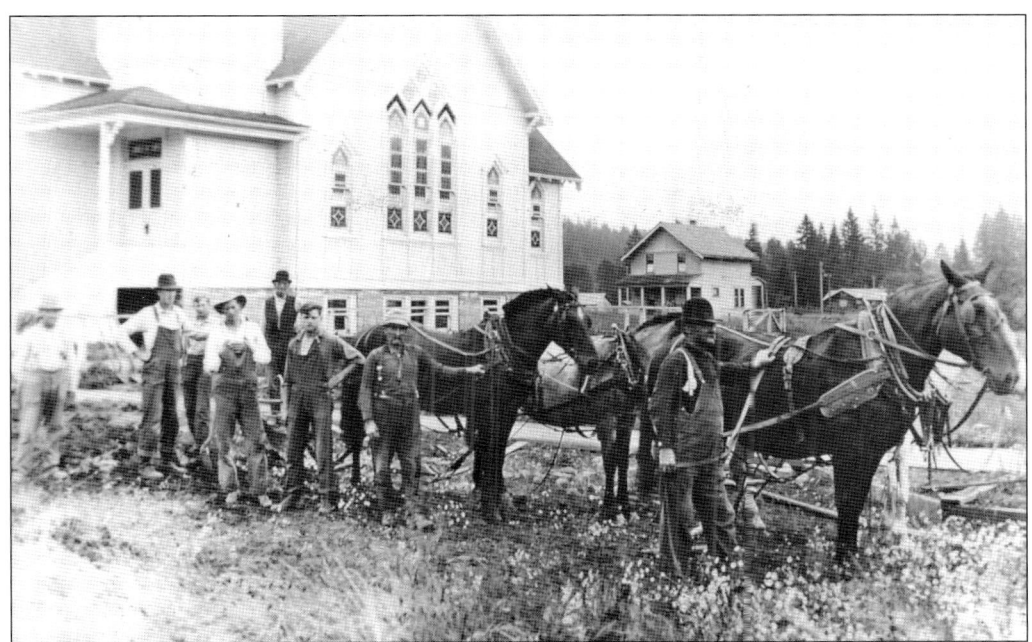

Because of the popularity of Chautauqua and other events held in Gladstone Park, some trolleys arrived at the Dartmouth Depot towing as many as two extra cars filled with passengers. There, a full and waiting park trolley would hook on the extra cars and tow the entire load to Gladstone Park. Above, in 1919, men from the Gladstone Christian Church plow Dartmouth Street, not only to improve the roadway in front of the church but also to make lanes for both wagons and automobiles on either side of the trolley track. Fred Haywood is third from left. Below, Gladstone Park's trolley ran from 1893 to 1901 and from 1907 into the 1930s. In the 1970s, the trolley tracks were removed from Dartmouth Street.

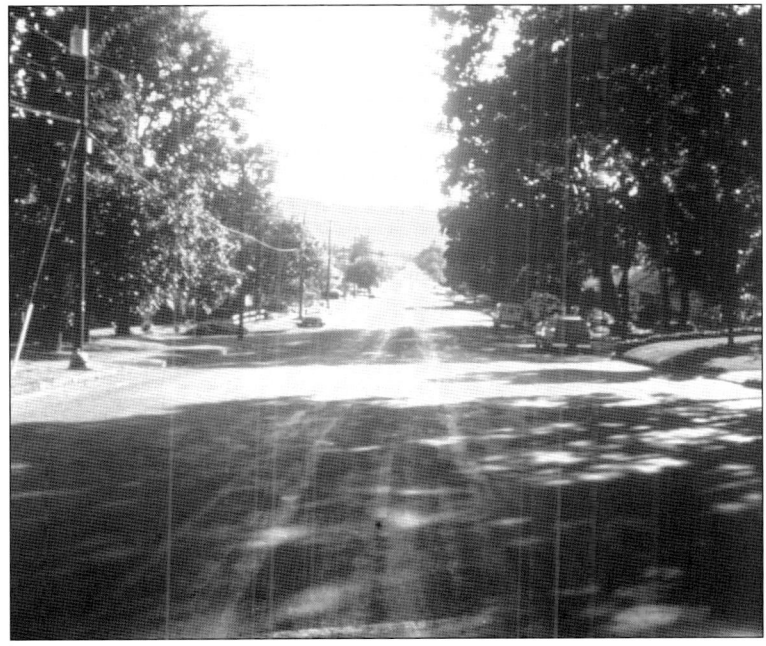

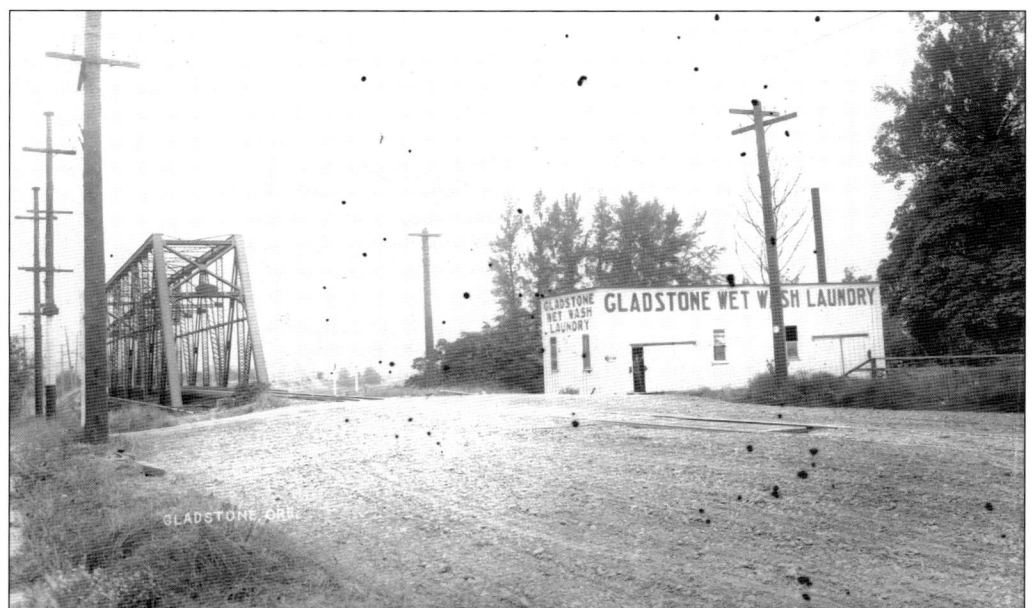

A flood in 1907 seriously damaged the 1893 trolley bridge. Even though the bridge was repaired, its reliability was questioned. In 1908, the first trolley bridge was taken down and a new one was built at the same location. Seen here in 1912 is the second trolley bridge.

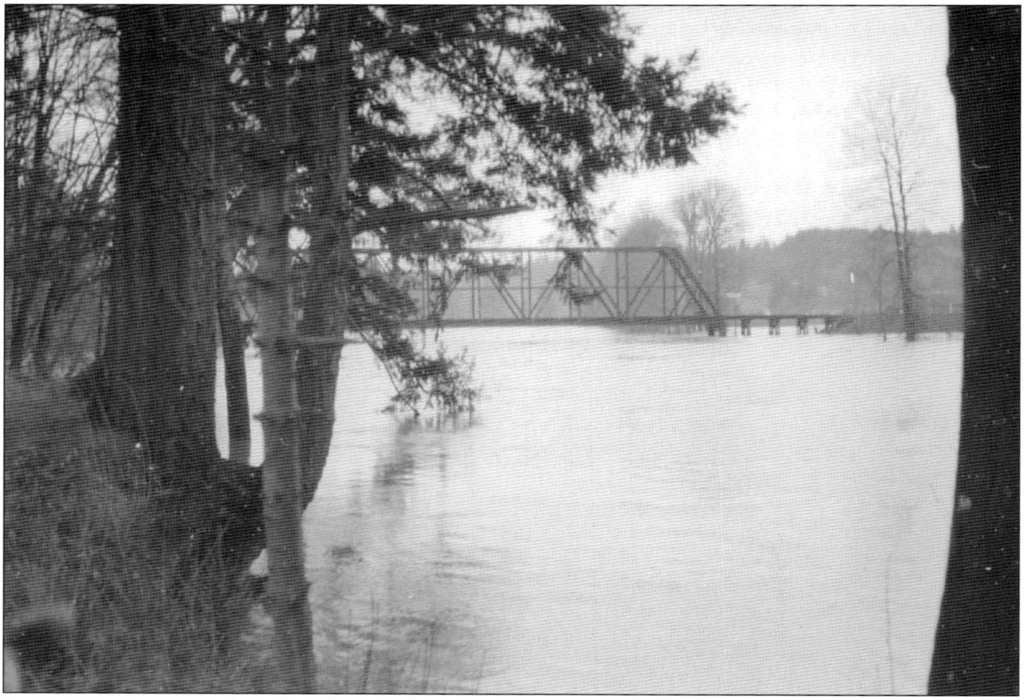

During the 1921 flood, the second trolley bridge nearly went underwater. The water came so close to the tracks that trolley personnel thought the bridge unsafe to use. Men needing to go to work in the Oregon City mills crossed the Clackamas River in rowboats until the water went down. Park Place can be seen in the background.

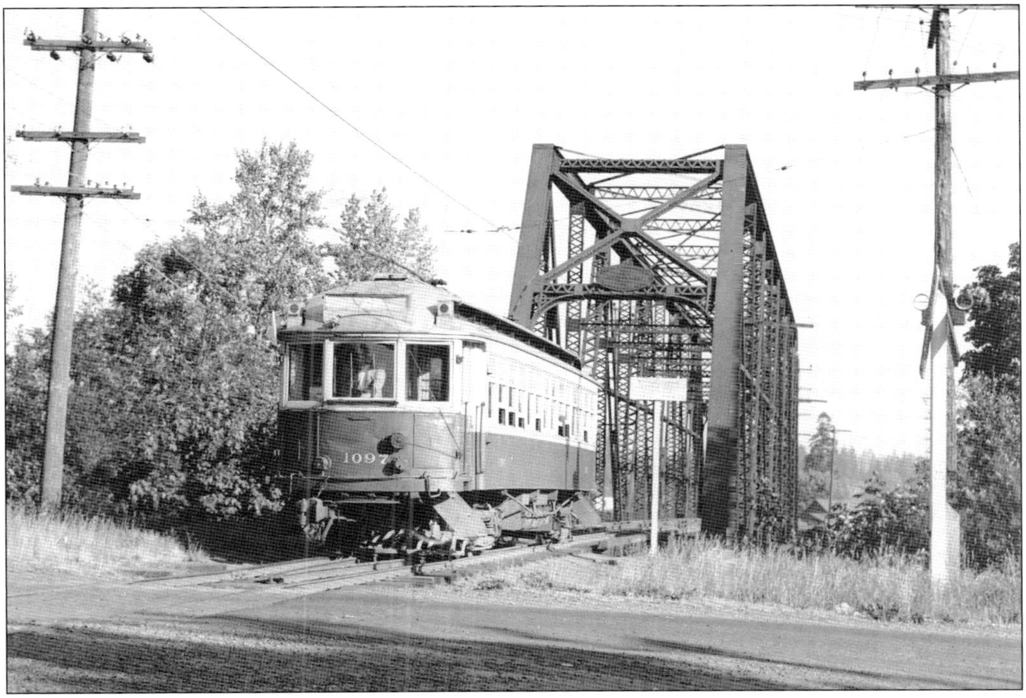

Beginning in the late 1880s, the paper and woolen mills at Willamette Falls in Oregon City were the largest employers in the surrounding area, and most employees rode the trolley to work. However, by the 1920s, cars and buses were gaining in popularity. Bus stops were replacing trolley depots, and parking spaces were taking over roadways. While passenger numbers dwindled on other interurban lines, the Oregon City cars stayed full. For years, Gladstone residents relied on the trolley as a valuable means of transportation. Above, in the late 1920s–early 1930s, a trolley arrives in Gladstone from Oregon City. By the 1940s, trolleys resembled buses in shape and size (below).

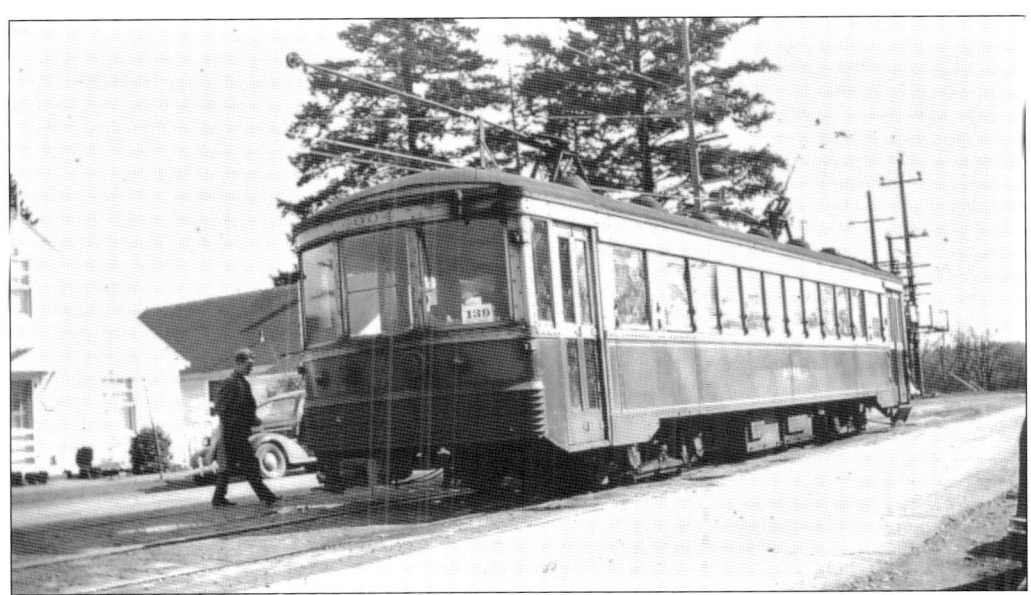

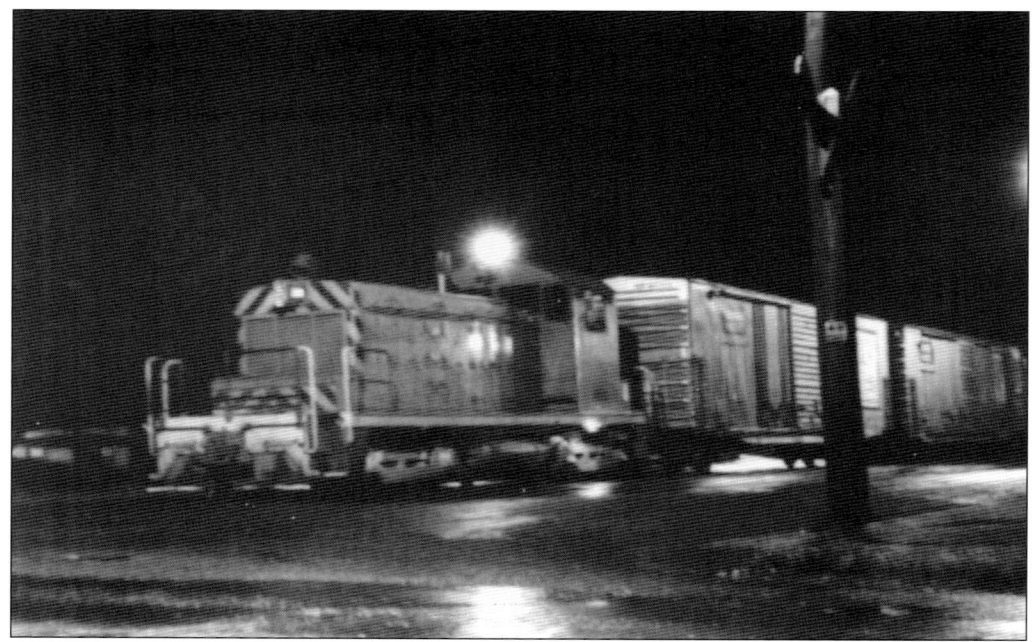

The Portland–Oregon City trolley made its final run on January 25, 1958. Unlike the park trolley, its tracks were not abandoned. The Portland Traction Company (PTC) began using the tracks for a regular nightly freight run from Portland to the paper mill in Oregon City. In 1968, the current owner of the trolley tracks, Southern Pacific Railroad, declared the Gladstone trolley bridge unsafe and not cost effective to replace. Mill deliveries were shifted to Southern Pacific freights, and the trolley bridge's tracks were removed. Above, the last freight train to come through Gladstone is shown on the night of its last run. In 2014, the 1908 trolley bridge began pulling away from its bank and was removed. (Above, courtesy of Oregon Pacific Railroad, Richard Samuels Collection; below, courtesy of Devon Huey.)

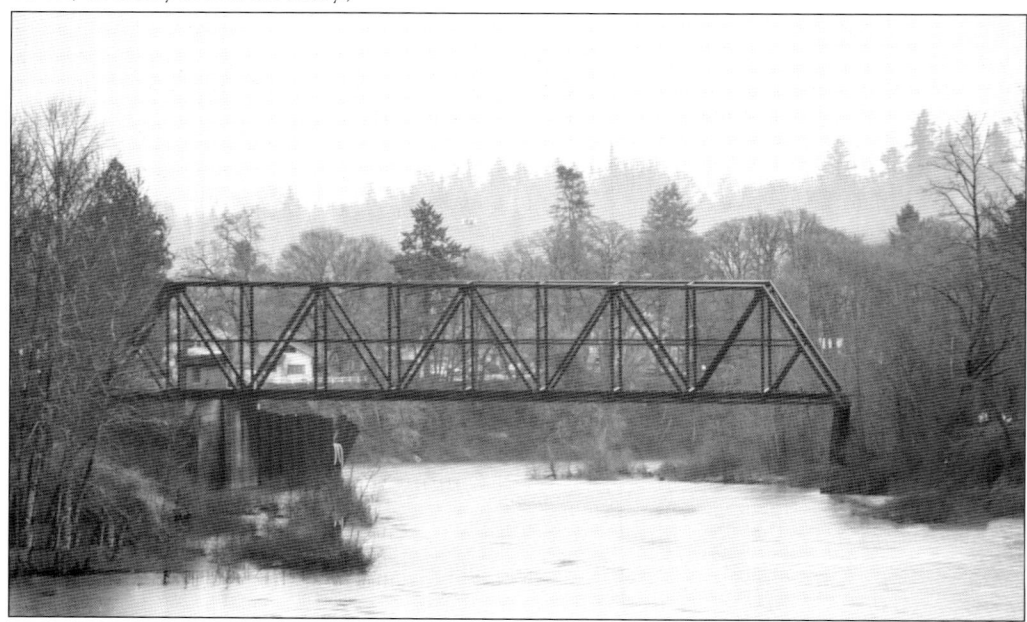

Seven

The Coming of Chautauqua

After its humble beginning as an outdoor Bible camp beside a quiet lake, the "Mother Chautauqua" in New York quickly grew to the size and structure of a university campus. Thousands came to partake of the "Four Es" that most benefitted the whole person: Education, Exercise, Evangelism, and Entertainment.

With more and more towns holding "Daughter Chautauquas," Rev. John Heyl Vincent, the founder of Chautauqua, determined that the general population of America must be eager for higher education. In 1878, he introduced a four-year home reading course called the Chautauqua Literary & Scientific Circle. Study materials were sent regularly by mail, after which students met in groups and discussed the reading assignments. At the end of four years, all students who had fulfilled the reading requirements were awarded a Chautauqua diploma.

In the early 1890s, Eva Emery Dye started a Chautauqua reading circle in her Oregon City home and soon became convinced that the community would welcome a Chautauqua. For some towns, Chautauqua was a circus tent pitched in a farmer's field where lectures were given by a local expert. For other towns, Chautauqua was a campground with a permanent auditorium and camping facilities. In 1894, Eva and Charles Dye, along with their friend Harvey Cross, formed the Willamette Valley Chautauqua Association, with Cross leasing Gladstone Park to the association for $1 per year.

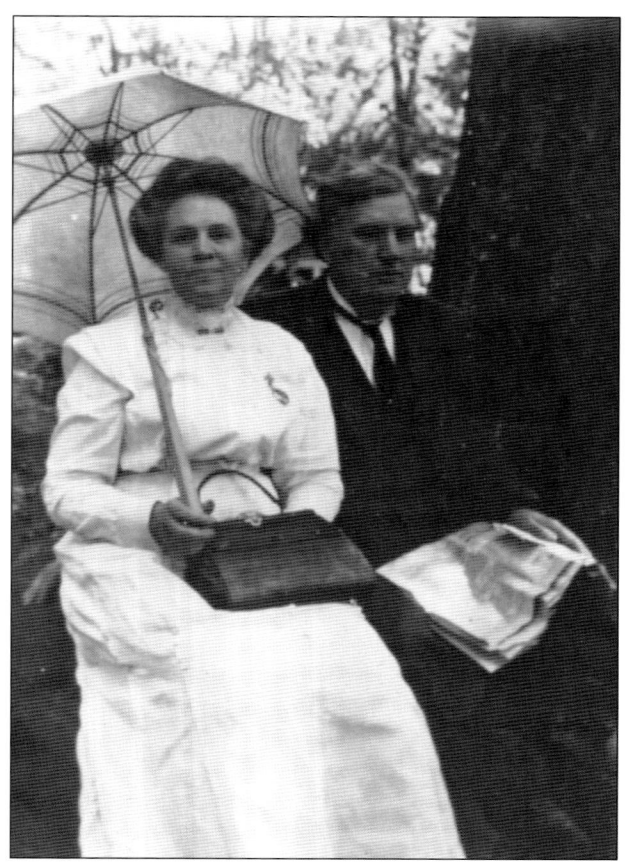

Eva Emery, born in 1856, and Charles Dye, born in 1855, met while both were attending Oberlin College in Ohio. Following graduation, they married and moved to Iowa, where both taught school for six years. In 1888, Charles returned to college and completed his law studies, after which the Dyes moved to Oregon City. While Charles built a thriving real estate and contract law practice, Eva devoted her time to raising four children and writing historical novels. At left, Charles and Eva Emery Dye are shown in 1900. Below, in 1900, Charles stands in front of his Oregon City law office.

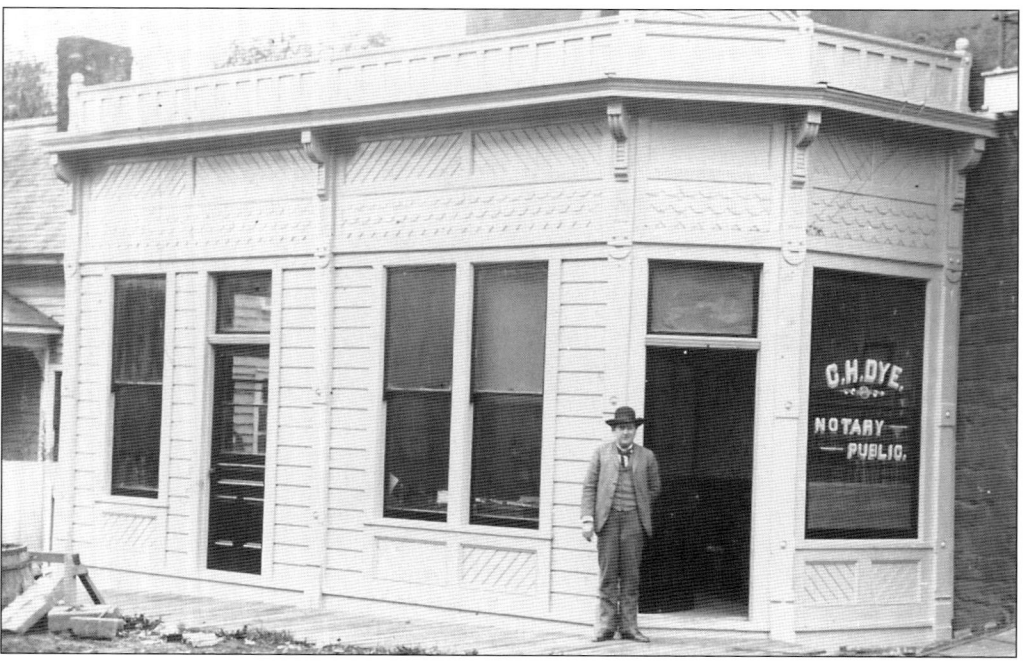

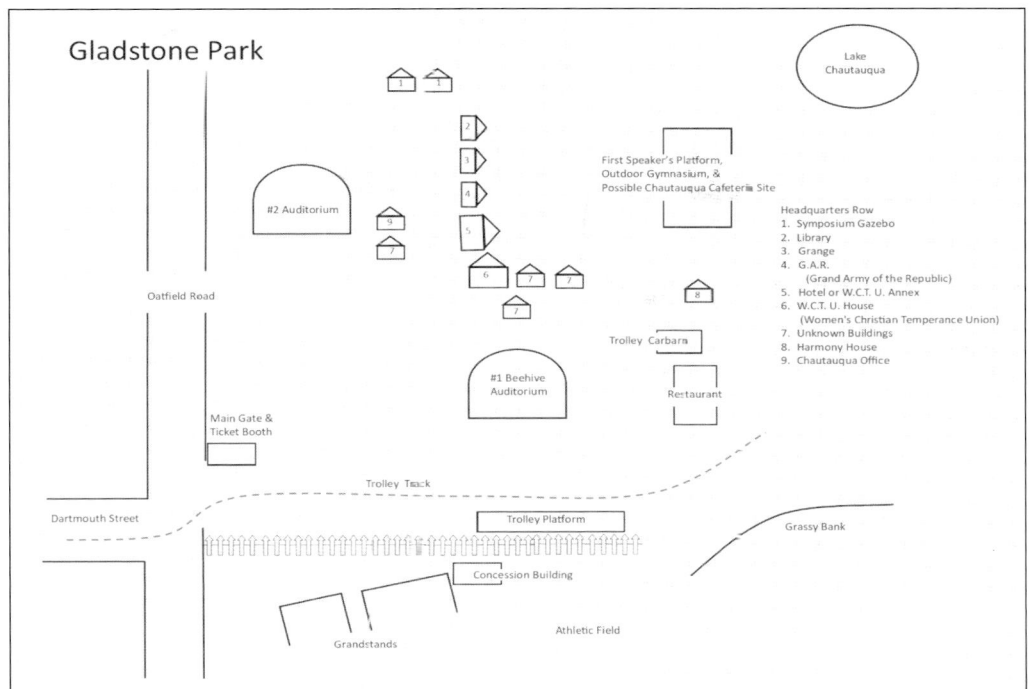

For the first Chautauqua, Gladstone Park had few amenities to offer. Each year, more conveniences and services were added until Gladstone Park became an event center that was ahead of its time. This map shows the layout of Gladstone Park during the Chautauqua years. (KAH.)

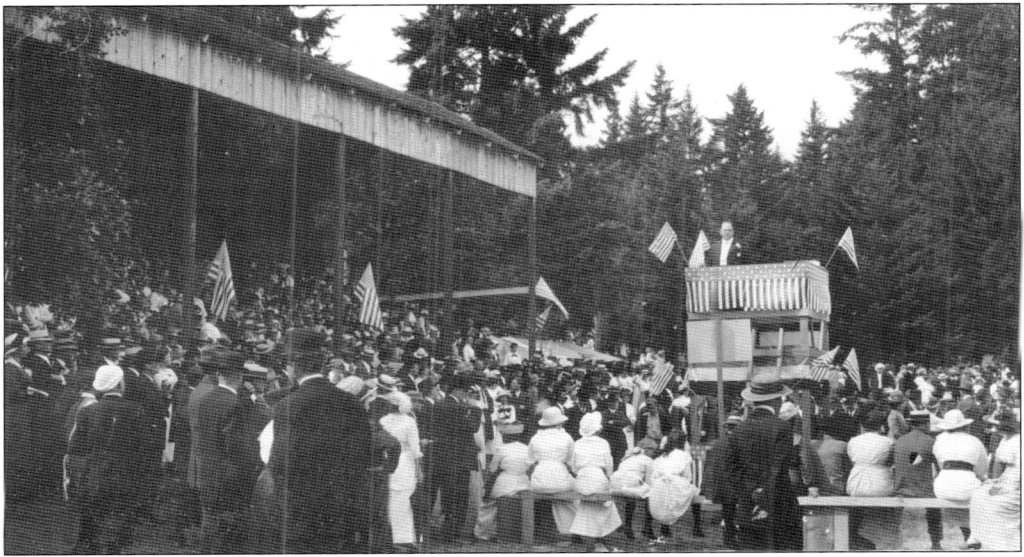

The first Chautauqua was held July 24–26, 1894, at a location near the lake, after which the lake became officially known as Lake Chautauqua. On opening night, all 1,000 seats surrounding the flag-draped speaker's platform were completely filled. This 1914 photograph of the Willamette Pulp and Paper Mill's Fourth of July celebration in Gladstone Park is reminiscent of the first Chautauqua.

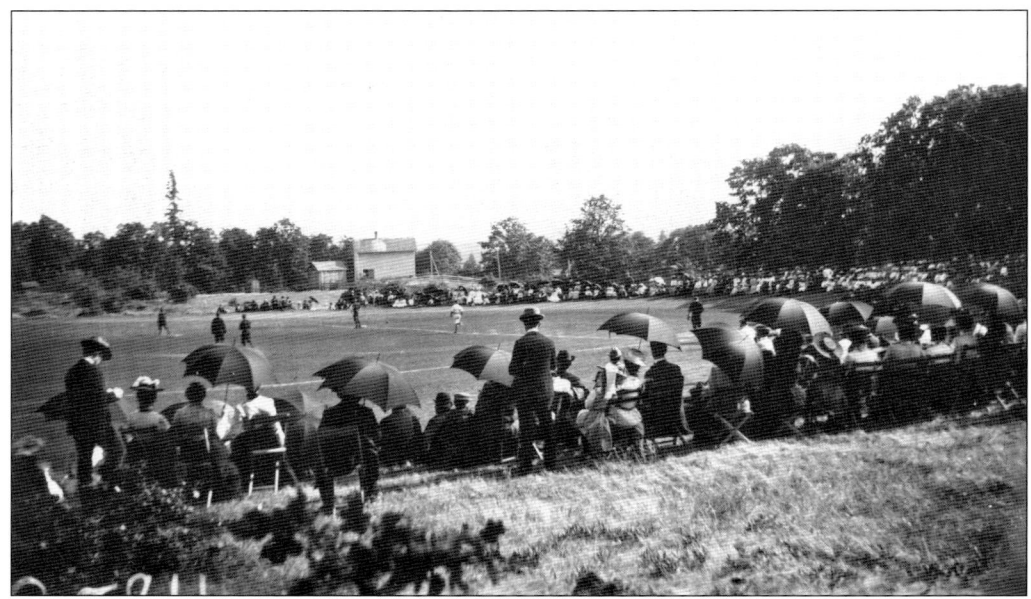

At the first Chautauqua, according to Eva Emery Dye, Dr. George A. Wallace gave the opening lecture on the 15th-century priest Savonarola. Mid-presentation, a downpour began. Asking the crowd if he should stop speaking, Dr. Wallace was unanimously urged to go on. The crowd then put up their umbrellas and continued to listen. Seen here in 1907, a crowd watches a Chautauqua baseball game from beneath umbrellas.

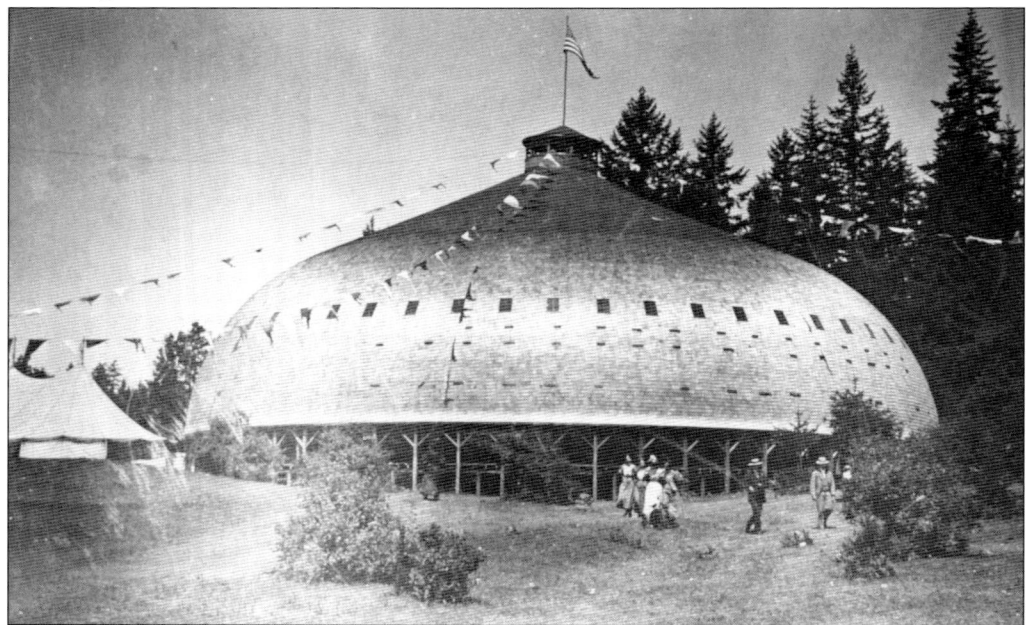

Over 3,500 people attended the first Chautauqua. Immediately, plans were made to hold another assembly the next year and to erect an open-air auditorium. Nicknamed "the Beehive" because of its unique shape, the auditorium, as shown here in 1895, accommodated 3,000 under its roof and an equal number around the outside. The auditorium was finished only moments before the first speaker stepped to the podium.

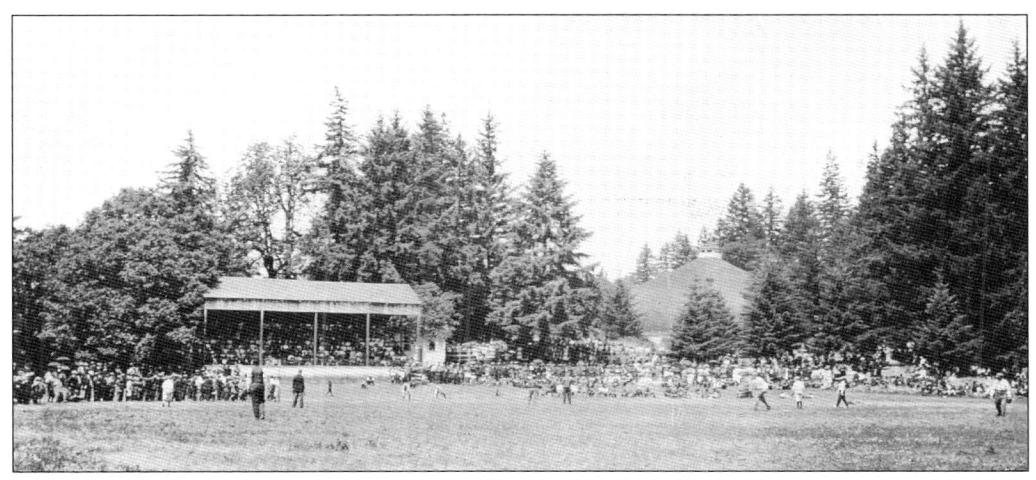

These two photographs show the area of Gladstone Park where Chautauqua activities first took place. Above, in 1911, a baseball game is played on the athletic field. To the far left of the 1904 grandstand and behind the trees is the main gate. In the center, a concession building sits beside the fence that lines the trolley platform. Next is the auditorium, and to the far right, behind the trees, is the restaurant. Below, in 1955, Gladstone Park's main gate is seen from Oatfield Road. The two large white buildings at center are the now-enclosed grandstands. At far left, the restaurant sits in the trees. To the right is a later bus stop with a strip of athletic field to its right. The Beehive is no longer standing. (Below, KAH.)

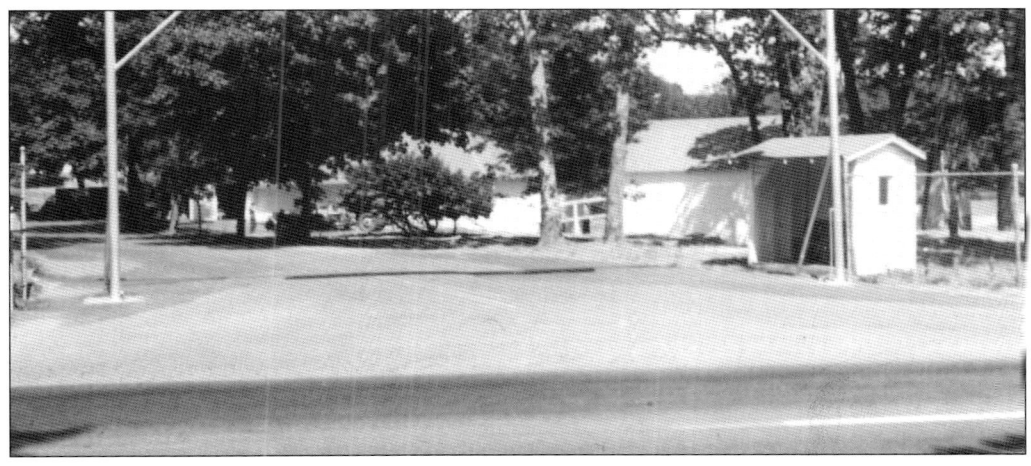

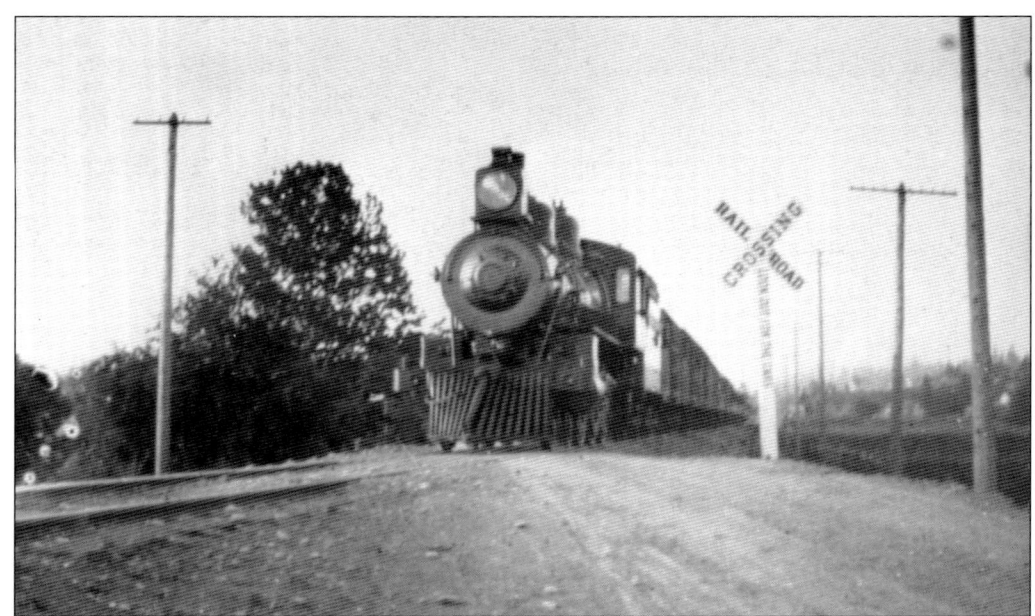

In 1895, adult season tickets for Chautauqua cost $1.50 and included all camping privileges, events, and most classes. Those who camped usually drove their own wagons loaded with camp furnishings. However, for those unable to bring their own camping supplies, the steamboats, Southern Pacific, and trolley all advertised special accommodations for Chautauqua passengers needing to transport excess and oversize baggage. The park trolley even offered freight delivery directly into Gladstone Park. Above, in 1910, a Southern Pacific train approaches Gladstone from Portland. This crossing was about a third of a mile east and the last intersection before the Gladstone (Chautauqua) Southern Pacific Depot. Below, in 1895, a steamboat filled with passengers travels up the Willamette River. Steamboats regularly sailed between Eugene or Corvallis and Portland, with stops at Oregon City.

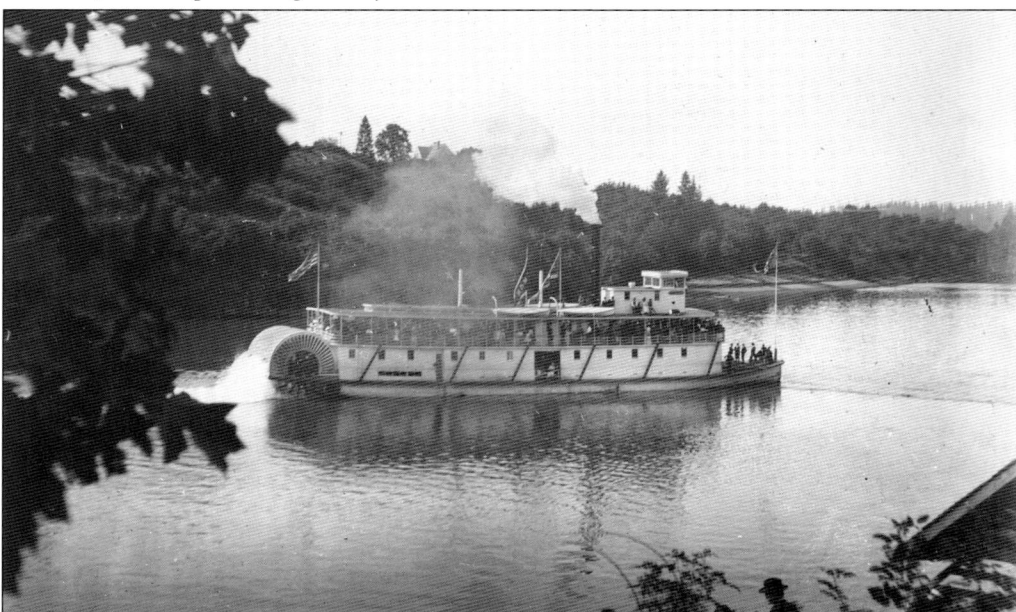

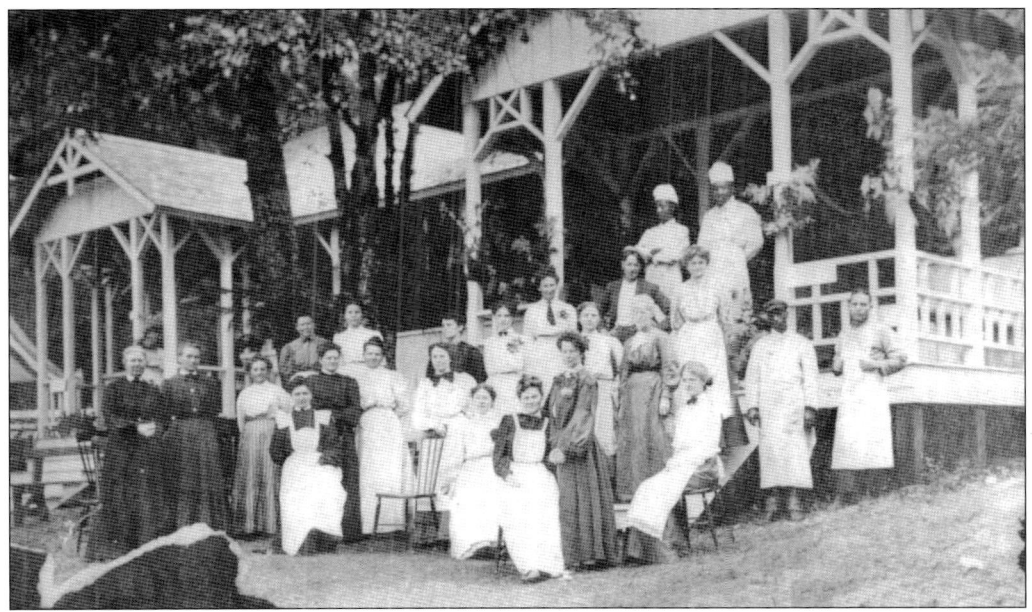

In 1896, the Chautauqua opened an open-air restaurant first managed by W.M. Robinson of the Electric Hotel in Oregon City. In 1900, due to the restaurant's popularity, a building with one dining room and a cooking platform was constructed. A second wing and second stove were added in 1905. In 1913, to accommodate all the diners, a cafeteria was operated along with the restaurant. Above, during the 1910 Chautauqua, members of the Oregon City Presbyterian church staffed the restaurant and are seen gathered around the building's original wing. At far left is the trolley car barn. Below, in 1926, a woman stands on the front porch of the Turel House. Operating as a grocery store, café, and boardinghouse, the Turel House was popular with Chautauqua attendees not wanting to camp in Gladstone Park.

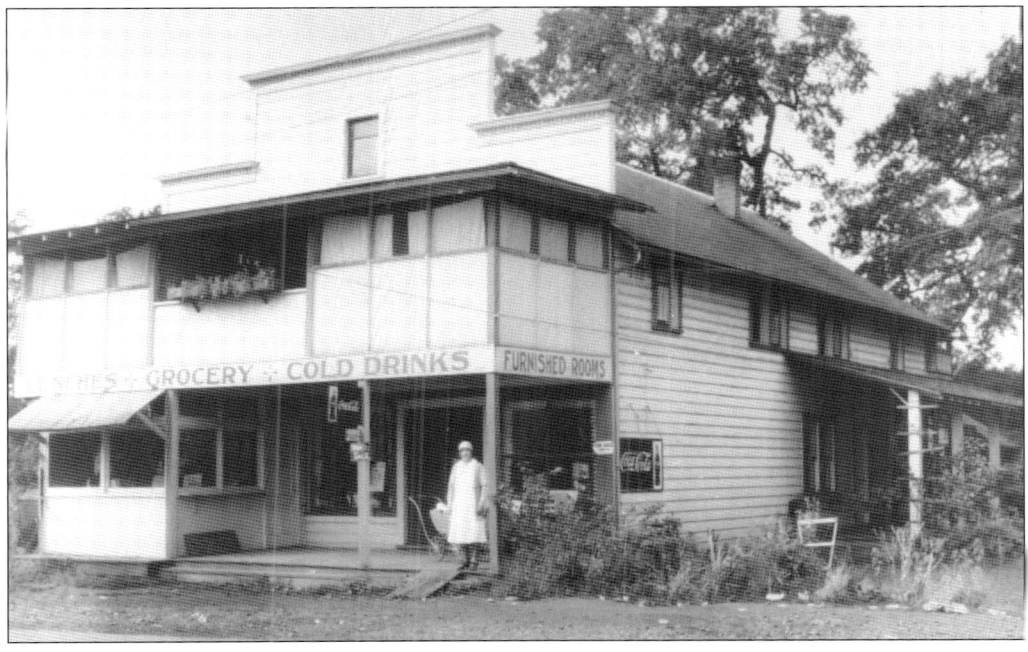

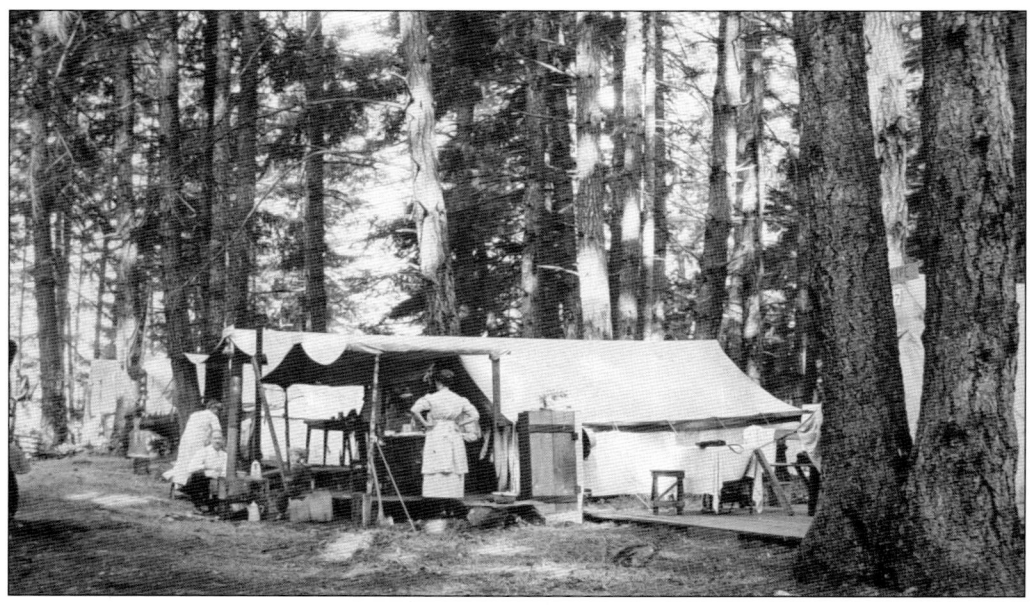

Food was plentiful at Chautauqua. Besides the restaurant, cafeteria, and concessions, cold lunch counters were scattered throughout the park. Limited to 20 customers per seating, these small open-air or tent diners served sandwiches. However, some campers preferred to cook, which meant bringing their own cooking stoves and buying food from vendors who toured the grounds daily. Some Oregon City markets also offered grocery delivery to Gladstone Park. Later, the Chautauqua would operate its own store. Above, in 1905, two women cook breakfast for their families. The woman on the right is standing on a cooking platform in front of her tent. Later, the Chautauqua offered furnished communal cooking shacks. Below, in 1905, these women sip tea from china cups and nibble on thick slices of cake between classes.

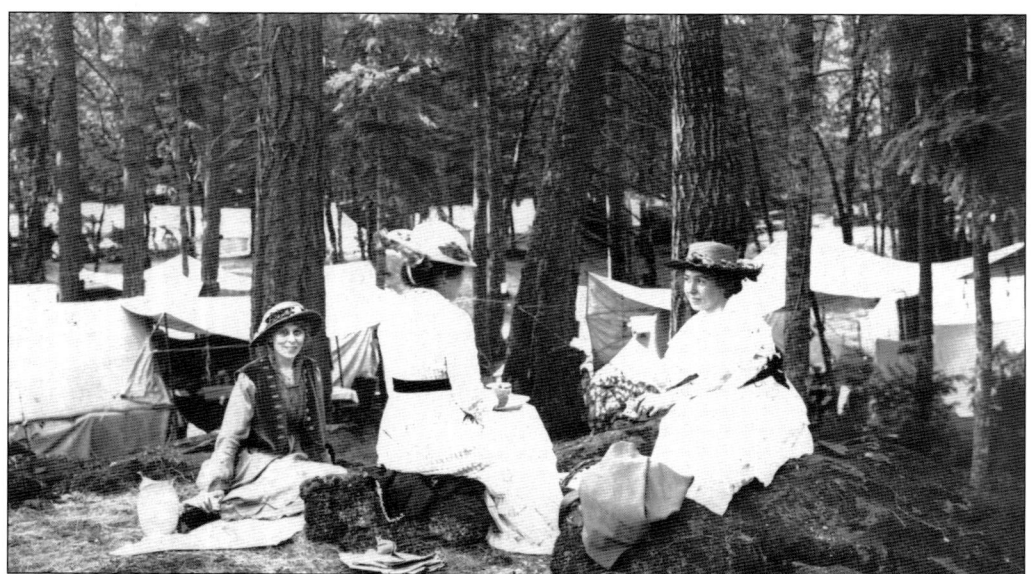

For the campers' enjoyment, Japanese lanterns were strung among the park's trees. Reports were that "Gladstone Park of an evening looked like a fairy forest and the effect was most enchanting." Other camper services included a bell that rang the time and announced events, US Signal Corps flags that forecasted the weather, and the daily delivery of the morning newspaper. At right, in 1925, Lena Charmin admires the Japanese lantern hanging at her campsite. Below, in 1949, the Chautauqua bell was still in use by Gladstone Park's new owners. Behind the bell tower is the 1905 drinking fountain and the 1930 cafeteria, which was possibly the Chautauqua cafeteria enclosed and extended over the athletic platform. The Chautauqua store can be seen at far left. (Below courtesy of Louise Newland Clark.)

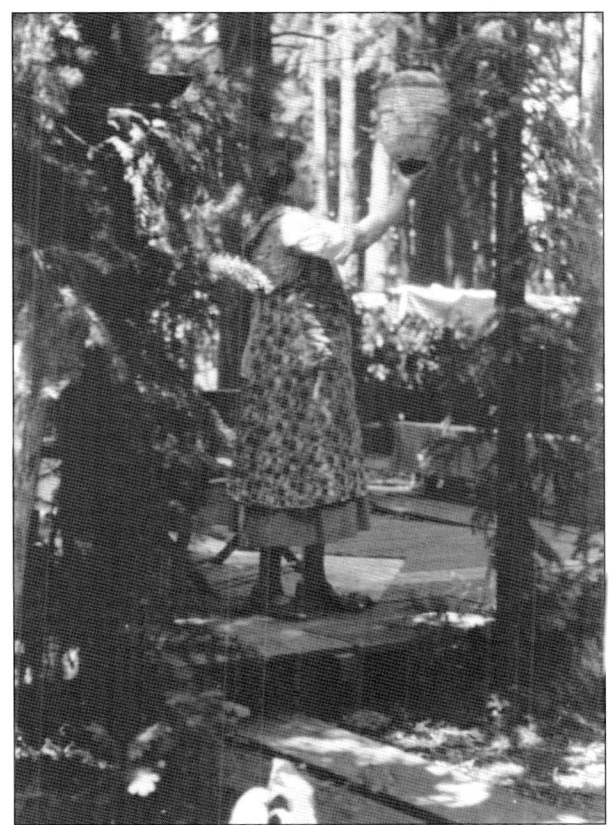

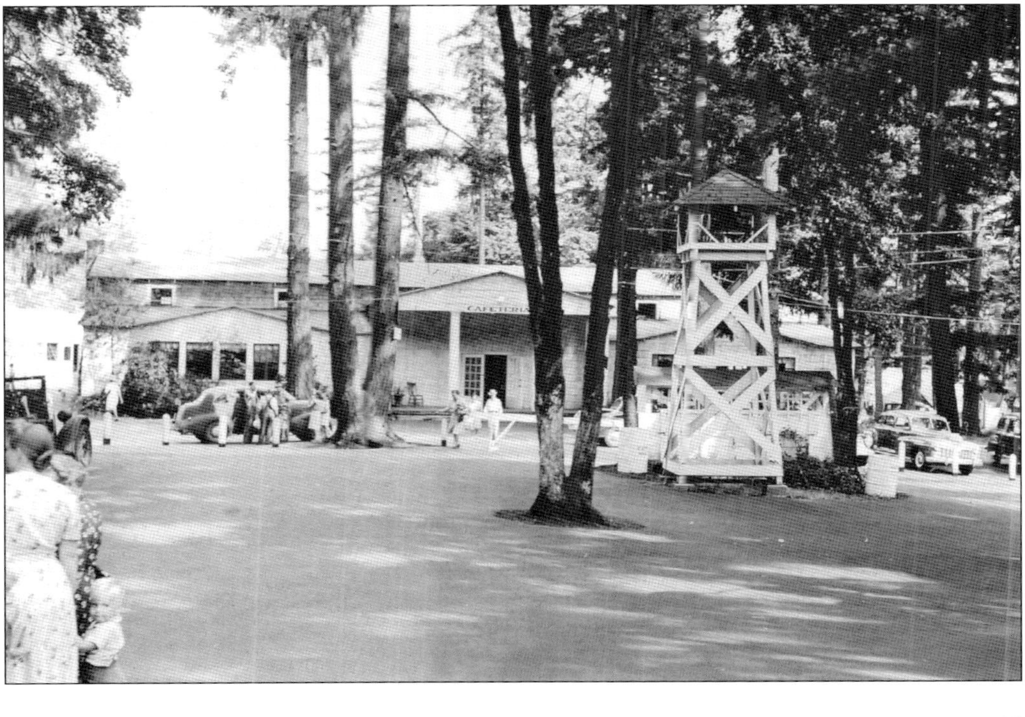

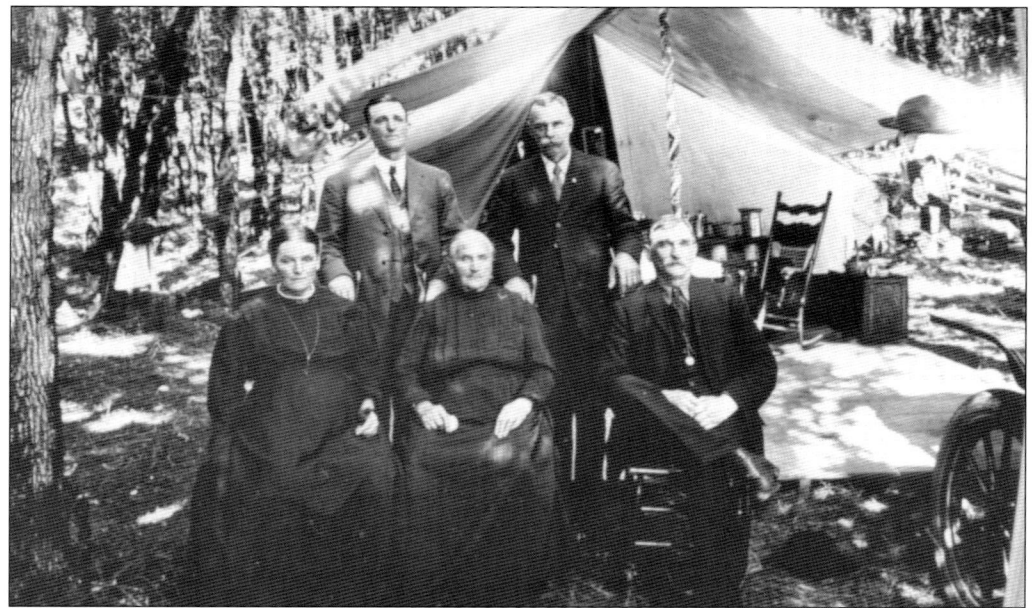

Families, schools, churches, organizations, and clubs all planned annual get-togethers at Chautauqua. One grassy knoll above the lake was considered so pleasant for picnicking and so crowded with group gatherings it became known as "Reunion Hill." Above, in 1910, the Schuebel family, prominent residents of the Oregon City area, held a family reunion at Chautauqua. Five members of the Gustav Schuebel family posed for this photograph. From left to right are (first row) Hedwig (daughter) Rosamonde (mother), and Gustav (father); (second row, standing) sons Christian and Robert. Many extended family groups camped together, and women with children camped alone until their husbands could join them for the weekends. Below, in 1900, May Mark, (far right) camped with her married daughter (far left), and her granddaughter.

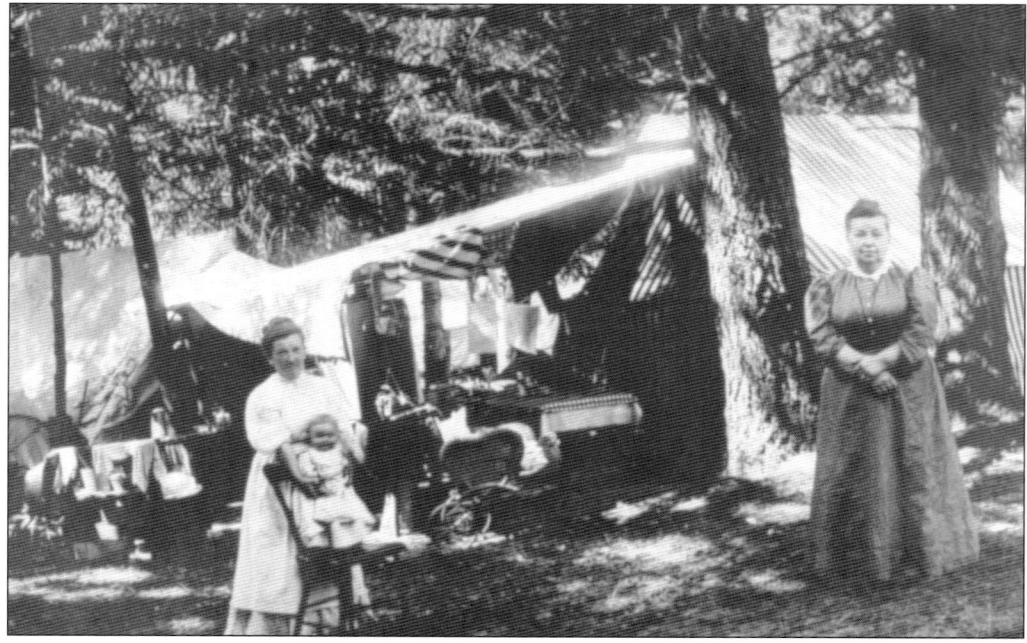

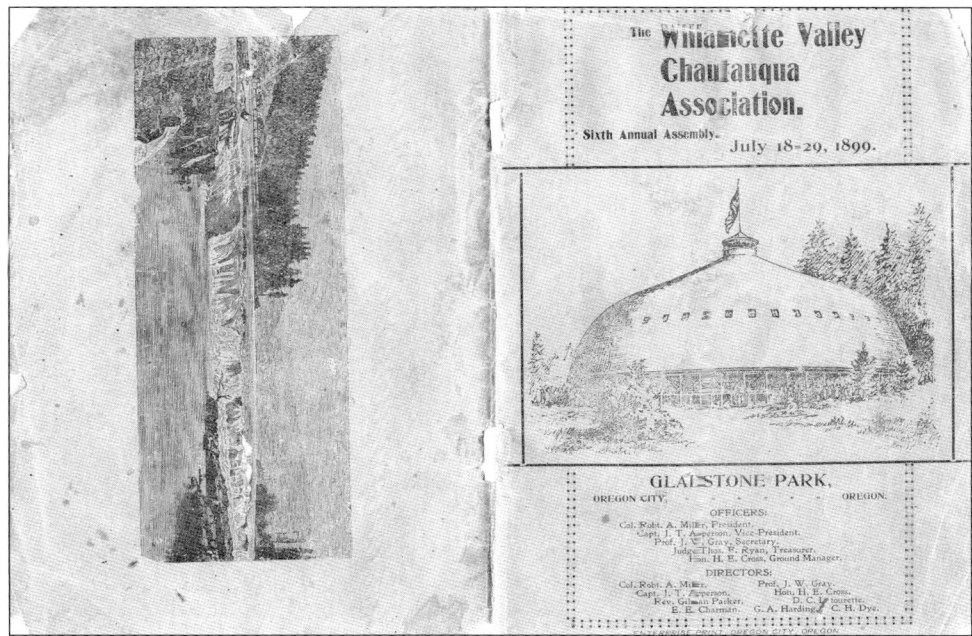

The primary goal of Chautauqua was to improve both the mind and the body. Each year, events generally followed the same schedule. Educational classes and lectures from 8:00 a.m. to 11:00 a.m., followed by a one-hour presentation of general interest in the main auditorium. At 1:30 p.m., a band concert took place in the main auditorium, followed by a ballgame played on the athletic field. Group meetings or round tables lasted from 5:00 p.m. until supper, and at 7:30 p.m., an orchestral concert preceded the evening's special event in the main auditorium. Over the years, Chautauqua lasted anywhere from 11 to 14 days. Shown above is the cover of the July 18–29, 1899, Chautauqua program. Below are pages 22 and 23 of the same program. (Both, GHS.)

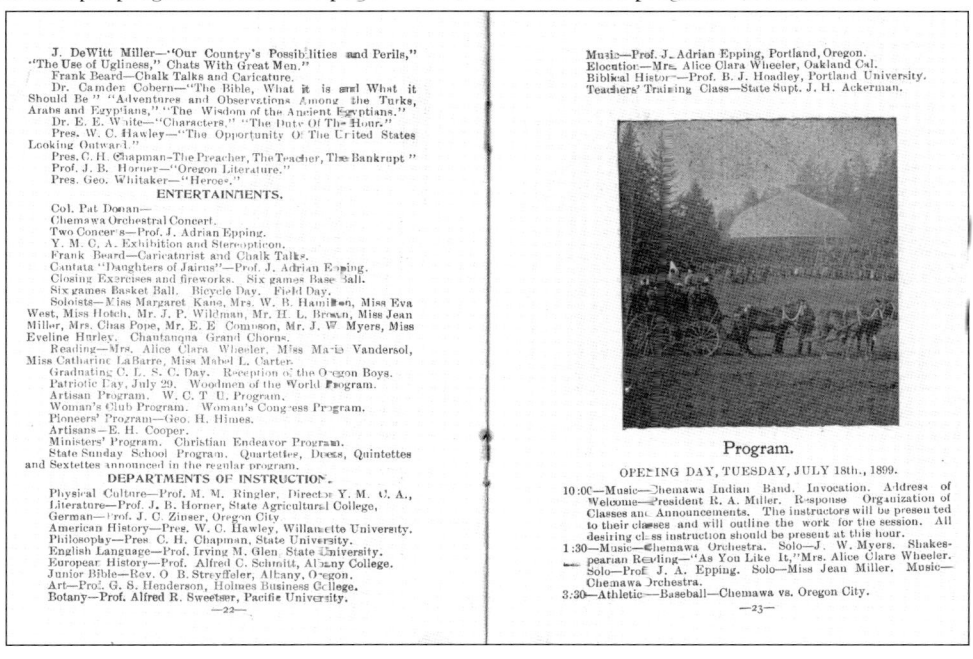

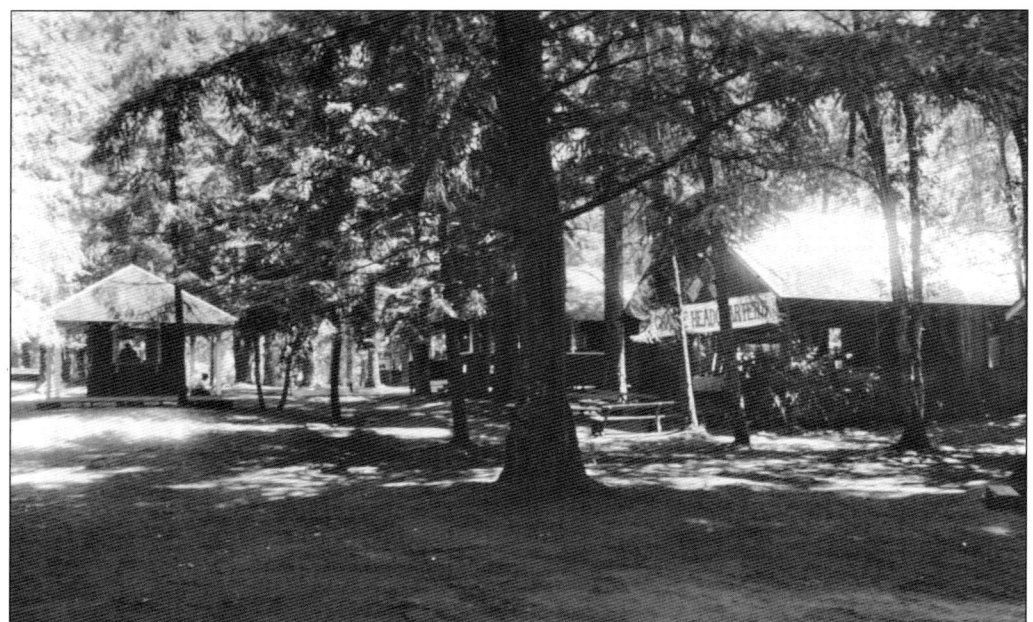

As Chautauqua grew, so did the desire for more buildings and fewer tents. Besides needing classrooms, some groups wanted permanent structures where they could establish a headquarters. Three hundred feet north of the Beehive auditorium, a semi-circle of buildings and gazebos were constructed and designated "Headquarters Row." The Oregon State Grange was one of the first organizations to occupy a new building, as shown above in 1922. Other buildings, from left to right, are the Chautauqua office, the symposium gazebo (in the trees), and the library built in 1921. The library, which included both an inside fireplace reading room and an open-air reading porch, was managed by the Salem State Library. Lola Belle Bellinger, a state librarian, supervised the 700 books. Below, the west side of Headquarters Row is seen as it appeared in the winter of 1910.

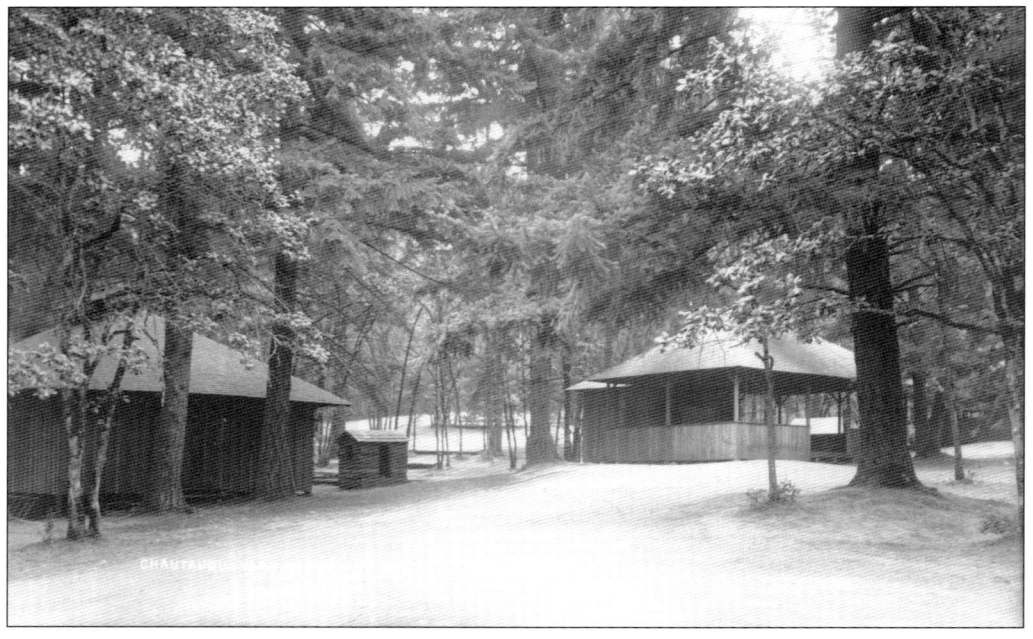

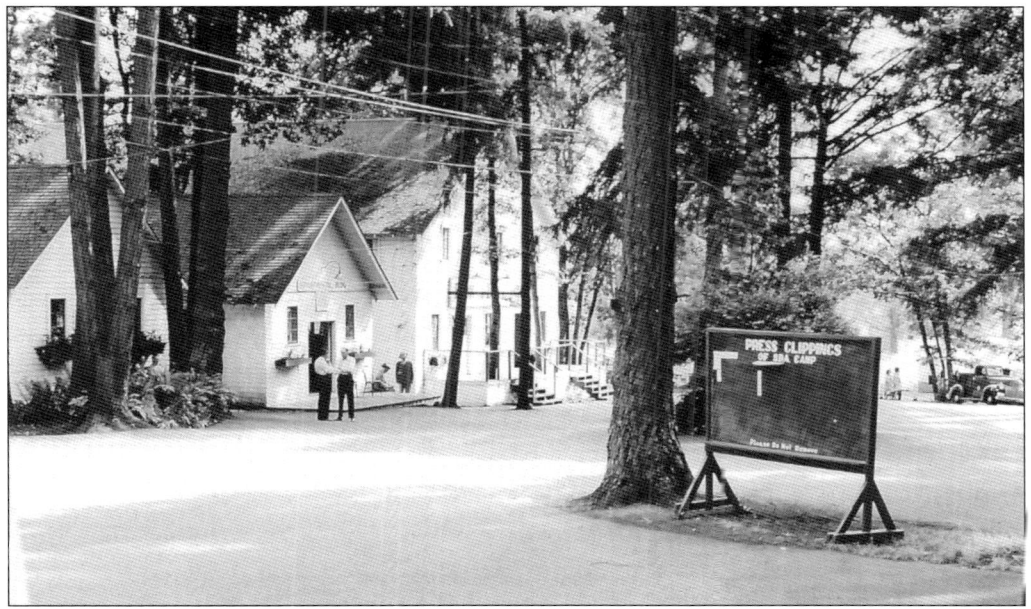

This 1949 photograph, taken facing south, shows Headquarters Row now in use by Gladstone Park's new owners. The buildings, from left to right, belonged to the Grange, the Grand Old Army of the Republic, and the third building is believed to have been either a hotel or the dormitory annex of the Women's Christian Temperance Union house, which sits behind it. (Courtesy of Louise Newland Clark.)

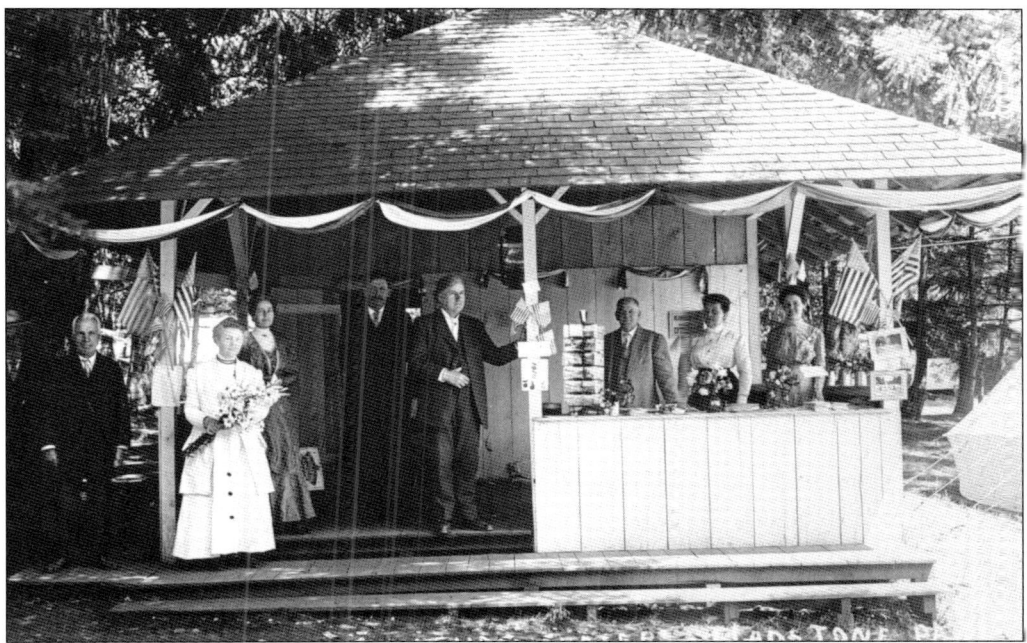

Officers and spouses of the 1905 Chautauqua stand on the porch of the Chautauqua administration gazebo. From left to right are unidentified, Eva Emery Dye, Orpha Cross, Harvey Cross, Charles Dye, and three unidentified. Both Harvey Cross and Charles Dye served as Chautauqua president and took other leadership roles throughout the Chautauqua years.

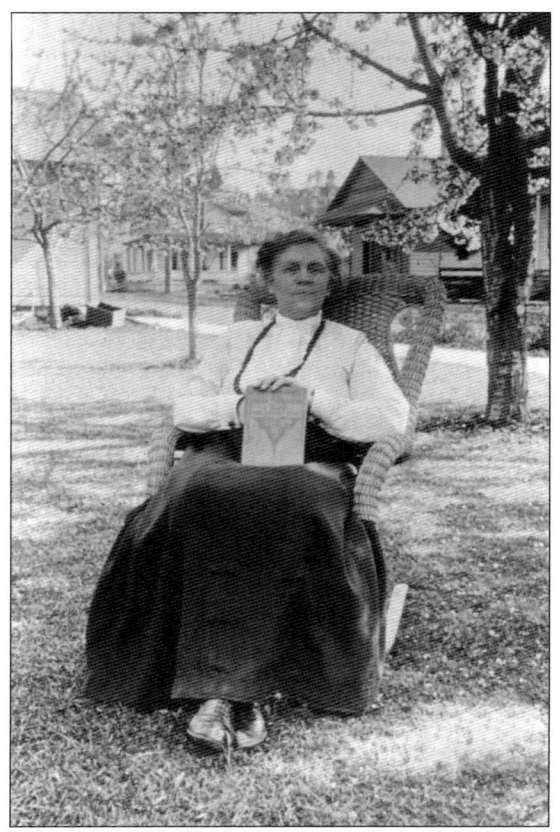

Seen at left in 1925, Eva Emery Dye poses with her *McLoughlin and Old Oregon* book in Gladstone Park, with several headquarters buildings behind her. On the left is the Harmony Improvement Club, where refreshments and 16 curtained-off cots were available to Harmony residents. The large white house in the background belonged to the Women's Christian Temperance Union and included a kitchen, parlor, dining room, and upstairs dormitory for use by women who were attending Chautauqua alone. Below, some groups never built headquarters buildings. In 1908, faculty and students of the Monmouth Normal College eat ice-cream cones at their headquarters tent. The child at far left is Hazel Gard Robinson Stone. Her father, Lewis Robinson, was a 1902–1910 Monmouth Normal College faculty member. (Below, courtesy of Nancy Stone Brown.)

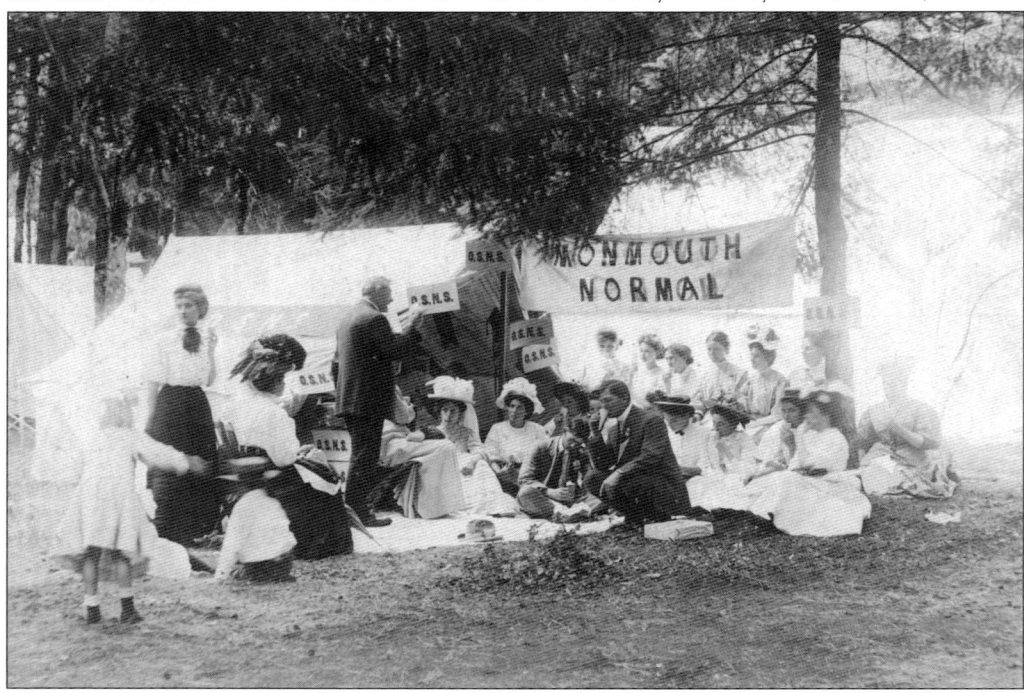

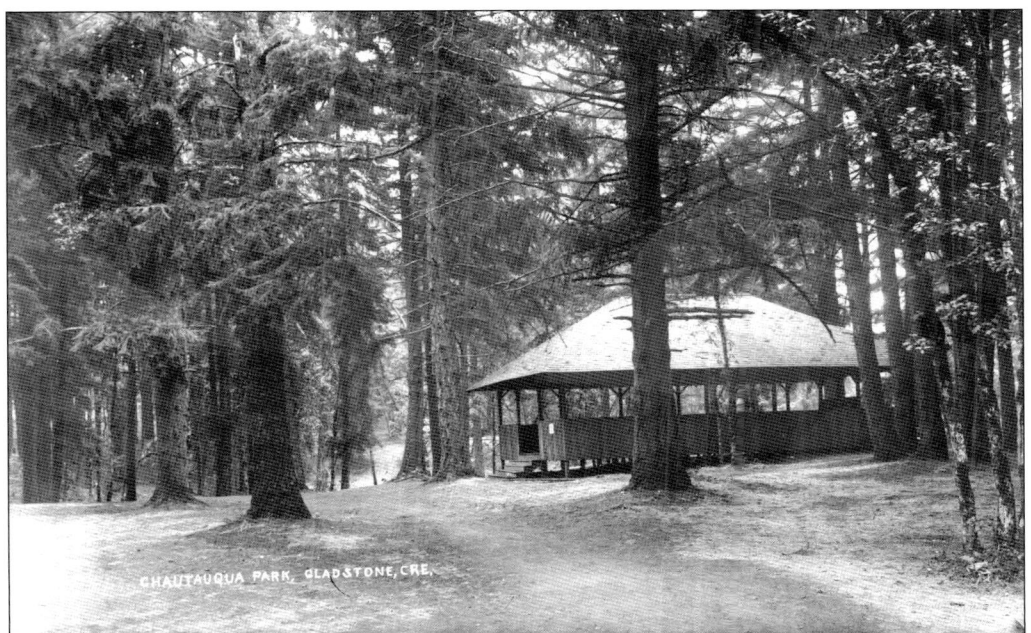

Headquarters Row grew to include services such as a bank, post office, icehouse, hospital, and grocery store. By 1904, E.L. Johnson was operating a camp barbershop. Elsewhere in Gladstone Park were a livestock pasture, free wood supply, restrooms, drinking fountains, and a bathhouse. Pictured in 1900, a lecture pavilion sits on a knoll above Lake Chautauqua.

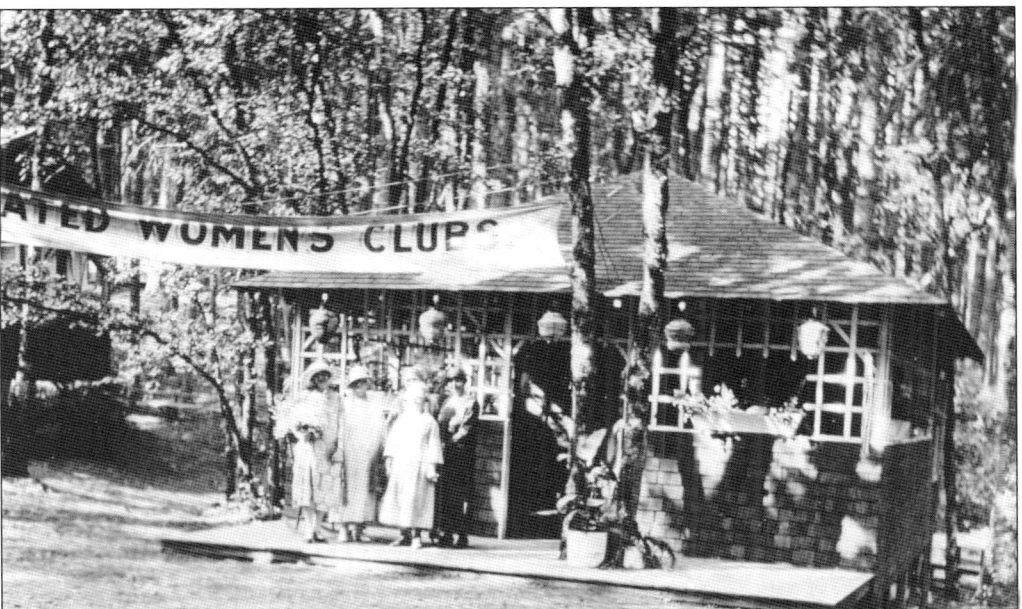

Eva Emery Dye hosted a symposium hour that was unique to the Gladstone Chautauqua. Conducted at the Women's Club pavilion in Headquarters Row, these popular sessions discussed topics that included arts, literature, and current women's issues. The symposium was visited regularly by suffragettes Susan B. Anthony and Abigale Scott Duniway. In the 1920s, these women stand in front of the Women's Club pavilion.

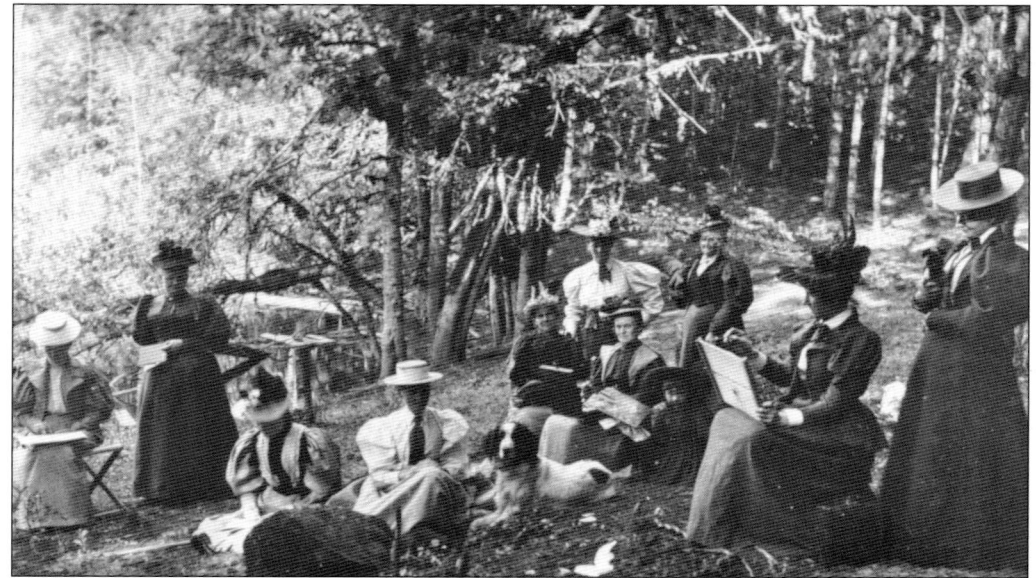

Not all classes were held indoors. Field lectures, bird watching, and geology classes took place throughout Gladstone Park. In 1897, the botany class discovered 70 different varieties of wildflowers growing in the park. As shown here in 1896, the lake was a popular place for art classes. Although it cannot be determined who is instructing here, the teacher that year was Alice Aubrey Weister, an art instructor at Portland University.

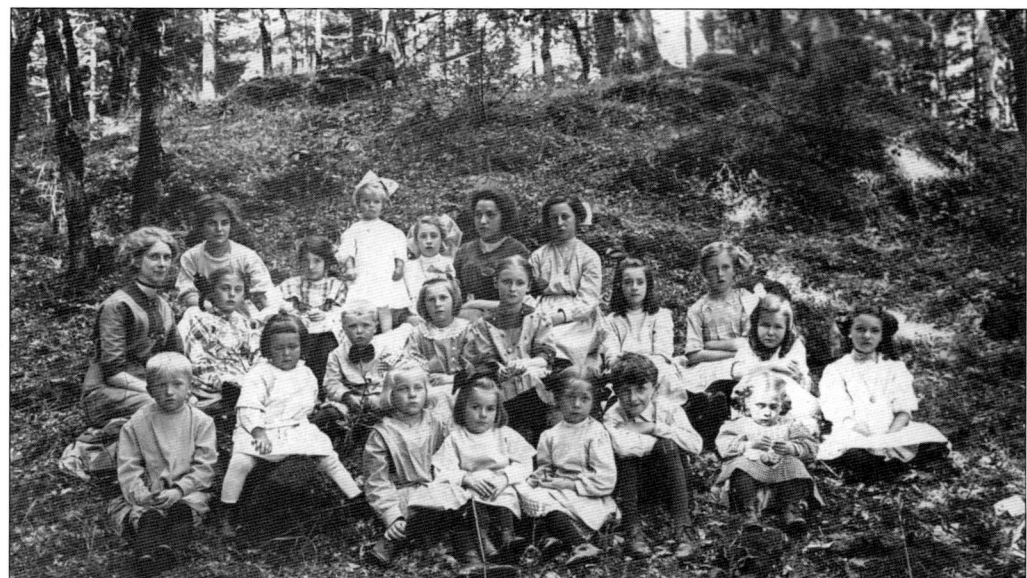

Chautauqua activities were also planned for children. At the nursery pavilion, a story lady took the younger children on imaginative strolls through Gladstone Park. At the kindergarten pavilion, children were taught art, music, and Bible. All children spent time in the supervised play area. Shown here between 1910 and 1913, Sylvia Phillips, one of the playground assistants (back row, second from left) sits with her young charges. (Courtesy of C. Riddell.)

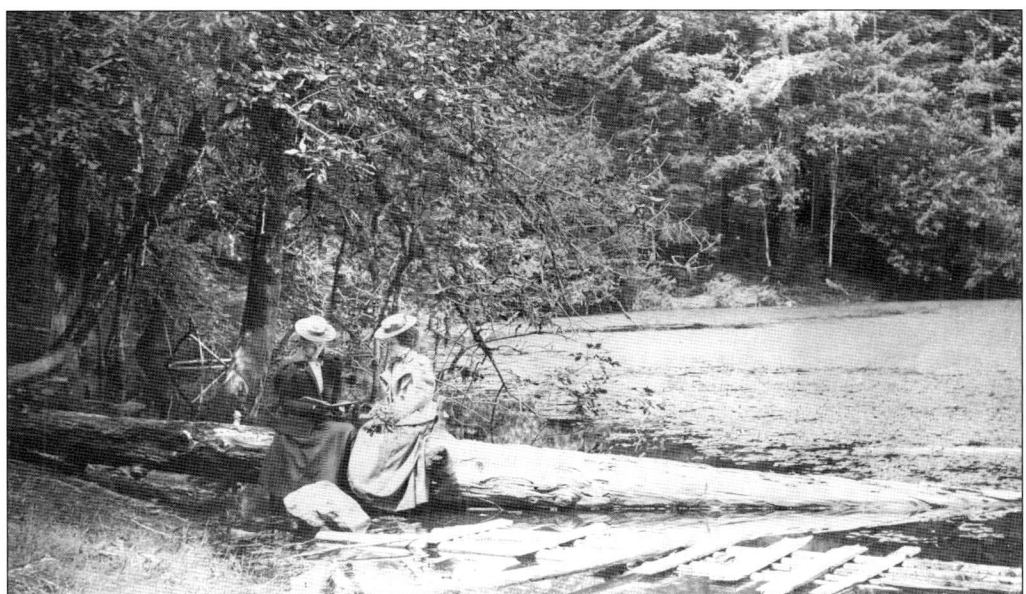

While daily Bible study was an important feature of Chautauqua, on Sundays, all regular instructional classes were suspended and as many as three non-denominational sermons were presented throughout the day. Evangelists who came to speak before record-breaking crowds were William Spurgeon from London, Dr. Charles F. Aked of New York, and the Rev. Billy Sunday of baseball fame. Above, in 1897, two women enjoy early morning Bible study beside the lake. Below, in 1919, a large crowd overflowed the auditorium, and many sat outside under the trees during a Sunday morning church service. Harvey Cross stands at far right, holding an open songbook.

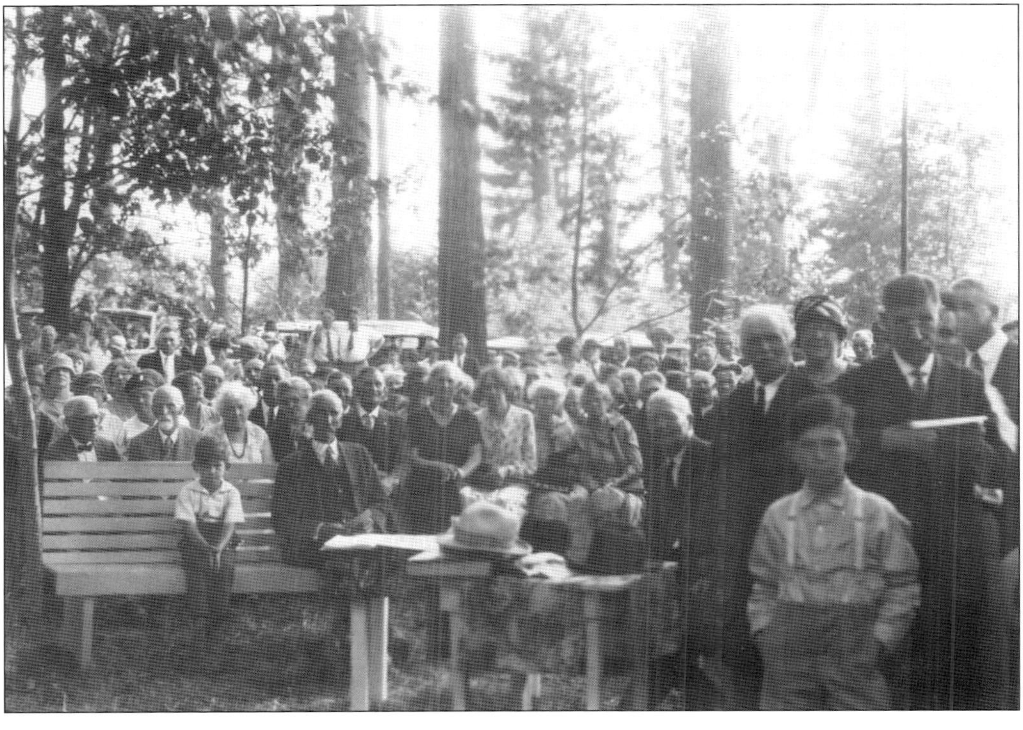

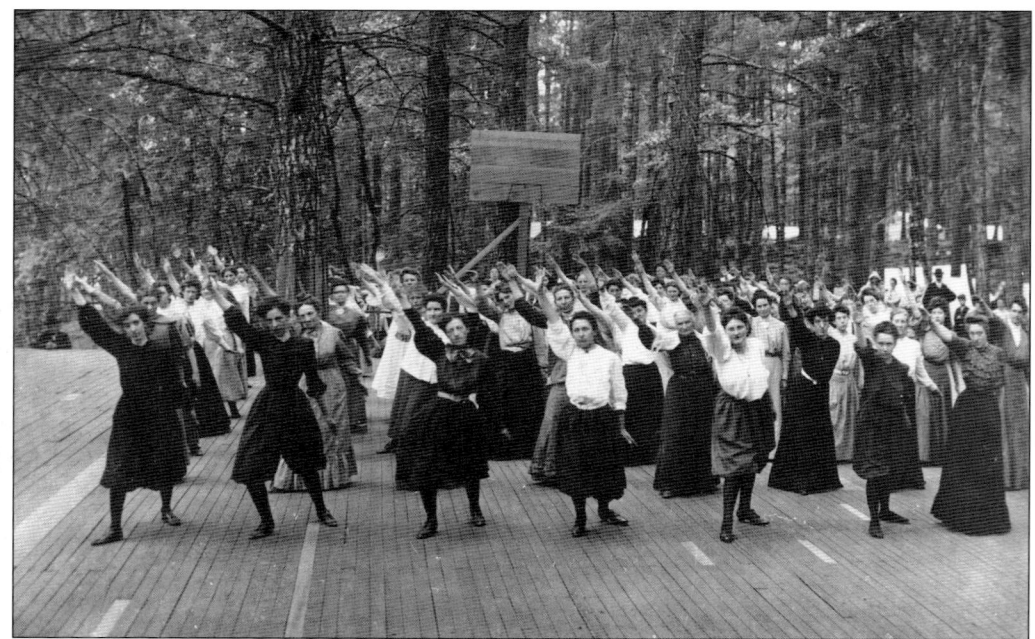

Exercise was as important as intellectual studies. In 1905, Prof. J.R. Wetherbee of the University of Oregon took charge of the physical culture program. Men's exercise class started at 8:00 a.m., followed by women's exercise class at 9:00 a.m. In 1909, an exercise class was added for 9- to 16-year-olds. All swimming classes were taught at the Clackamas River. The outdoor gymnasium, seen above in 1904, was a 50-by-90-foot wooden platform that somehow incorporated the 1894 speaker's platform. Described as being constructed closer to the lake, the outdoor gymnasium was most likely located 300 feet northeast of Headquarters Row. Later, the gymnasium was given a cement floor. As seen below in 1914, women were encouraged to wear blouse waists and split skirts, or bloomers, for modest and beneficial exercising.

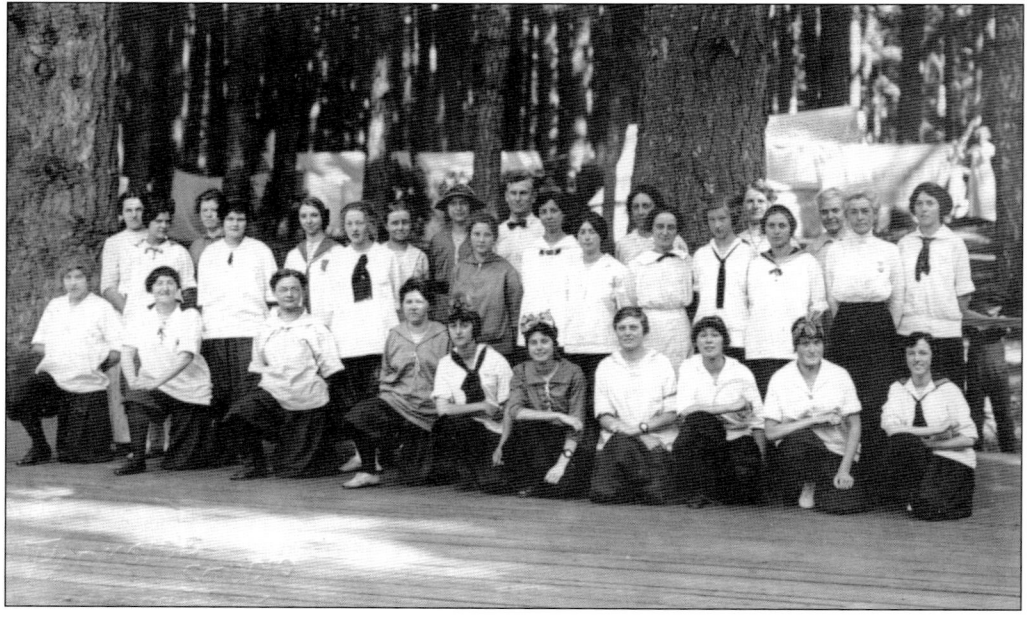

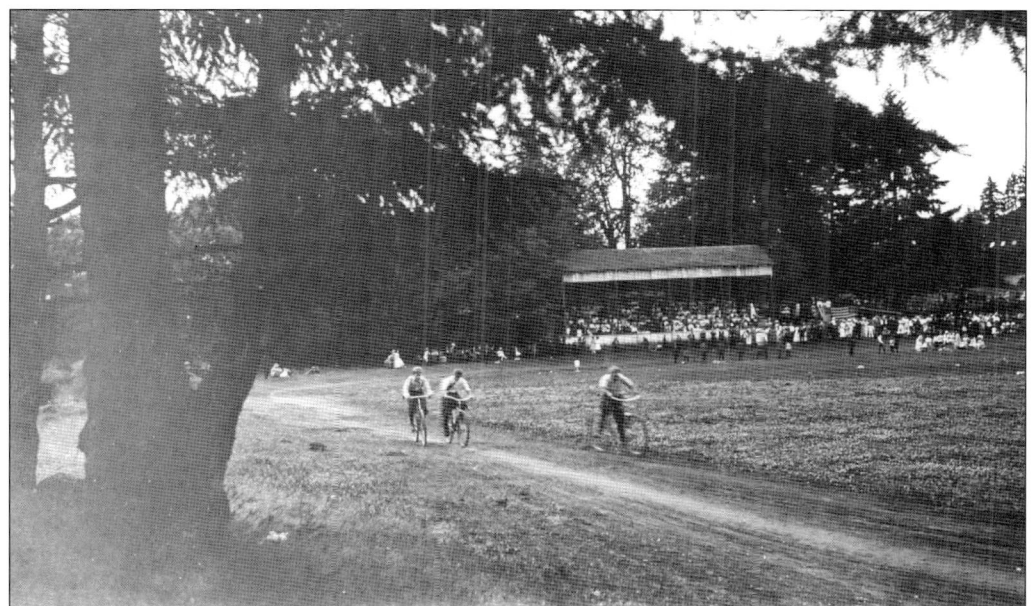

The athletic field's sloped north bank created amphitheater seating that was perfect for viewing sporting events. In 1896, Harvey Cross scraped and graded a quarter-mile racetrack around the perimeter of the baseball diamond where foot races, bicycle races, and even a horse race took place. In 1910, one of the Children's Day events was a boys' bicycle race. (GHS.)

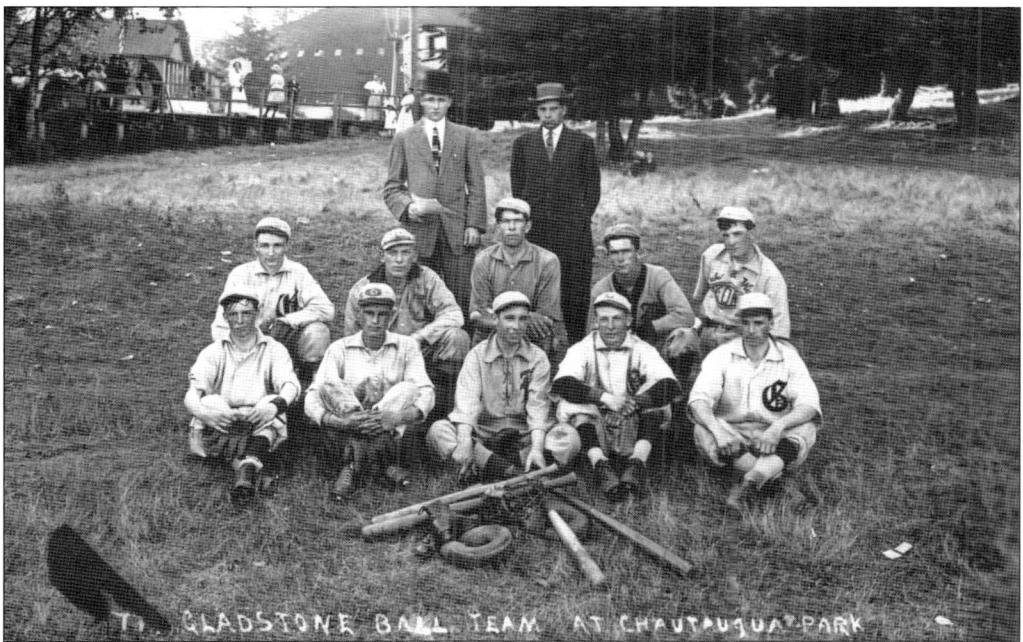

While track and field events were popular, baseball games drew the biggest crowds. Every year, a five-team baseball tournament was held at Chautauqua with the winning team taking home a grand prize. In 1912, the Gladstone team played against Mount Angel and lost. Charles Sievers is standing in back at far right. (GHS.)

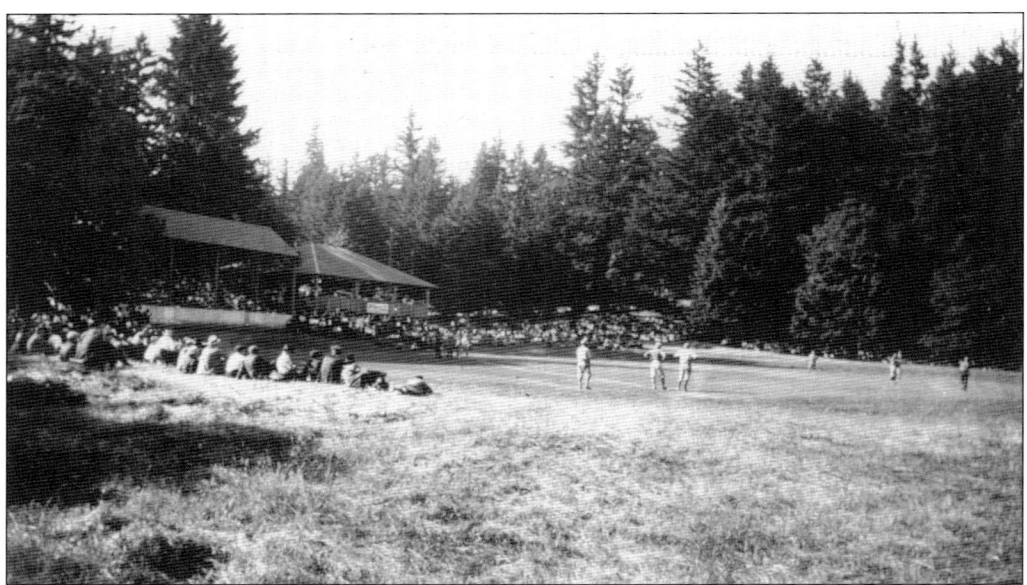

One of the most exciting ballgames ever played at Chautauqua took place in 1917 between the town of Wilsonville and the Kirkpatricks of Portland. Right-fielder Henry Hasselbrink, called the "one-arm phenomenon," amazed the crowd by achieving two putouts, one assist, five singles, three stolen bases, and two of his team's four home runs. With only one arm, Hasselbrink single-handedly won the game for Wilsonville.

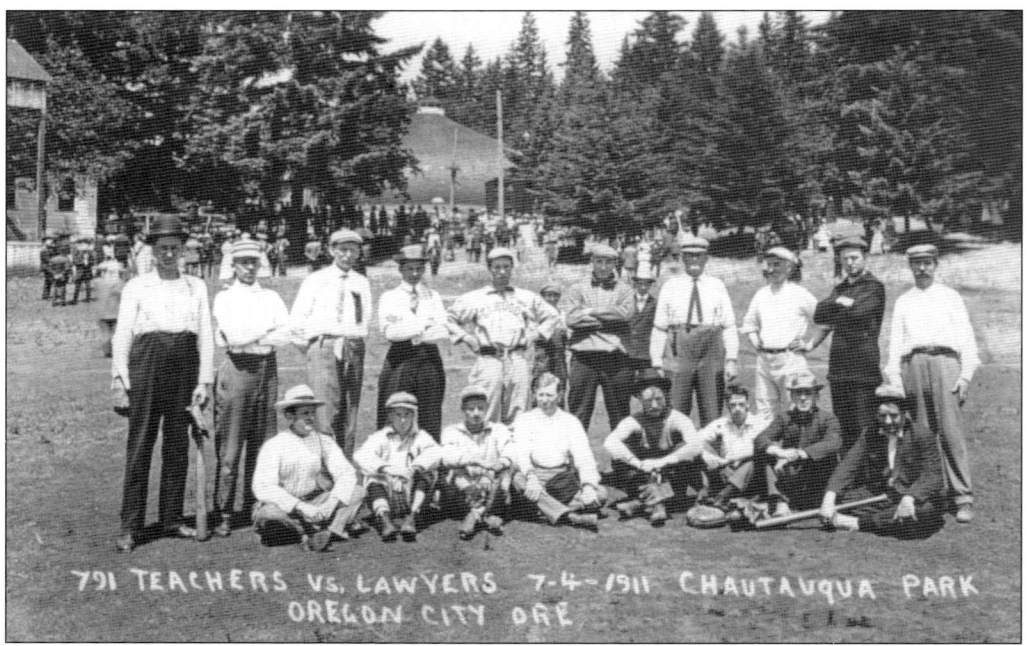

In 1911, an exhibition baseball game was played between the Oregon City teachers and a team chosen from among the local lawyers, ministers, physicians, and dentists baseball teams. The teachers chose the lawyers and won. Shown in this photograph is the winning teachers team. In the background, a trolley sits on the track.

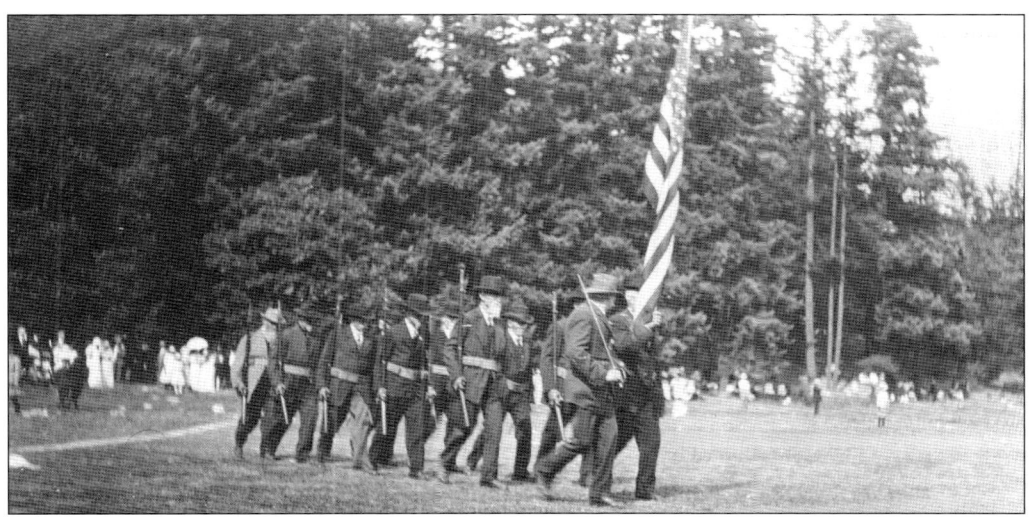

Every year, Chautauqua celebrated theme days, such as Pioneer Day, Audubon Day, and Clackamas County Day. Patriotic Day was an annual event. Festivities included band concerts, speeches, a pageant or parade, and a grand finale of fireworks. In 1911, the opening day of Chautauqua occurred on the Fourth of July, resulting in a huge patriotic celebration. That year, members of the Grand Old Army of the Republic, seen above, were the honored guests and marched in the parade that took place in the athletic field. Over the years, the Oregon Naval Militia band was a favorite performer. As seen below during the 1911 Chautauqua, the band performed daily, giving as many as two concerts in one day.

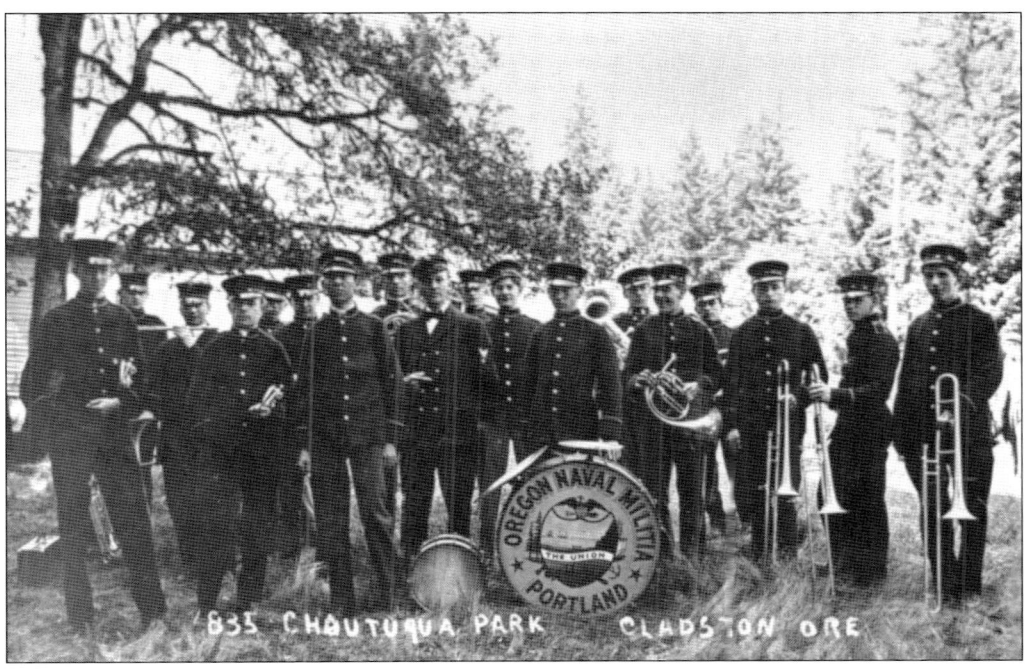

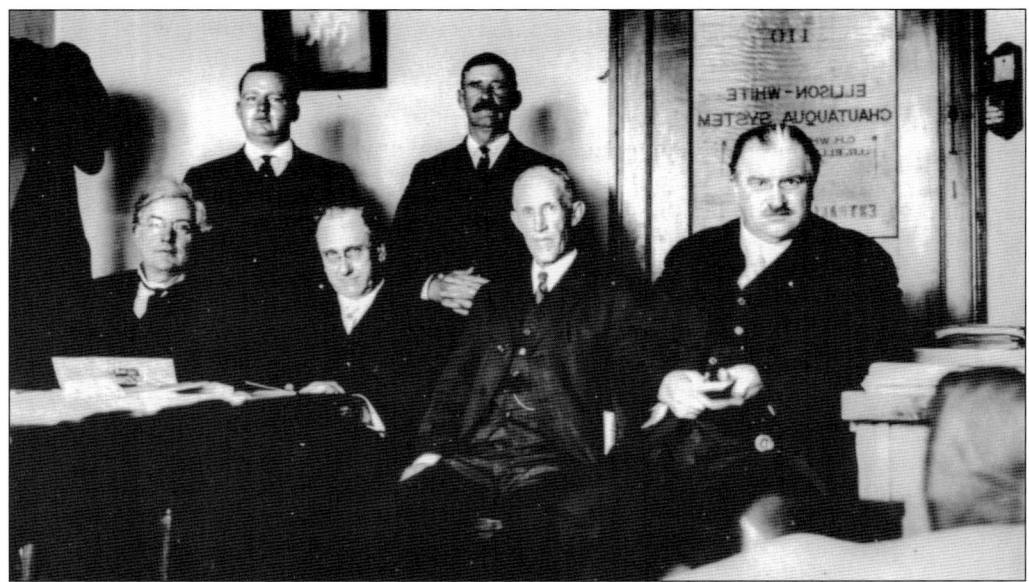

In 1915, Ellison-White Chautauqua System, an international booking agency for traveling lyceum performers, was contracted to provide talent for the Chautauqua's evening events. Ellison-White brought recognized figures to Gladstone Park, which increased the attendance but resulted in shifting the assembly's focus away from education and more toward entertainment. By 1916, Gladstone Park had reached national prominence as the third largest permanent Chautauqua in the United States and was known as the "Mother Chautauqua of the West." Overflowing crowds were now trying to squeeze into an auditorium that was literally coming apart at the seams. Above, in 1915, the Willamette Valley Chautauqua Board is shown in the Portland office of Ellison-White. From left to right are (first row) Charles Dye and three unidentified; (second row) Thomas Burke and Harvey Cross. Below, in 1911, members of the Rinearson family leave a crowded Beehive auditorium. (Above, OHS.)

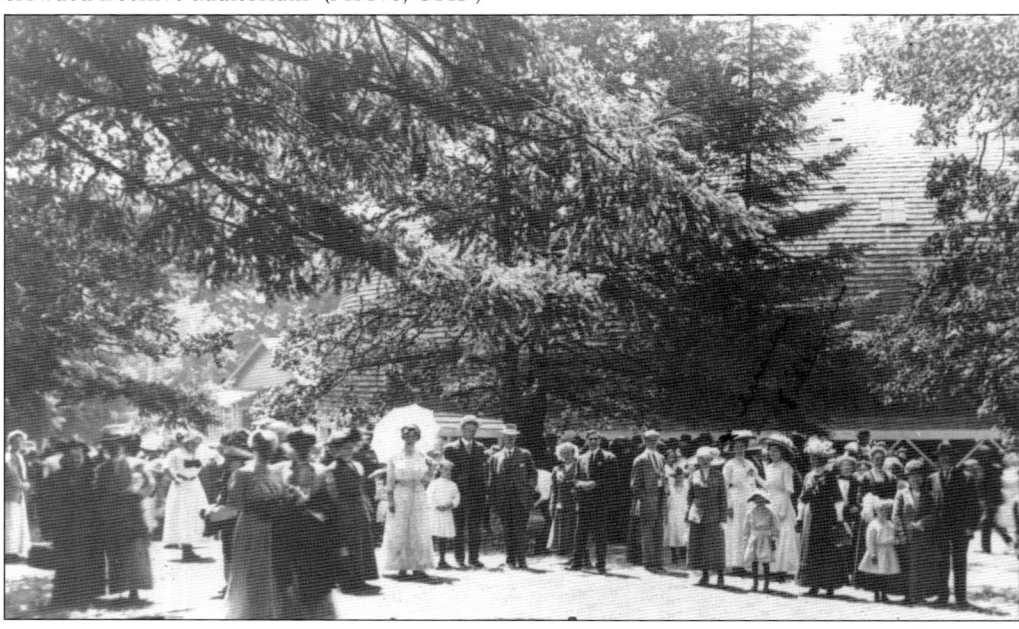

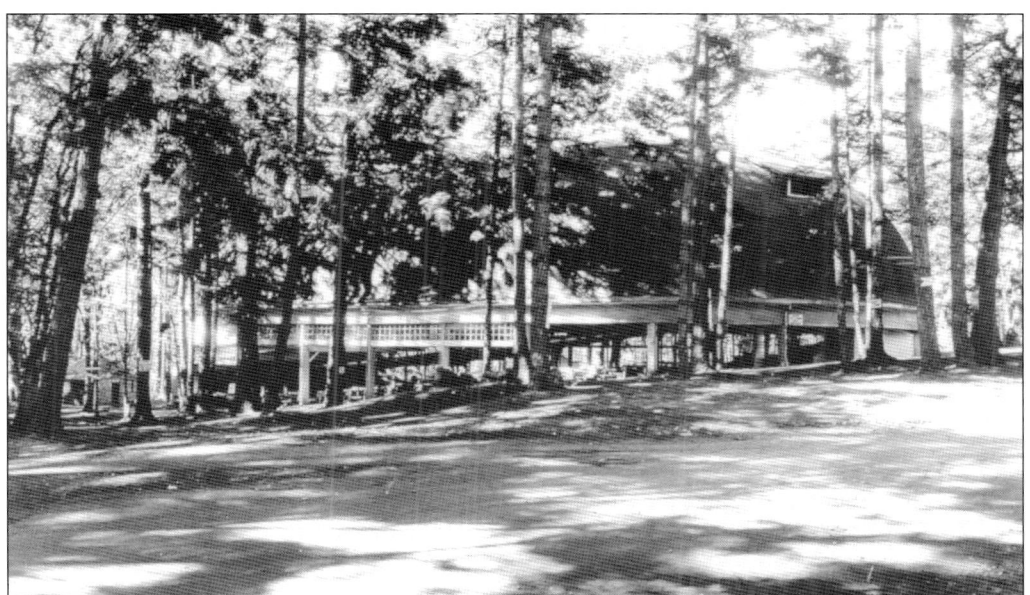

In 1917, a new open-air auditorium was built 200 feet north of the Beehive. Costing $5,000, this auditorium accommodated 5,000 under its roof and an equal number around the outside. Inside was a partial balcony, a 200-seat choir loft, and a 100-seat stage. Though not finished for use during the 1917 Chautauqua, it was decided to dedicate the new auditorium anyway. On the last Sunday of the assembly, over 10,000 people attended Rev. Billy Sunday's dedication sermon. Impressed with the Gladstone Park Chautauqua, Reverend Sunday refused his $1,500 speaker's fee, which was then used to make the final payment on the auditorium. Above, the new auditorium is seen as it appeared during the 1918 Chautauqua. Below, in 1955, a camp meeting crowd overflows the main floor and balcony of the second auditorium. (Above, OSL; below, KAH.)

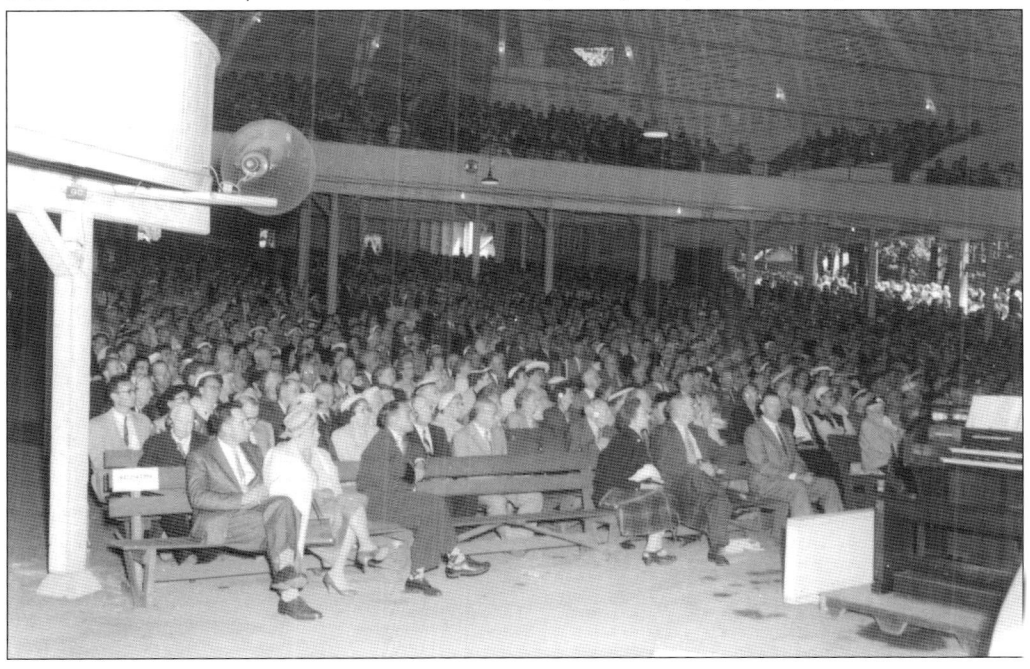

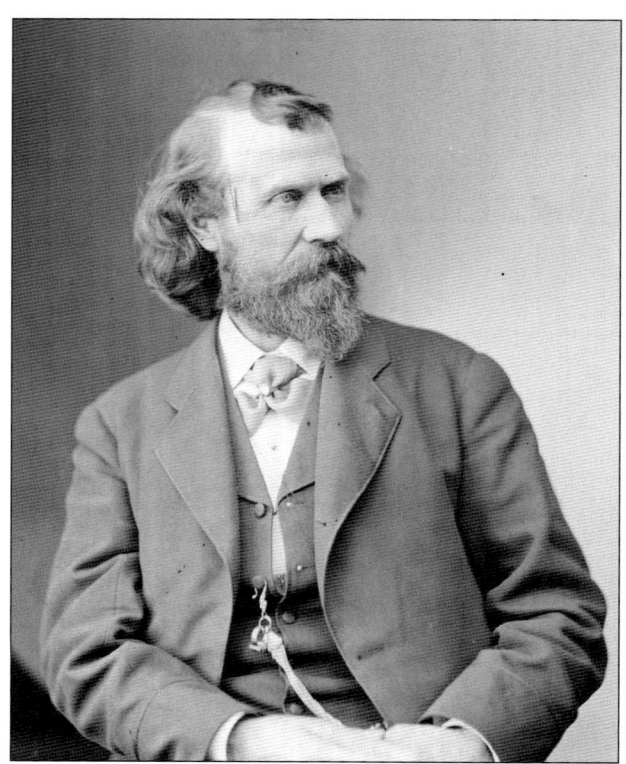

By today's standards, many who appeared at the Gladstone Park Chautauqua would not be considered famous. However, at the time, most were celebrities. Joaquin Miller (left) visited Gladstone's Chautauqua twice. Touted as a teller of tall tales that were mostly true, Miller was a former Pony Express rider, a published poet, friend of Bret Harte, and the man who taught Buffalo Bill how to dress. The most popular of all Chautauqua speakers was William Jennings Bryan (below). A three-time presidential candidate, former US representative, and US secretary of state, Bryan appeared in Gladstone in 1896, 1897, and 1919. At his last appearance, he spoke to his largest audience ever: over 10,000 day attendees plus those camping. (Both, Brady-Handy Collection, Prints and Photographs Division, Library of Congress.)

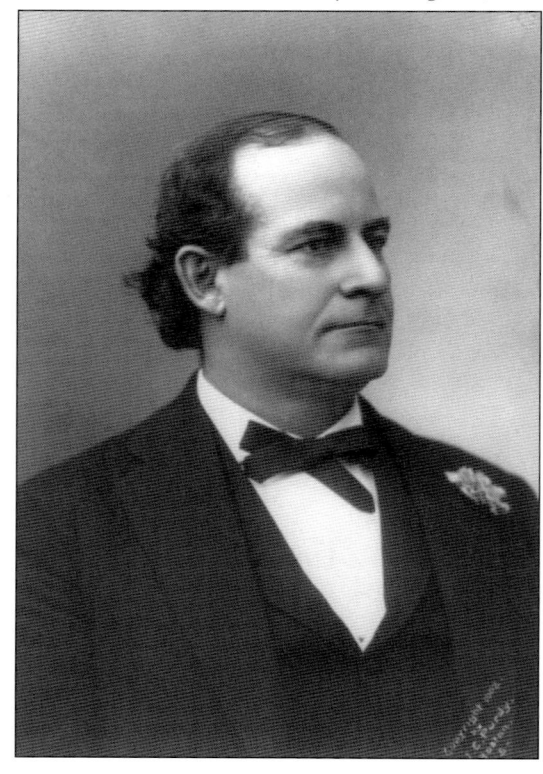

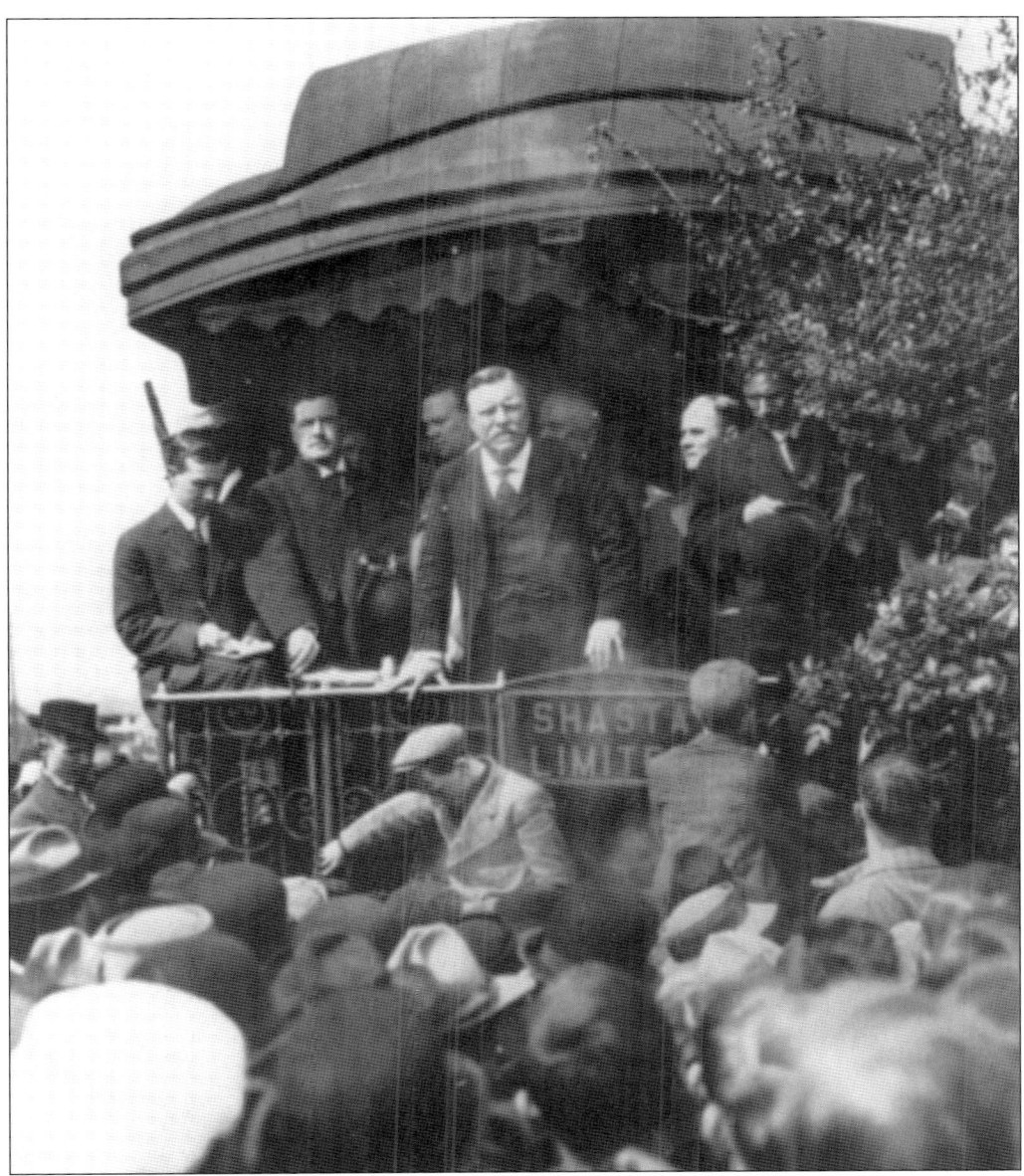

Tradition has it that several US presidents visited the Gladstone Park Chautauqua, but only one can be verified. While making a whistle-stop tour of the Willamette Valley, as seen here in 1911, Theodore Roosevelt stopped at Gladstone Park. Other notables who appeared at Chautauqua were socialist Eugene V. Debbs, author Upton Sinclair, world traveler Lou Beauchamp, publisher Charlotte Gilman Perkins, revivalist Sam Jones, suffragette Rev. Anna Shaw, humorist Jahu Dewitt Miller, Rachel Frank (the first female rabbi), actress Maude Wills, Temple University founder Russel Conwell, engineer Montraville M. Wood (inventor of Harry Houdini's illusions and escape tricks), and educator Booker T. Washington. In the early 1920s, dancer Isadora Duncan became a friend of Eva Emery Dye and visited Gladstone with the idea of establishing a dance school. She also hoped to teach dance classes at Chautauqua. Reluctantly, she gave up her plan when she determined that the Oregon City area wasn't ready for her style of interpretive dance. (Courtesy of Prints and Photograph Division, Library of Congress.)

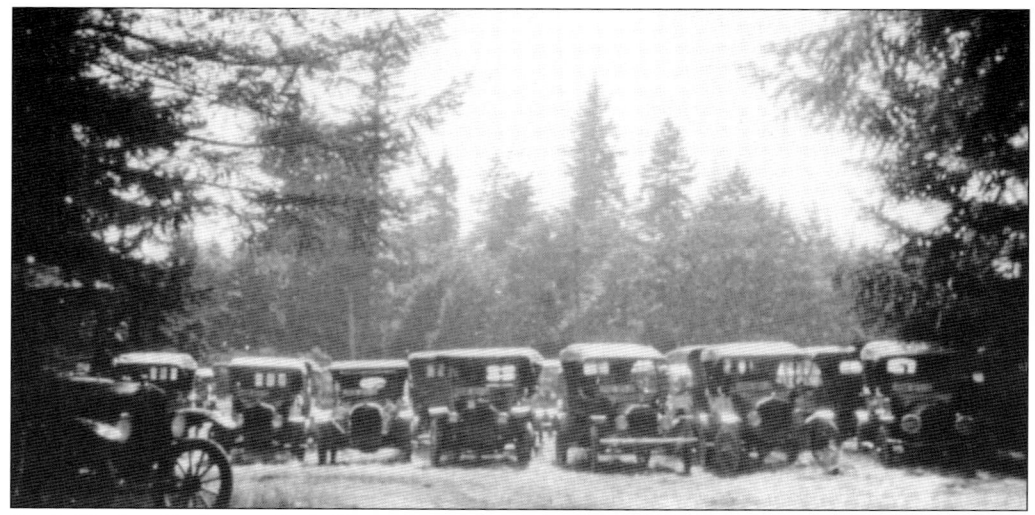

By 1927, the Gladstone Park Chautauqua was failing. Instead of 50,000 attendees, only a few thousand came through the gates. Having continually kept entrance fees low to ensure a larger attendance, the assembly could no longer meet expenses. Many things contributed to Chautauqua ending. Numerous small Chautauquas partnered with the Lyceum circuit, enticing attendees to stop traveling and attend locally. Automobiles, radio, and moving pictures offered new ways to experience the world. The Chautauqua Reading Circle, which had inspired many to obtain a higher education, was now overlooked for traditional colleges. Above, in 1919, automobiles have replaced horses in Gladstone Park's pasture. In 1929, Gladstone Park was sold to the Western Oregon Conference of the Seventh-Day Adventist Church as a permanent location for its annual camp meetings, as seen below in 1955. (Below, KAH.)

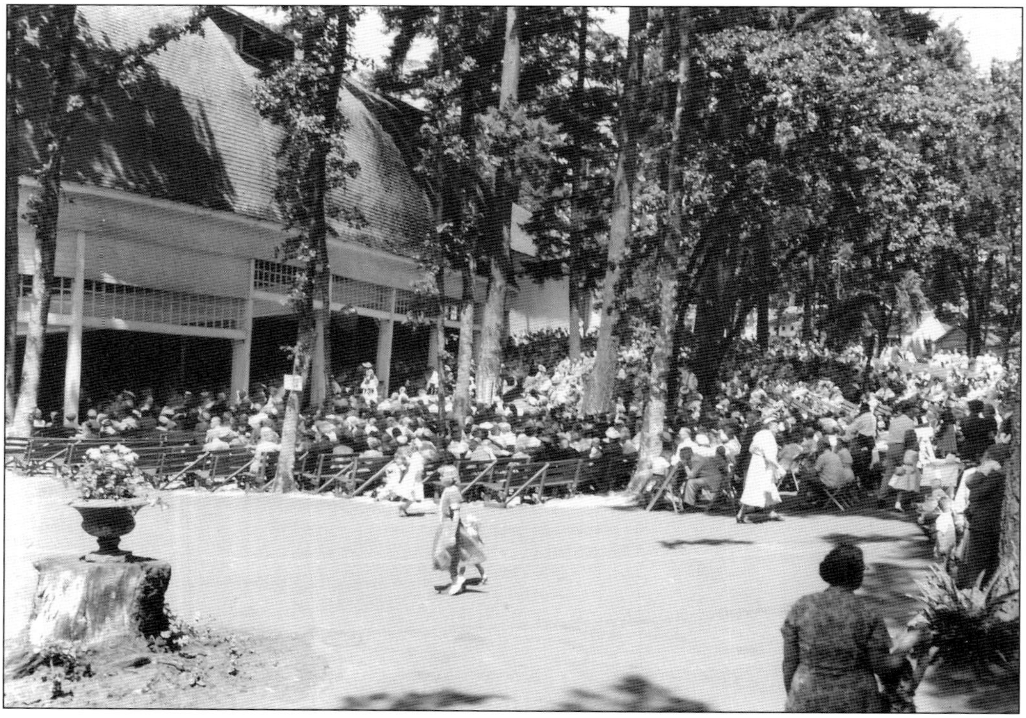

Eight

GLADSTONE BECOMES A TOWN

In 1893, there was a flurry of activity to plat the town of Gladstone, with two different filings platted as West Gladstone. Both acreages had been purchased from Peter Rinearson in the 1880s, and both appropriated the name Gladstone from Harvey Cross. But neither of these would-be town founders had the farsightedness, perseverance, and benevolence to nurture a small community into a productive town.

On September 10, 1894, Cross filed his own town plat and Gladstone was born. Named after Great Britain's prime minister William Ewart Gladstone, a man Cross admired, the town of Gladstone came to symbolize education. Prime Minister Gladstone revolutionized England's elementary school system, and Cross, having once been a teacher, shared that same desire for all to have the opportunity to learn.

Education was the great motivator for Cross so quickly agreeing to bring the Chautauqua to Gladstone Park. Education was why he so generously donated land to build a school before Gladstone became a town. And education was the reason he so sentimentally kept alive the memory of Ad Cason's Little Red Schoolhouse. To keep a focus on education and higher learning, Cross named nearly all of Gladstone's streets and avenues after colleges.

In 1927, after 33 years of extraordinary summer assemblies and attendances as high as 50,000, the Chautauqua closed. In August 1929, at age 73 and a life well-lived, Harvey Cross died, preceded a month earlier by his good friend Charles Dye and the following December by his wife, Orpha. Eva Emery Dye continued her work in women's causes until her death in 1947. And all the while, Gladstone continued to grow.

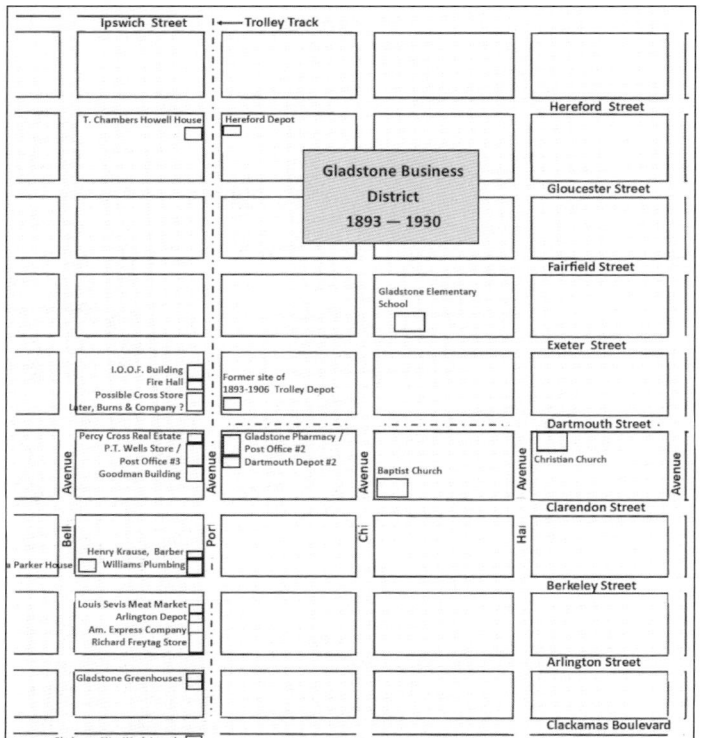

In 1889, Harvey Cross formed the Gladstone Real Estate Association and began selling home lots. The first building erected in future downtown Gladstone was a grocery store (1890) managed by Mitt Cross, Harvey Cross's brother. The store's location is unknown. This map shows early downtown Gladstone.

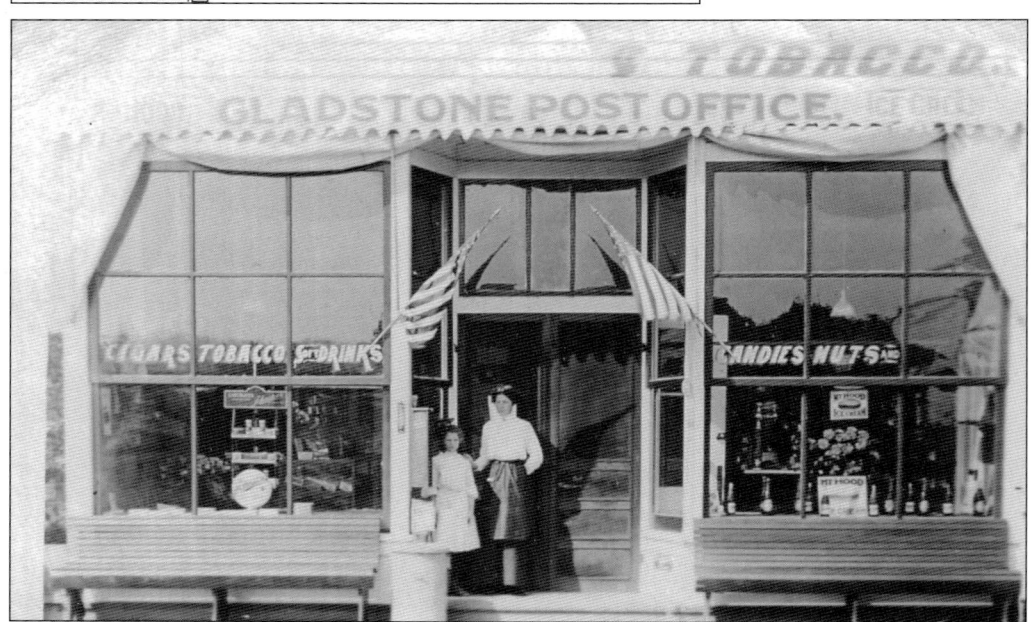

In 1890, the first Gladstone post office was located inside Mitt Cross's store with Elmer Cross, another of Harvey Cross's brothers, acting as postmaster. Later, the post office was moved to the Gladstone Pharmacy, with Asa Parker as postmaster. In this c. 1900–1905 photograph, a woman and girl stand in front of the pharmacy building on the southeast corner of Dartmouth Street and Portland Avenue.

Harvey Cross, a strict Baptist, wrote an unusual restriction into the deeds of his sold properties. No alcohol could be manufactured, vended, used, served, or given away, or the property would revert to Cross. There is no record of Cross repossessing any properties for alcohol violations. As early as 1893, houses began appearing in Gladstone. The first was built by Asa Parker or his son Rev. Gilliam Parker. Seen at right, the Pudabauhgh house is pictured on East Clarendon Street between 1893 and 1895, before the street was plowed. Around the same time, Cross built the house pictured below on Arlington Street for his wife's parents. From left to right in this 1904 photograph are Orpha Cross, Julia Tingle (mother), unidentified, and Nathan Tingle (father). (Both, GHS.)

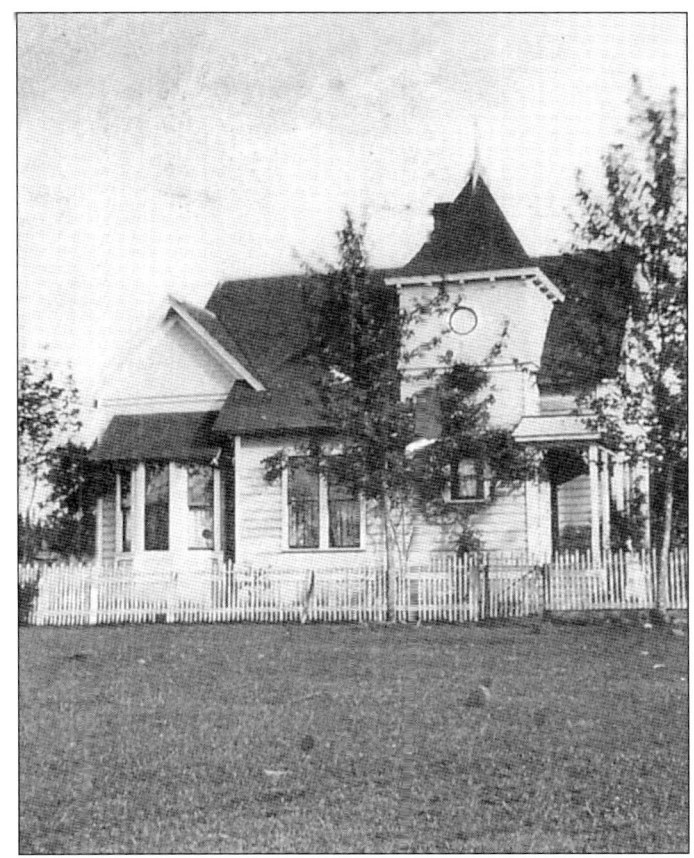

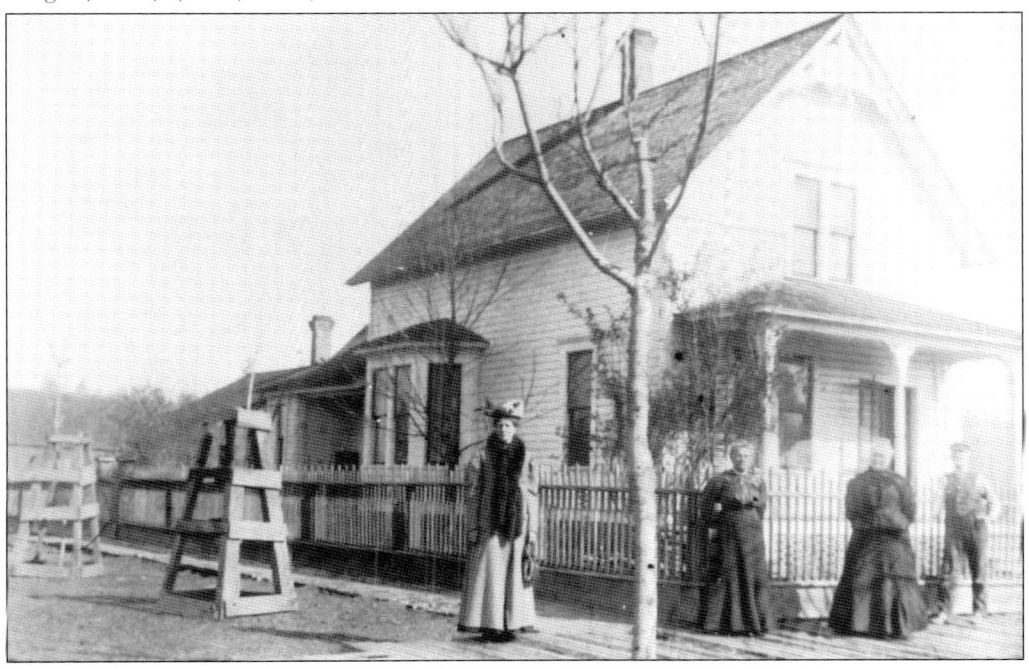

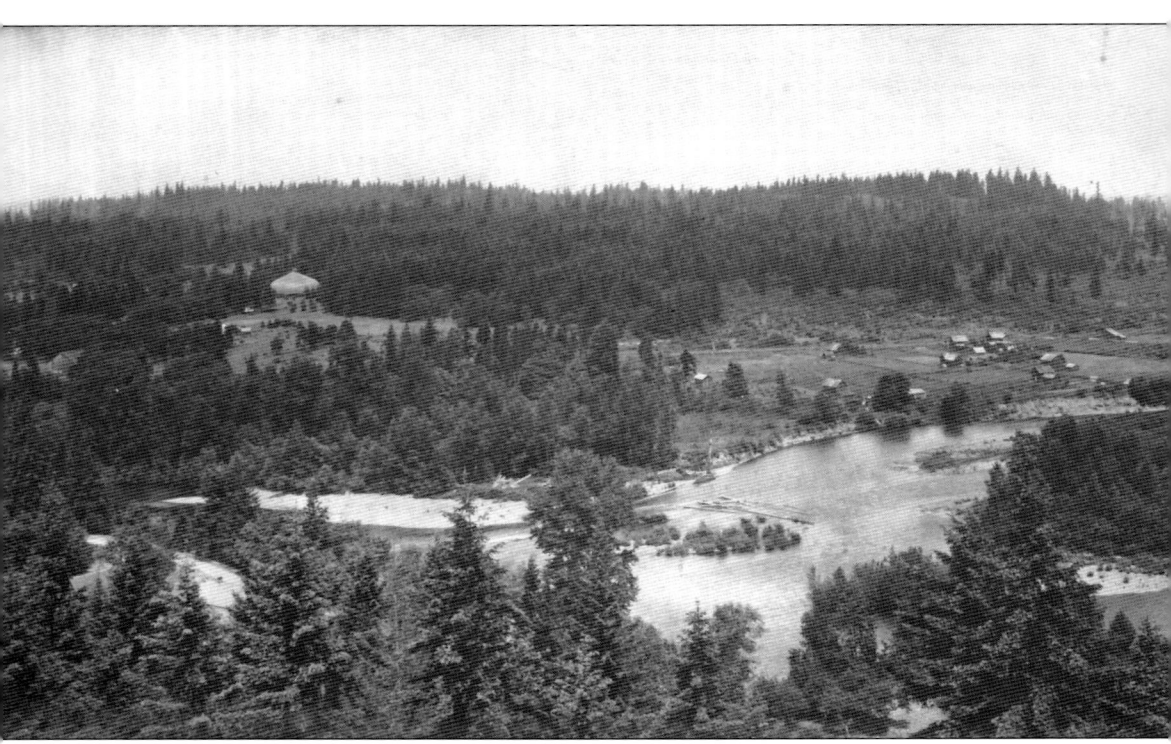

No sooner were rules made than they were broken. In 1906, August Erickson, owner of the notorious Erickson's Saloon in Portland, sold his business and bought Lot 123 at the far southeast corner of future Gladstone. There, he built his new Clackamas Tavern and Health Resort (also called the Roadhouse) next to the Clackamas River. Offering fried chicken dinners and car service to and from the Gladstone trolley line, guests were invited to swim in the river, stroll the orchard, skate at Gladstone's first roller-skating rink, and drink soda pop. Gladstone residents enjoyed going to Erickson's, with local groups holding banquets in the tavern's dining hall and ladies' church clubs having picnic teas in the outdoor gazebo. The cluster of buildings at far right in this early 1900s photograph is Erickson's Clackamas Tavern. Also shown is the 1895 Chautauqua Beehive auditorium. In the foreground is the Clackamas River.

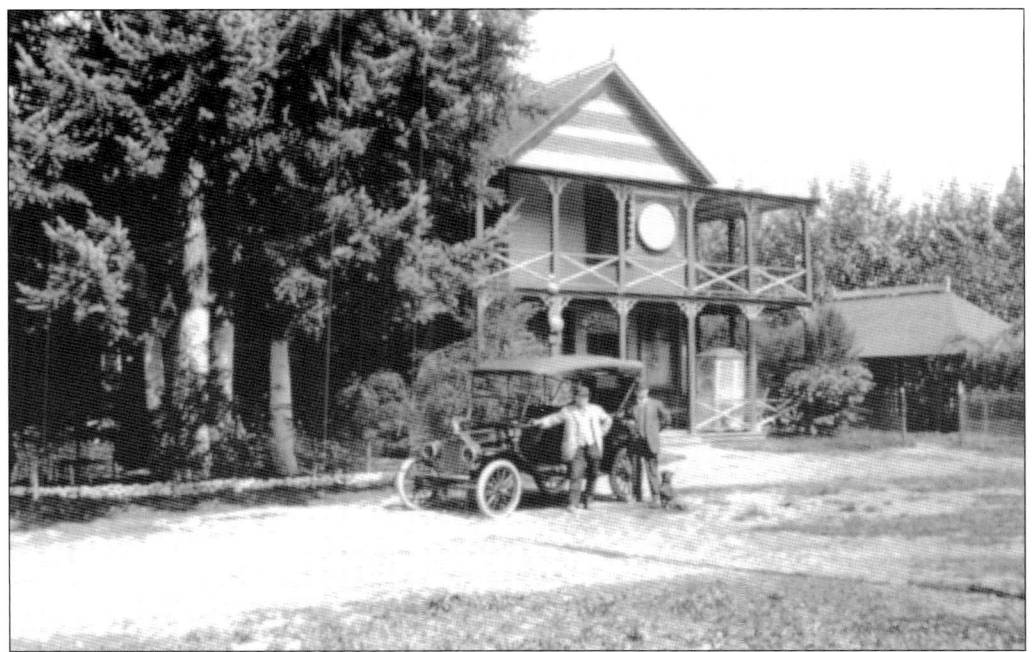

In 1908, Erickson ran afoul of the law. Somehow, alcohol got into his soda pop bottles. Following a stint in jail, he sold his orchard, added a hotel with Russian baths, and continued to serve illegal "soda pop." Seen above in 1912, Erickson (left) and his chauffeur pose in front of the Clackamas Tavern, which soon became a favorite of Portland's rich and reckless. Taking fast automobile spins to the Clackamas River for some illicit fun and frolic, tavern-goers filled their gas tanks at the 3-Way Inn, seen below in 1926. Located at the intersection of Clackamas Boulevard and the automobile bridge, the inn also featured a store and lunch counter. After two wives, too much liquor, and more jail, Erickson lost his business and most of his mind. (Above, OHS.)

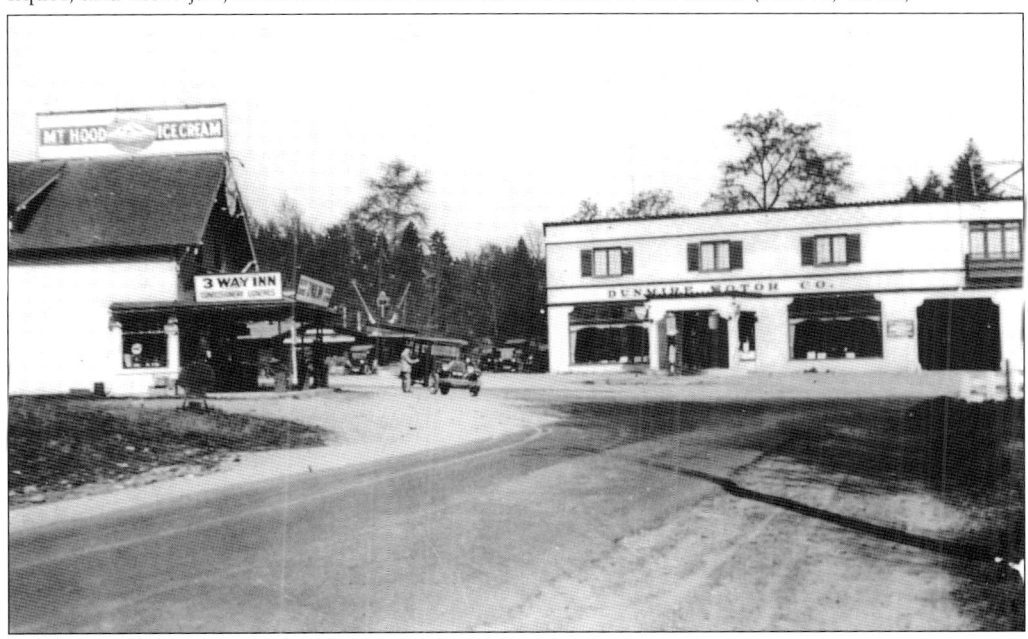

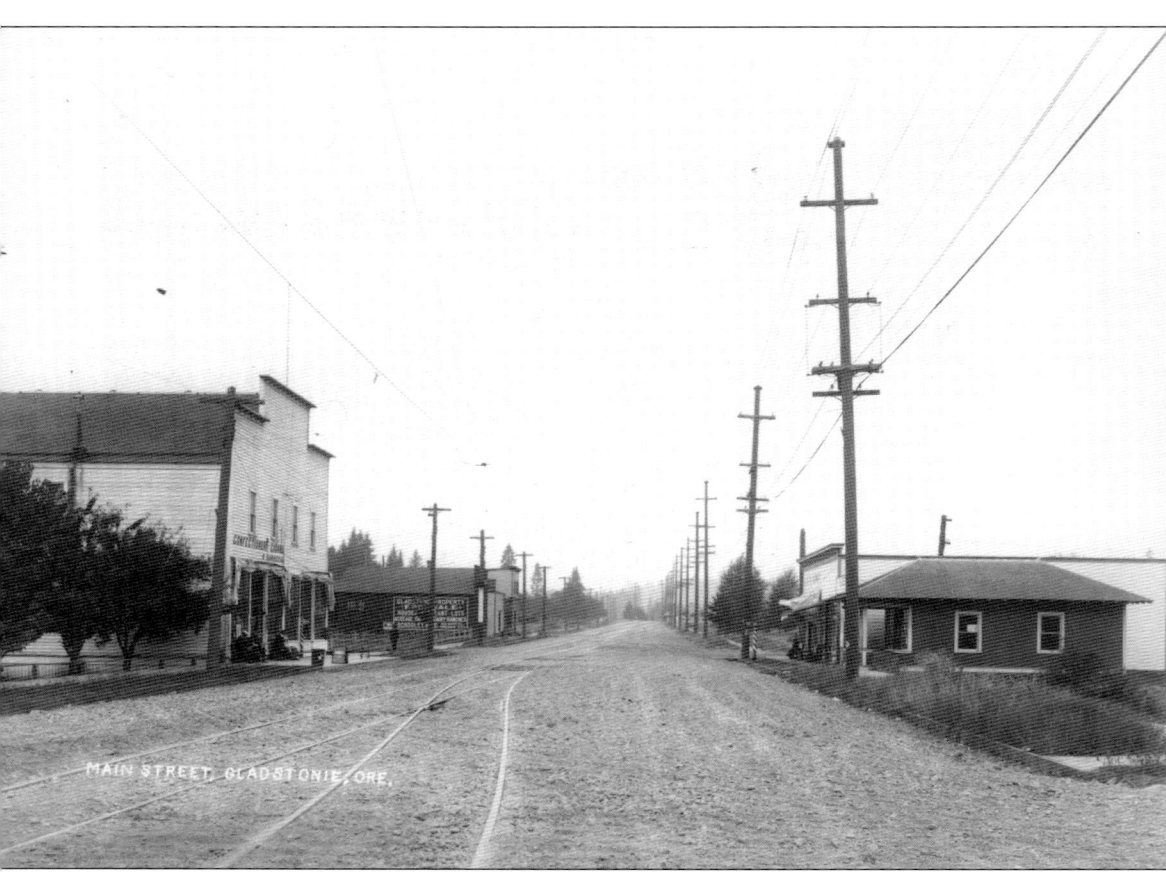

This 1912 photograph shows the north end of Portland Avenue, Gladstone's main street. Near the southwest corner of Dartmouth Street, the tall building on the left is a confectionery and delicatessen purchased by F.E. Goodman about 1912. Directly across the street is the Gladstone Pharmacy (white building), which is believed to have been built between 1900 and 1905 and was first owned by A.C. Sleight. The short, dark building next to the pharmacy is the Dartmouth trolley depot, built in 1906. Both the Goodman building and the pharmacy remain in present-day Gladstone. The Goodman building is greatly altered by the loss of its top floor, while the pharmacy is more recognizable. In the second block, from left to right, the dark building behind the large sign is possibly the Burns and Company store, the short building became the fire hall in 1913, and the tall two-color building belonged to the IOOF.

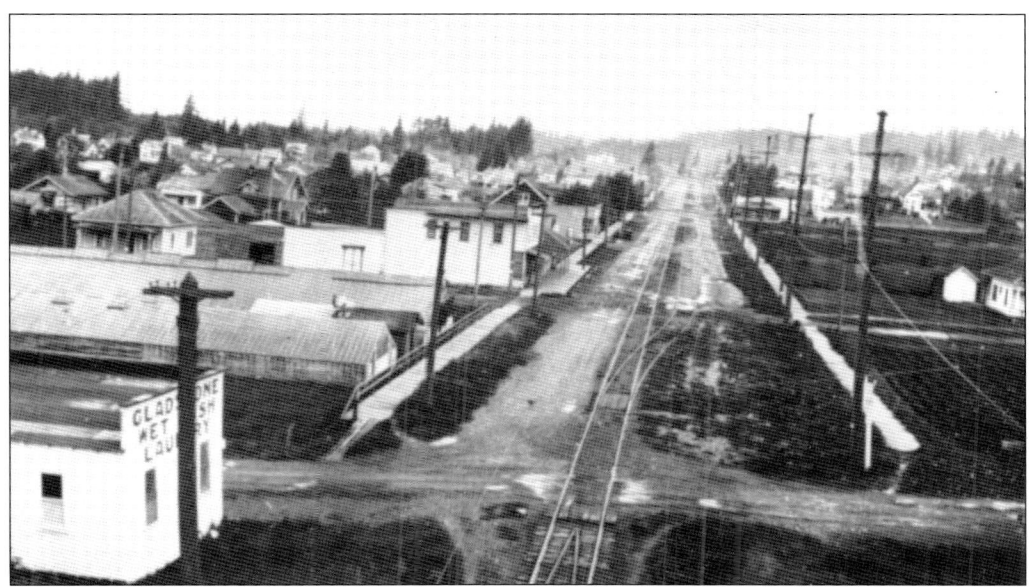

The 1912 photograph above shows the south end of Portland Avenue. At the far left is the Gladstone Wet Wash Laundry, built in 1912. Across Arlington Street are the Gladstone Greenhouses, the first business to take up residence in Gladstone after Harvey Cross's early enterprises. Built in 1893 by James Wilkinson Jr., the greenhouses claimed to offer "the finest collection of carnations ever grown in Oregon City." Below, across Arlington Street from the greenhouses are, from left to right, Richard Freytag's grocery store, the American Express Company, the Arlington trolley depot, and Louis Sevis's Meat Market. Freytag, who in 1908 moved his store from its original 1904 location to where it is shown now, is believed to be the man standing at left wearing suspenders.

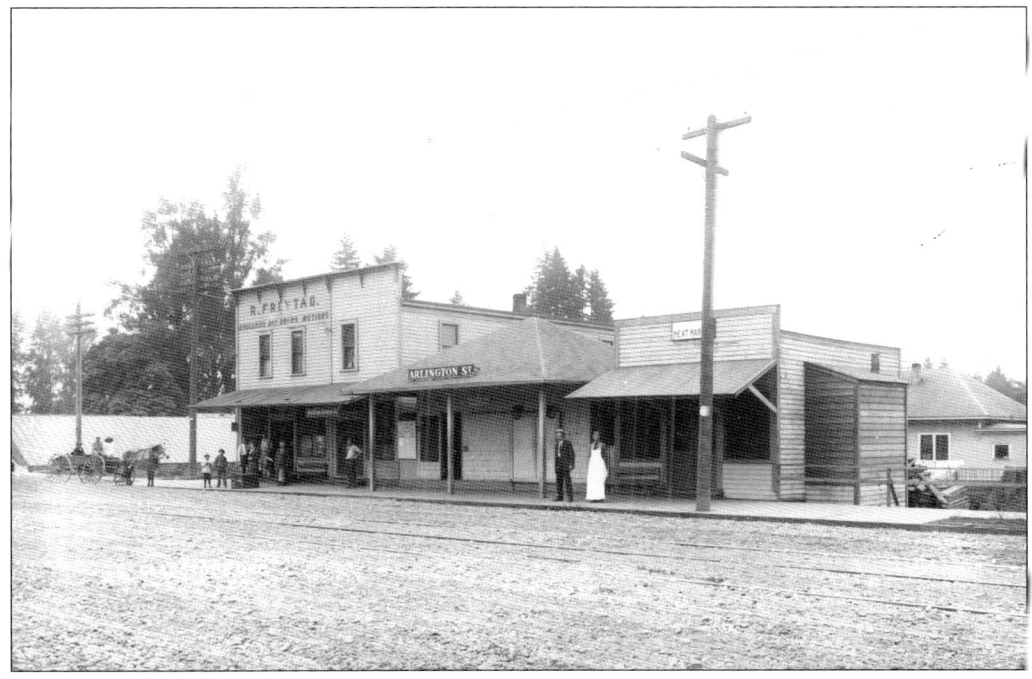

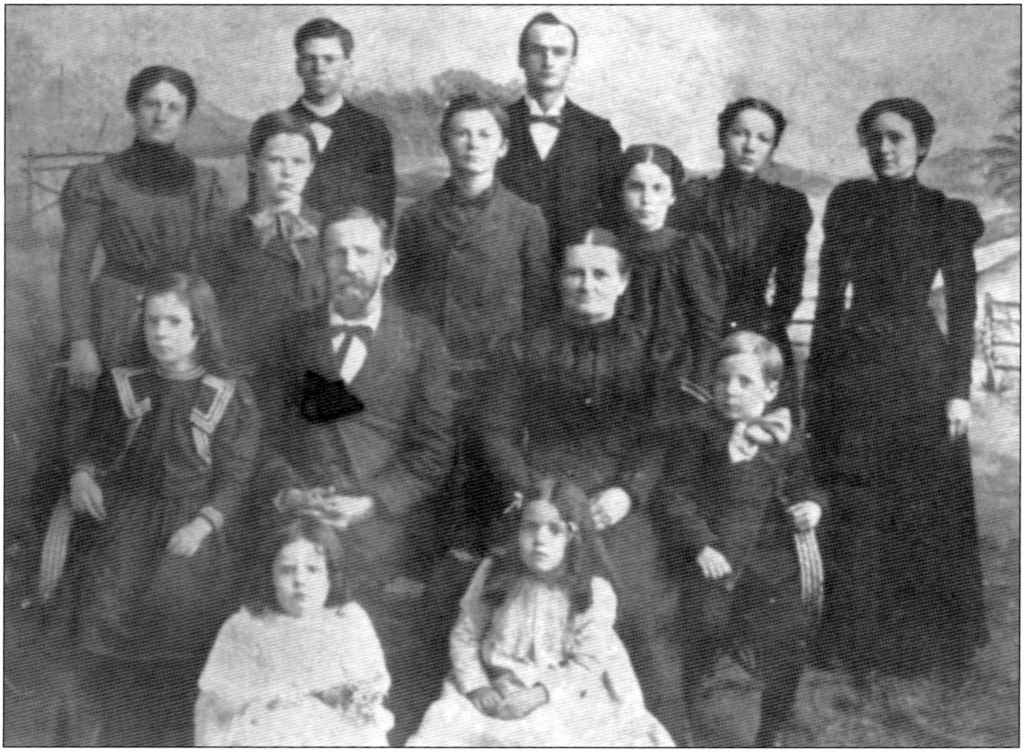

In 1908, Rev. Aaron Mulkey, his wife Josie, and their children came to Gladstone. With the help of his large family, Reverend Mulkey soon raised up a congregation of 55 charter members and established the first church in Gladstone. This family photograph, taken in 1890, shows Reverend Mulkey and his wife sitting in the center of the second row. The children are unidentified. (GCC.)

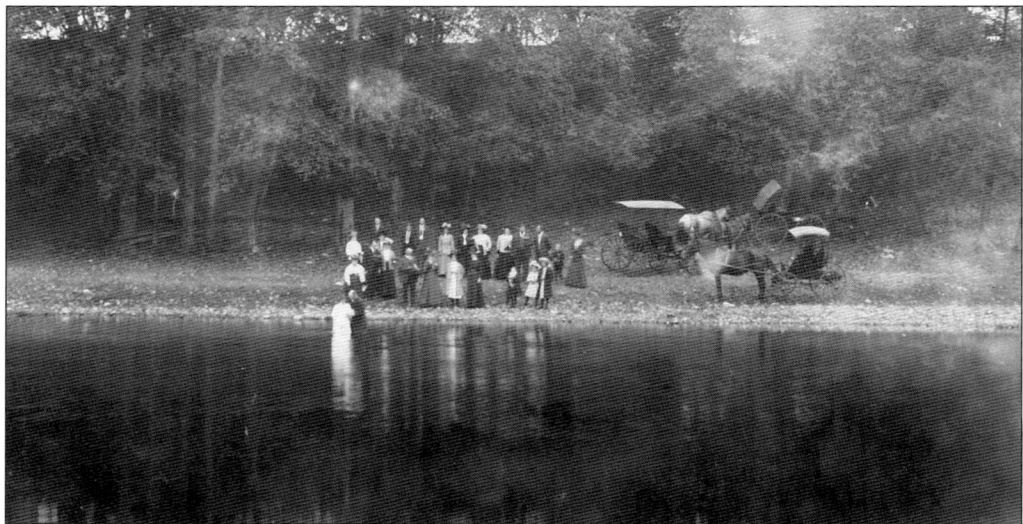

Reverend Mulkey worked tirelessly to increase his congregation, and his hard work reaped good results. In this 1908–1910 photograph, members of the Gladstone Christian Church attend a baptism held in the chilly waters of the Clackamas River. Reverend Mulkey, wearing a black robe, can be seen standing in the water. (GCC.)

In 1908, Harvey Cross donated the Christian church's fledgling congregation a piece of land on the southeast corner of Dartmouth Street and Harvard Avenue. With little resources, the members constructed a crude building out of tarpaper and rough boards in which they held services until a permanent church could be built. In the background is the 1908 elementary school. (GCC.)

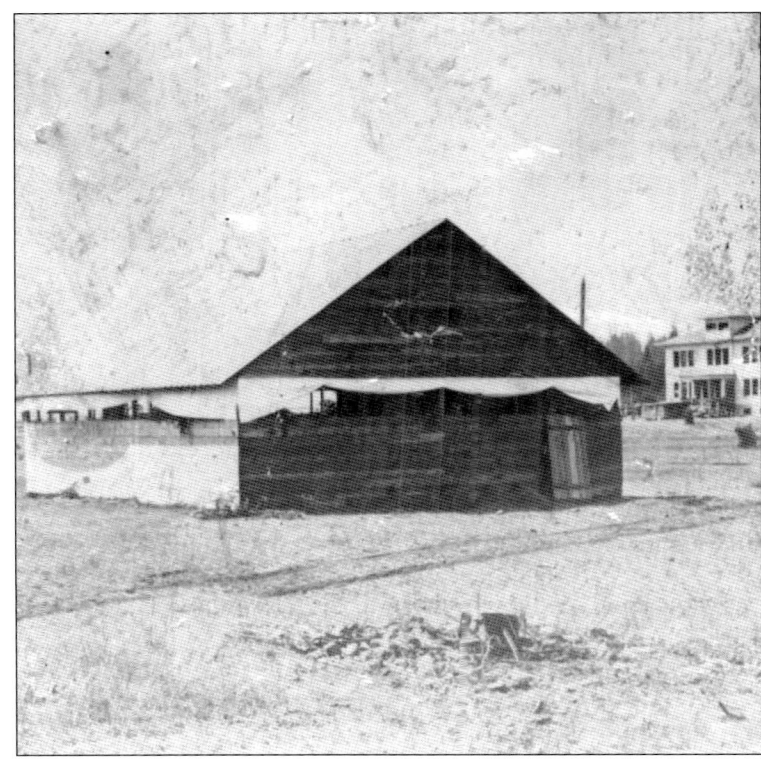

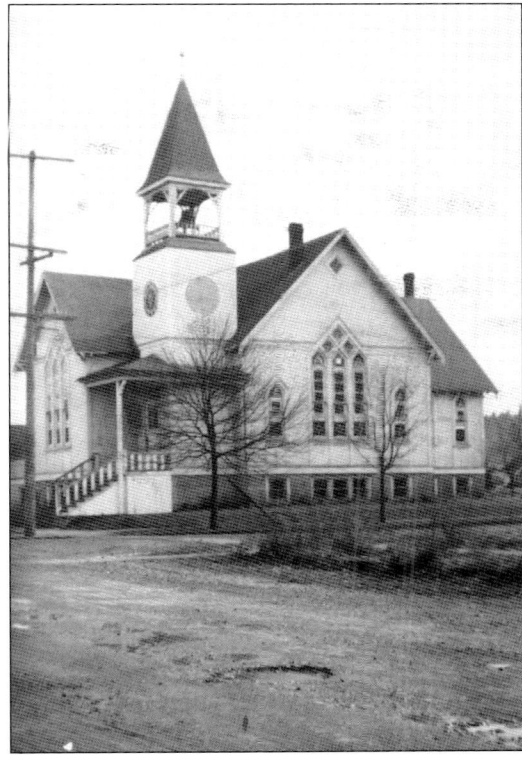

In July 1912, the new Christian church building was finished and dedicated. As seen here in 1920, the new church with its bell tower, stained-glass windows, and gothic styling was one of the most beautiful buildings in Gladstone. (GCC.)

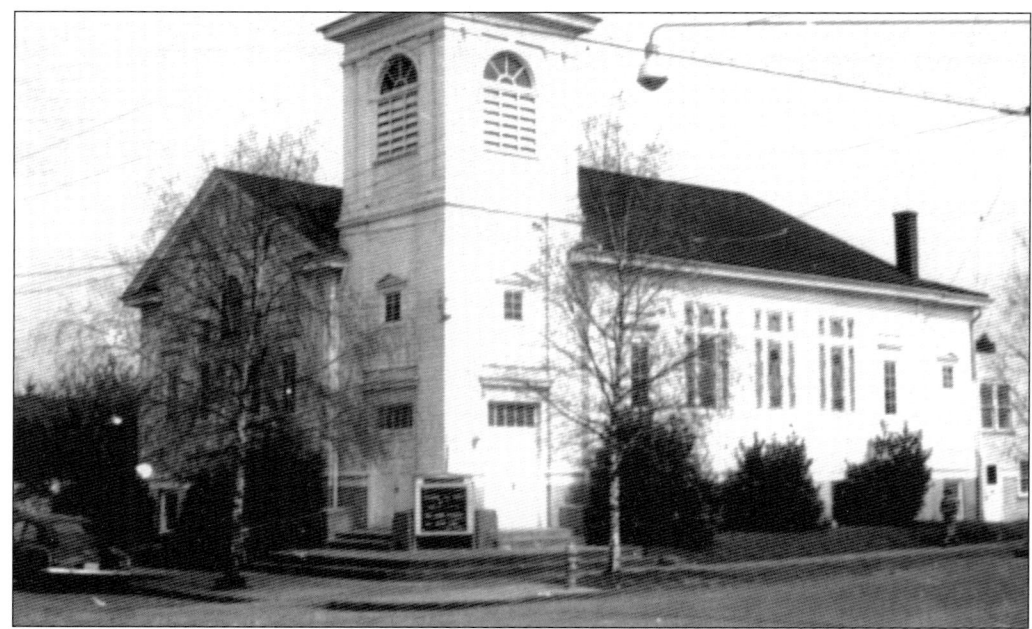

In 1913, members of the Oregon City Baptist Church formed a new congregation and moved to Gladstone. First meeting in a building on the northwest corner of Portland Avenue and Dartmouth Street, Harvey Cross soon donated the Baptists a piece of land on the northeast corner of Clarendon Street and Chicago Avenue. In 1915, the Baptists built an equally elegant church and dedicated it in 1924.

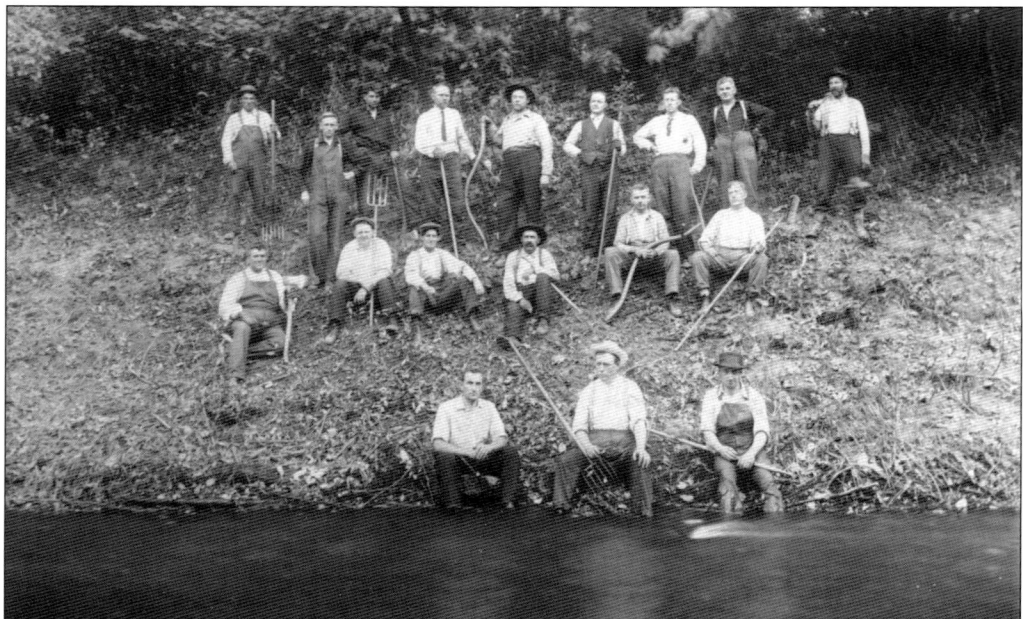

In 1908, a group called the Gladstone Improvement Club busied themselves with projects that involved enhancing the beauty and livability of Gladstone. One of the many undertakings of these club members, shown taking a break from their work, was to periodically clear brush and tidy the overgrown banks of the Clackamas River.

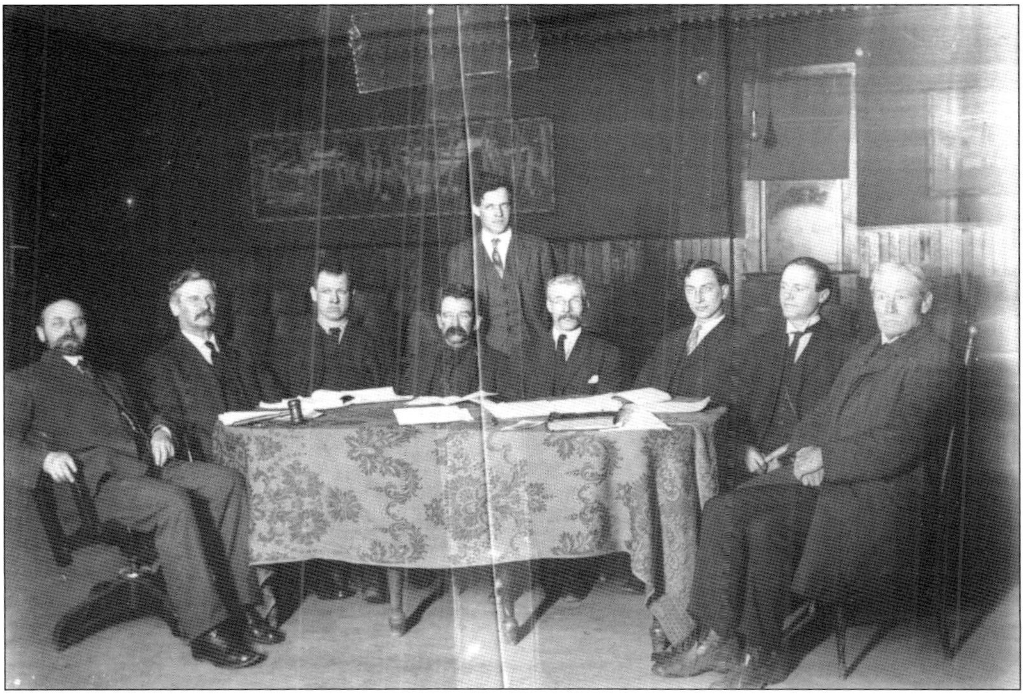

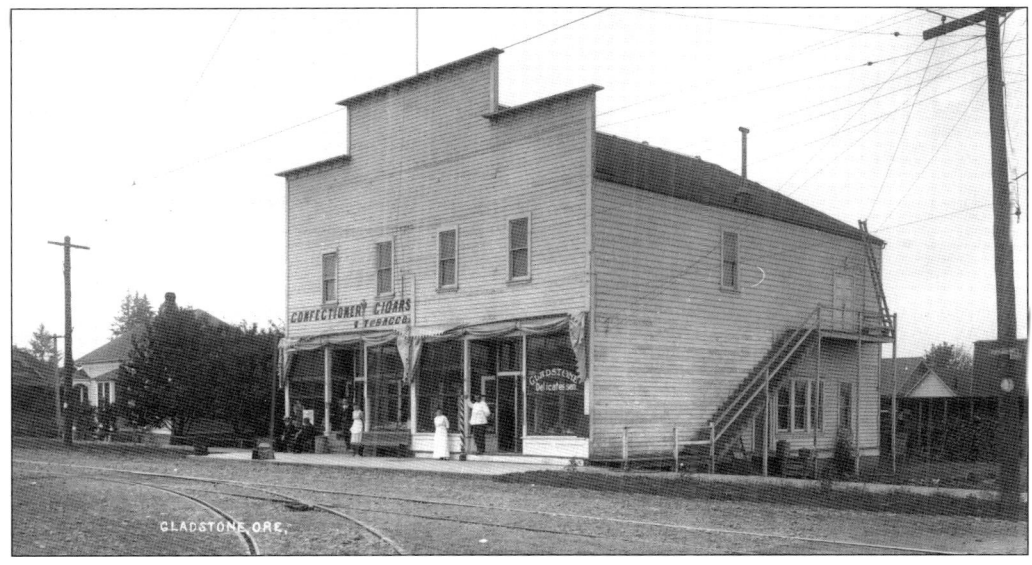

The Gladstone Improvement Club campaigned for Gladstone to incorporate, and by December 1910, Gladstone was an official town. Above, on January 10, 1911, the first Gladstone town council met in makeshift council chambers on the second floor of the Goodman Building. The first council included, from left to right, Mayor Oscar Freytag, four unidentified, Brendon Vedder, T. Chambers Howell, and F.S. Baker. William Hammond is standing. The council's first order of business was to vote on Harvey Cross's donation of land along the north bank of the Clackamas River, between the wagon bridge and the trolley bridge, for a town park. The gift was accepted. Not long afterward, the first town well was dug in Cross Park. In 1921, the park acquired its first comfort station.

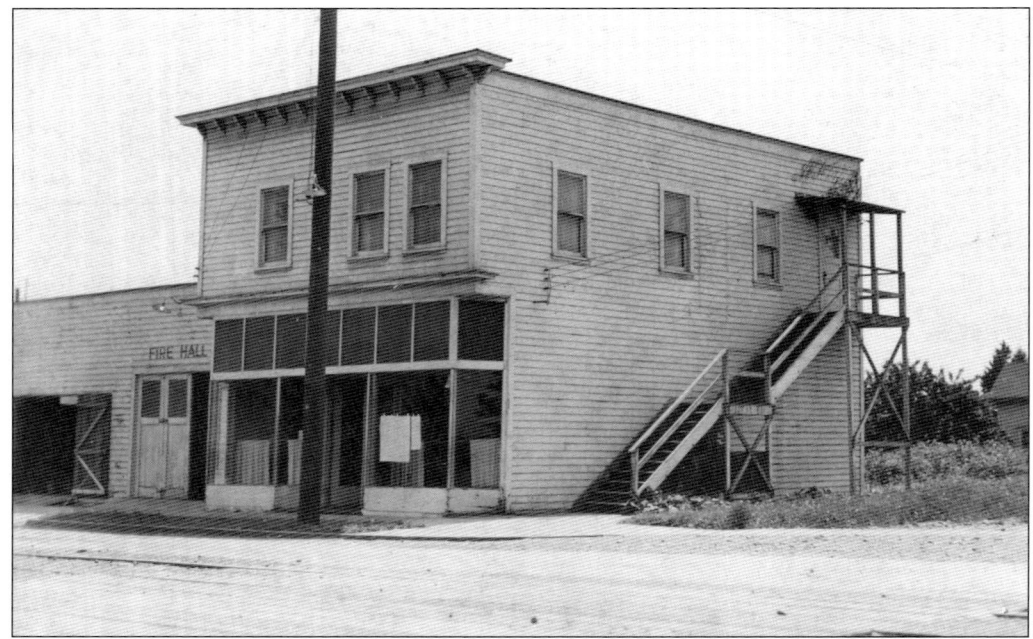

In 1913, the IOOF building was a commercial office building and storefront located on Portland Avenue between Dartmouth and Exeter Streets. During the late 1920s and into the 1930s, the building's second floor housed Gladstone's city hall, with the attached garage serving as the fire hall. The building no longer stands.

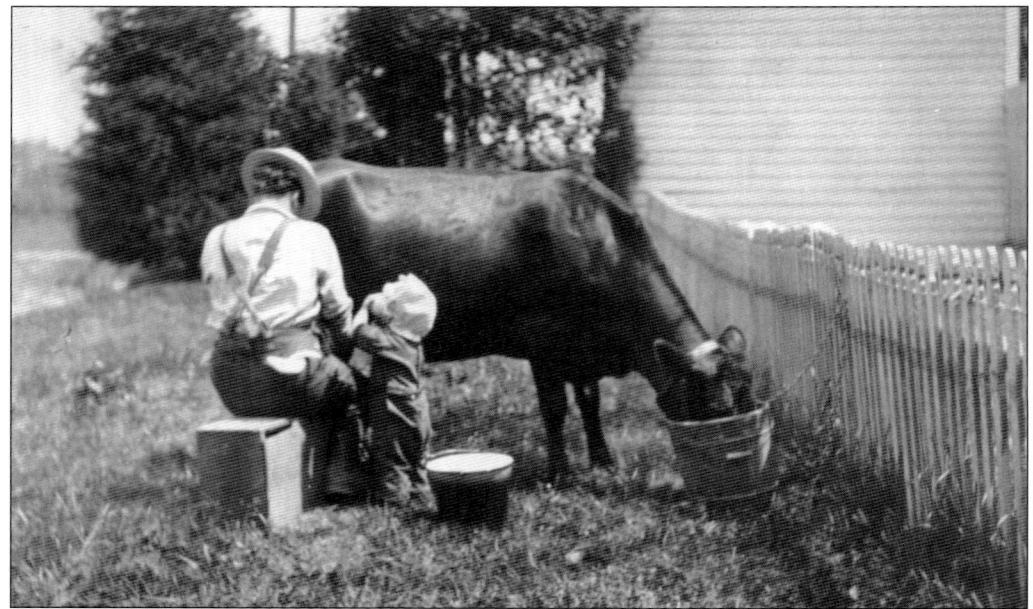

In early Gladstone, cows were allowed to graze wherever they liked. One pressing matter discussed by the new town council was whether the wandering bovines should have their cowbells removed. According to complaints, the continual bell ringing unnerved residents. In 1916, Charles Sievers milks his cow. The council's decision was unpublished, but notice that Bossy is not tied, nor is she wearing a bell.

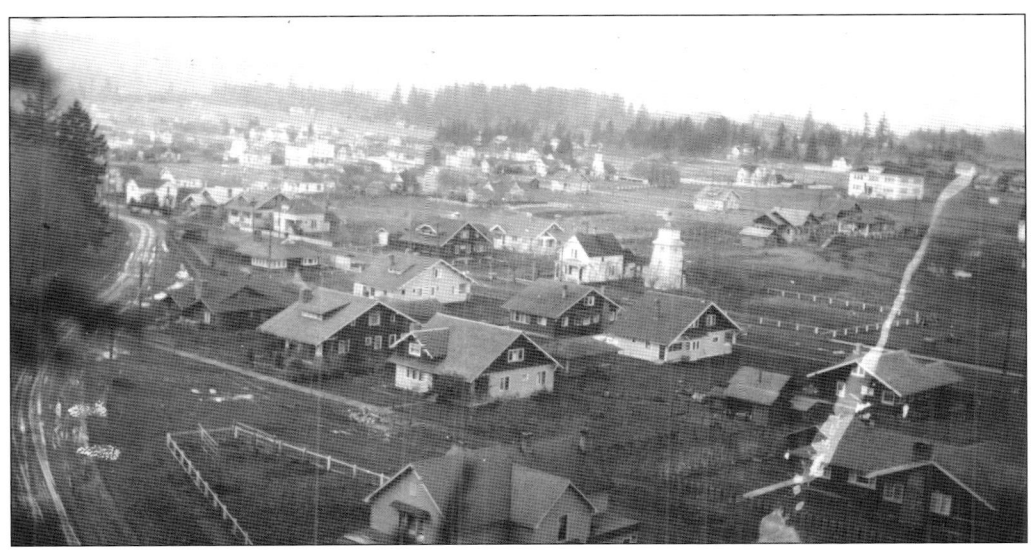

No sooner had Gladstone become a town than new houses began lining the streets and cars began filling them. Above, Bungalow Row, as seen in 1915, was the first "housing development" in Gladstone. Located along Arlington Street and Clackamas Boulevard, at least 13 similar houses were built, many by local architect Guy LaSalle. Besides being of a like design, many of these bungalows incorporated Clackamas River rocks in their construction, such as in the foundations and chimneys. The square towers in the background are private water storage tanks. Below, in 1919, men and boys from the Gladstone Christian Church get ready to leave on a fishing trip in their automobiles. Instead of walking to the Clackamas River, they are driving to the Pacific Ocean.

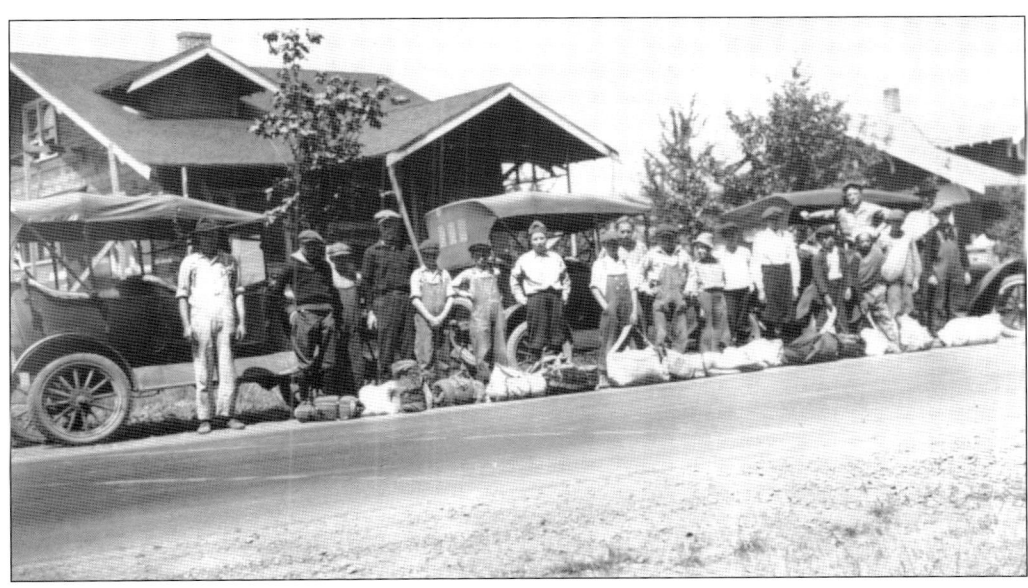

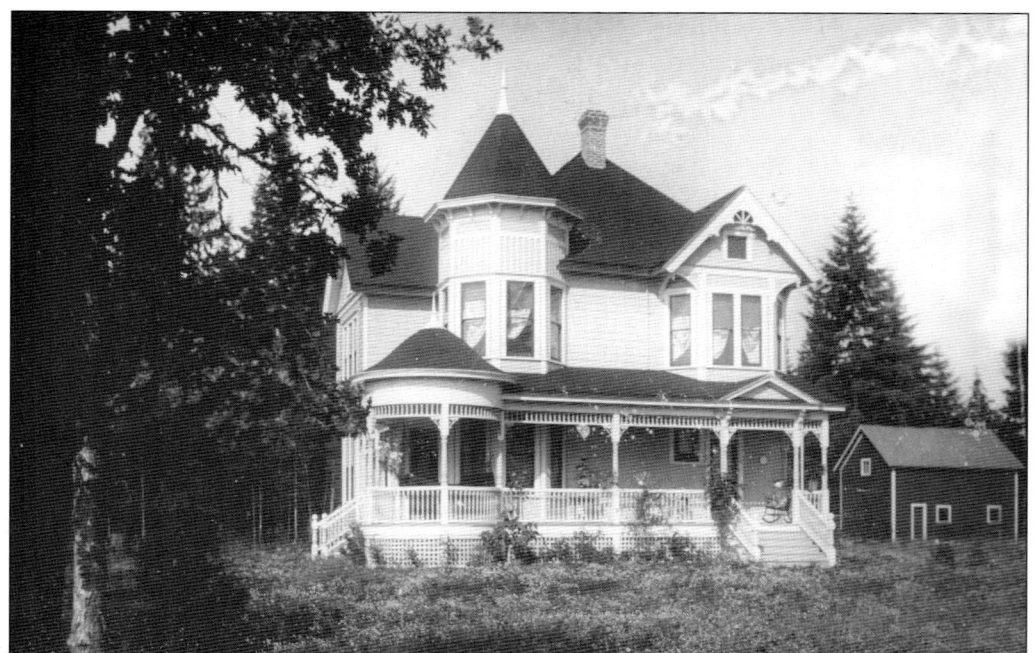

T. Chambers Howell, twice mayor of Gladstone, owned one of the first automobiles in town. In 1914, Howell purchased a 15-acre tract on the northwest corner of Portland Avenue and Herford Street where he built what was to be for many years the most expensive house in Gladstone. The Howell house, shown here, burned in the early 1920s and was replaced by an equally luxurious house.

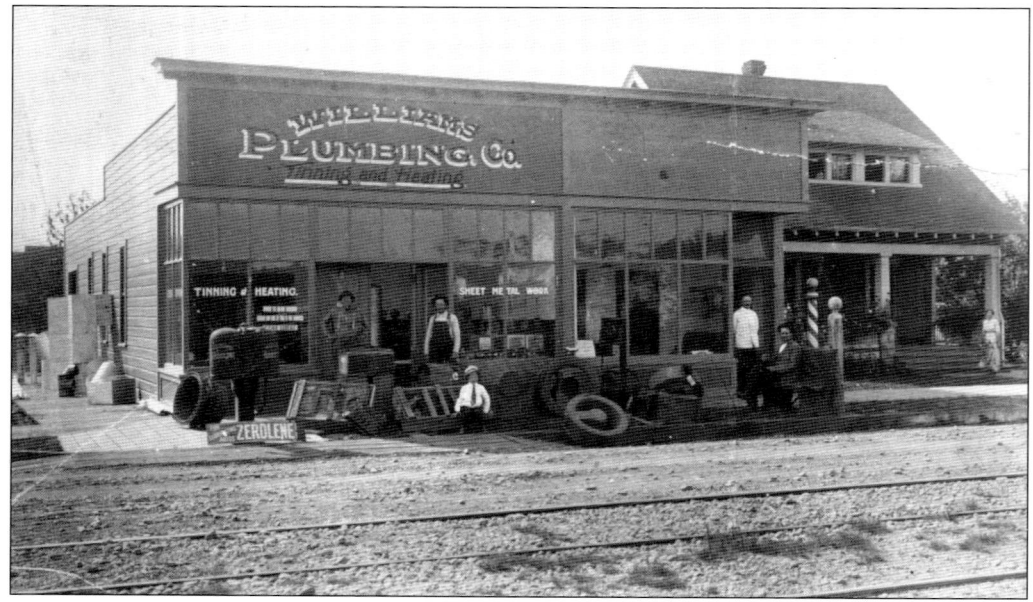

In 1903, the telephone arrived in Gladstone, followed by sidewalks in 1904, indoor plumbing in 1906, indoor electric lights in 1894–1906, electric streetlights in 1909–1912, and a new city water system in 1912. In 1915, T.J.B. Williams (standing at far left) opened the first plumbing company in Gladstone. Located on the northwest corner of Portland Avenue and Berkley Street, he shared a building with barber Henry Krause (standing at far right).

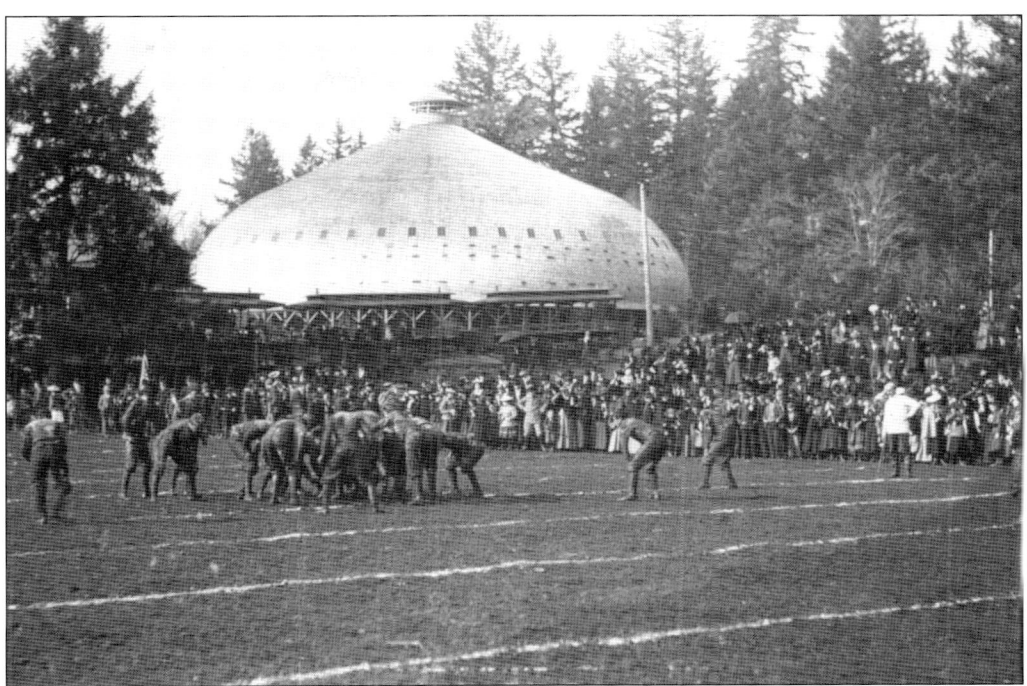

Even though Gladstone was busy working and growing, residents still found time to have fun. Above, on Thanksgiving Day 1897, as many as 1,000 spectators crowded the Gladstone Park athletic field to watch the big football game played between Oregon City National Guard Company F and the Oregon City Athletic Club. At one point, the game became so exciting, onlookers crowded the playing field and had to be pushed back before play could continue. The soldiers won 4-0. Below, in 1907, the second Clackamas County Fair was held in Gladstone Park. Organized by the newly founded Clackamas County Fair Association, nearly five decades had passed since the first agricultural event held on Rinearson land. Besides exhibits, a livestock show, and contests, attendees took rides on a Ferris wheel. (Below, GCC.)

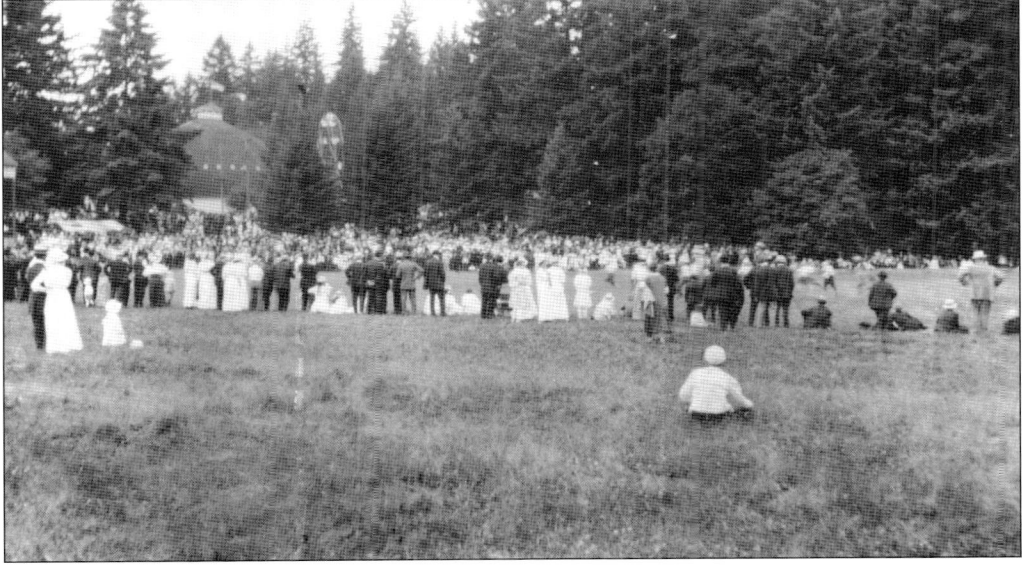

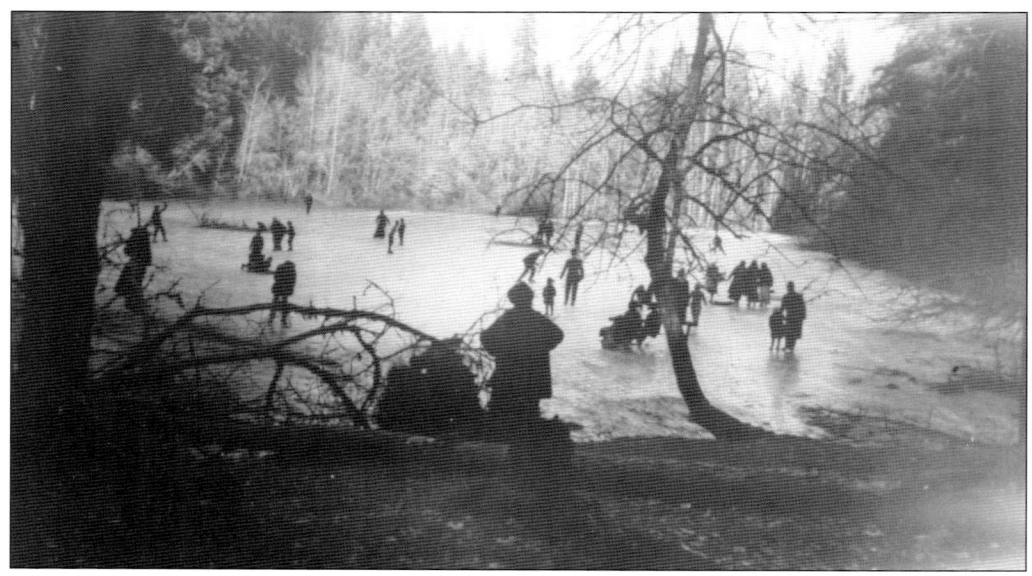

Whether winter or summer, Gladstone residents made good use of all the water that surrounded them. Above, in 1917, Lake Chautauqua froze solid. Gladstone residents braved the hilly climb and cold trek through the woods to enjoy a few hours of skating. Below, in 1931, the Gladstone town council decided to name the land that Harvey Cross had donated for a park the Gladstone Swimming Beach. Later, the park would be renamed for Harvey Cross, but at the time, the first name was appropriate. On hot summer days, the river overflowed with sunbathers, swimmers, boaters, and even a few fishermen, many of whom had come from as far away as Oregon City or Portland to enjoy the water. (Both, GCC.)

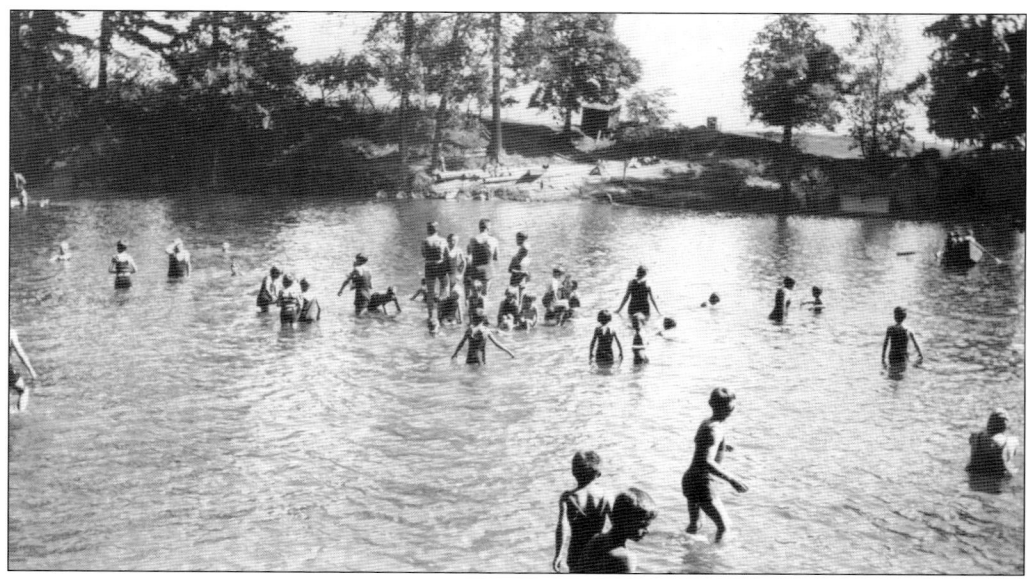

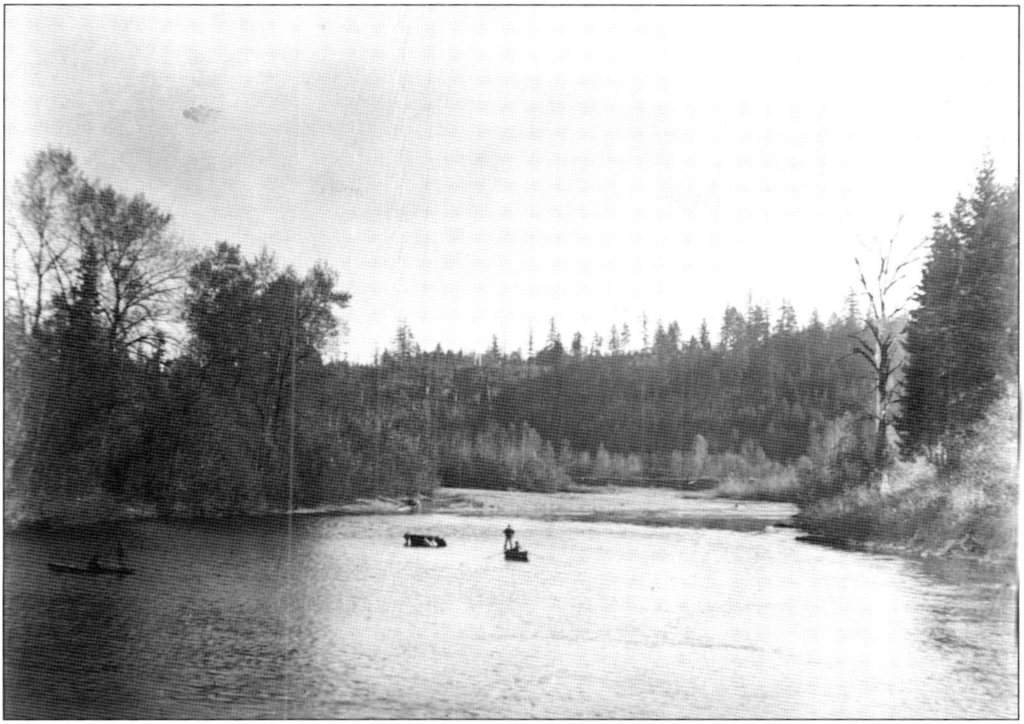

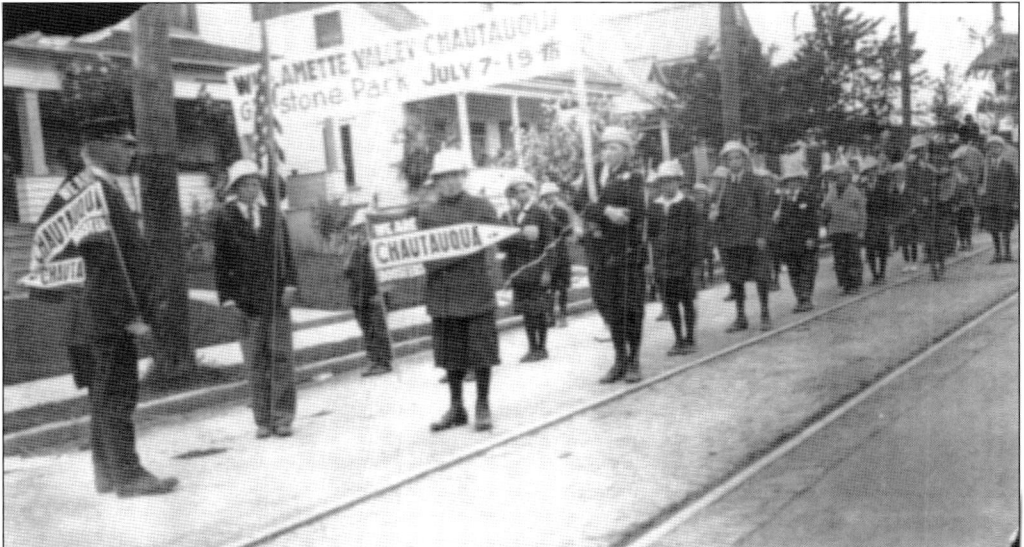

Some of the best fishing to be found on the Clackamas River was above High Rocks, and some believed that the cloudier the day, the better the fishing. In 1910, these men appear to be looking for the best place to drop their lines. In the background is the location of the Gladstone dam. In the far background, the hills overlook Bakers Ferry Road, later Clackamas River Drive.

Gladstone celebrated summer with parades and patriotism. In 1914, the Gladstone Boy's Chautauqua Booster Club marched through the streets of Gladstone to announce the upcoming Chautauqua assembly, the most important event of the season. In this image, the boys stand in formation on Dartmouth Street.

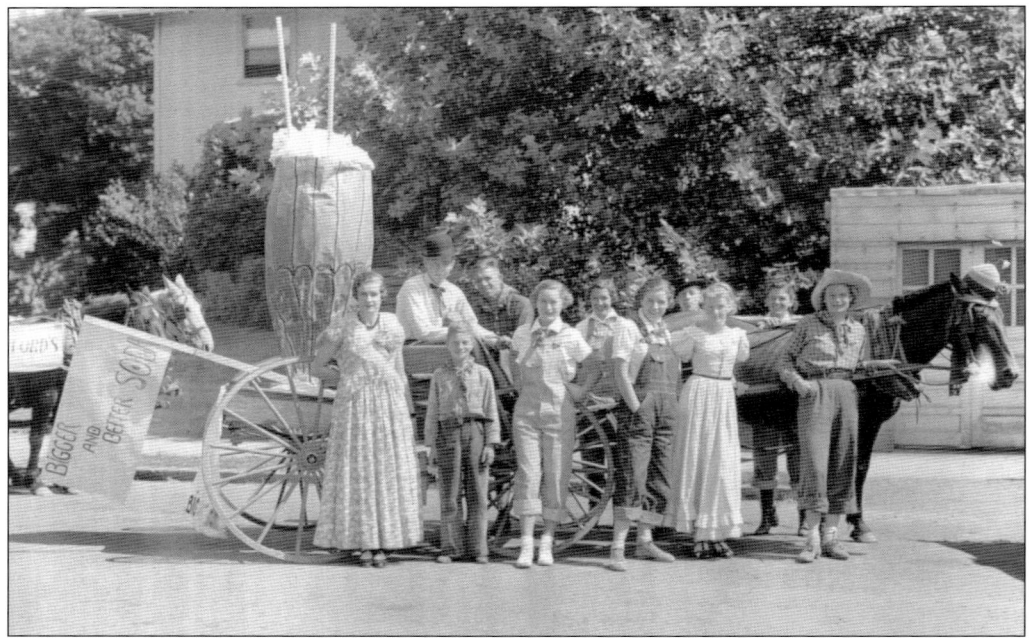

Parades were also about simply having fun. In the 1920s, a group of young Gladstone residents dressed in Western costumes proudly display an ice-cream soda atop a parade float. Dorothy Hammond is at far left. (Courtesy of Diane Nickerson Timmons.)

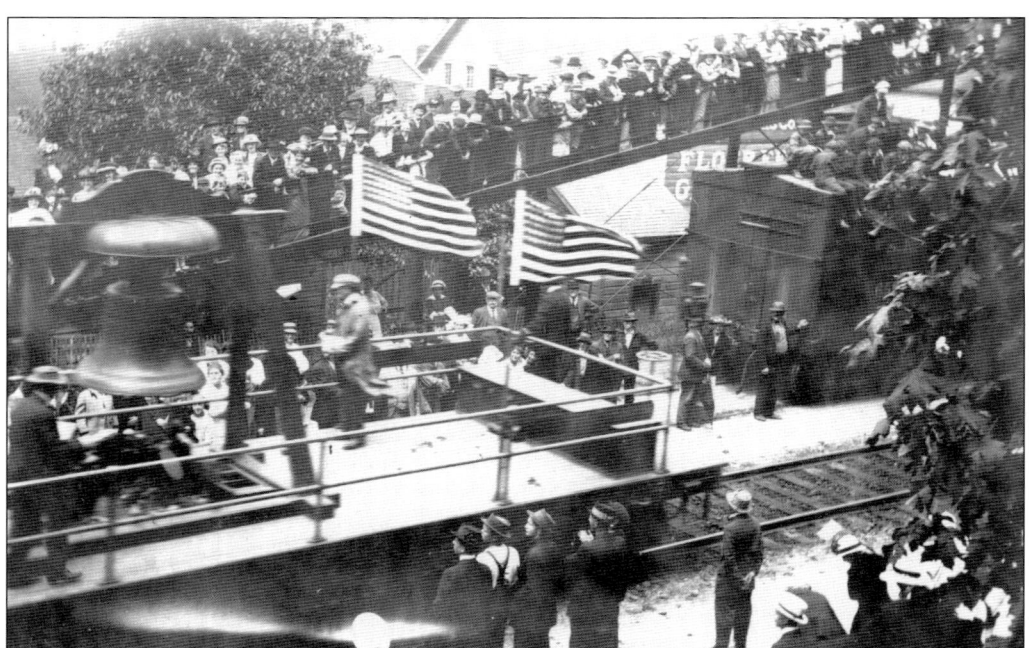

On July 14, 1915, during its 1915–1917 tour, the Liberty Bell, riding on a Southern Pacific flatbed car, stopped at Gladstone Park for a 10-minute viewing before proceeding south. As many as 40,000 people attended the event. As shown here, the bell was unable to stop in Oregon City, but those wanting to see it were allowed to line the tracks and watch as it slowly passed uncovered.

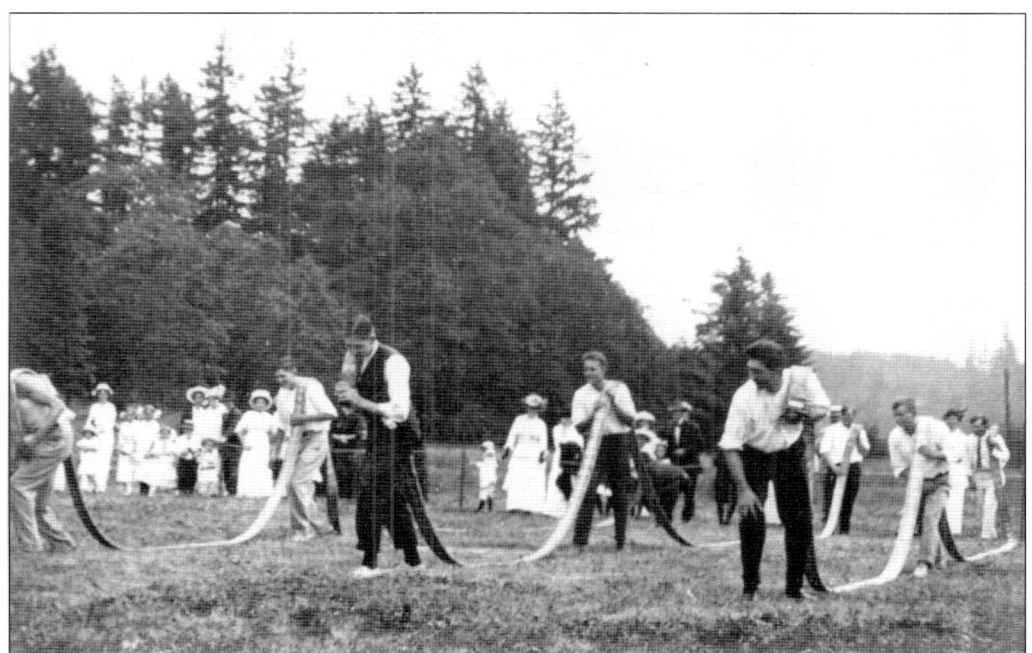

In 1895, only 17 Oregon City Pulp and Paper Mill (OCPPM) workers lived in Gladstone, but with the ease of trolley transportation, that number increased quickly. On July 10, 1914, the OCPPM hosted a company picnic in Gladstone Park for its employees and family members. Along with food and speeches, the day was filled with games, contests, and races. The fun was endless, as were the number of trolley cars hired to transport all the attendees to Gladstone Park. Reports were that shortly after the park gates opened at 8:20 a.m., 1,000 people descended upon the athletic field. Two of the most popular events were the men's firehose rolling race, above, and the ladies' hammering contest. Below, the woman at far right with the white feather in her hat really "nailed" the contest and won.

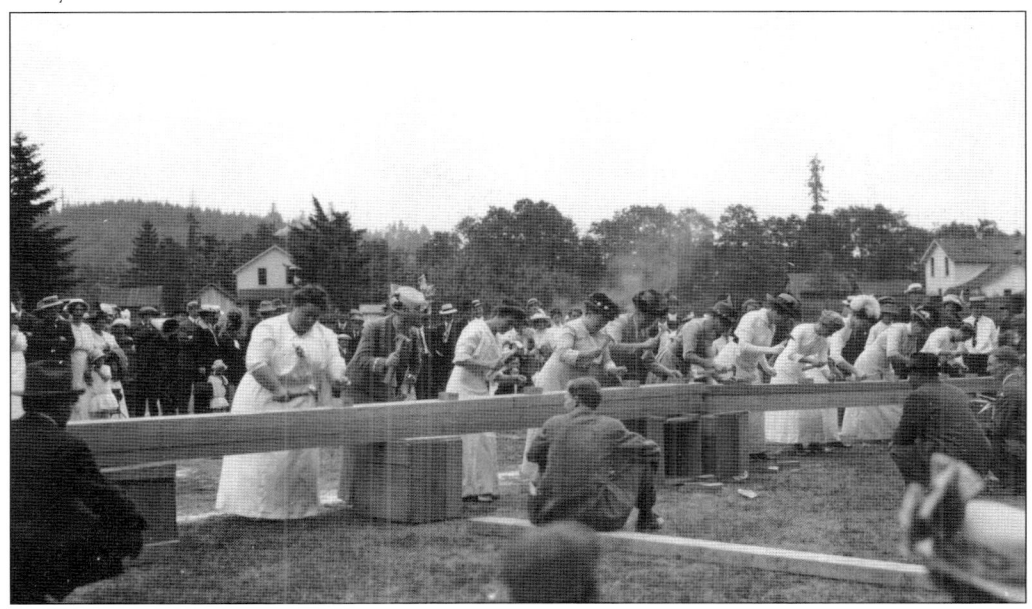

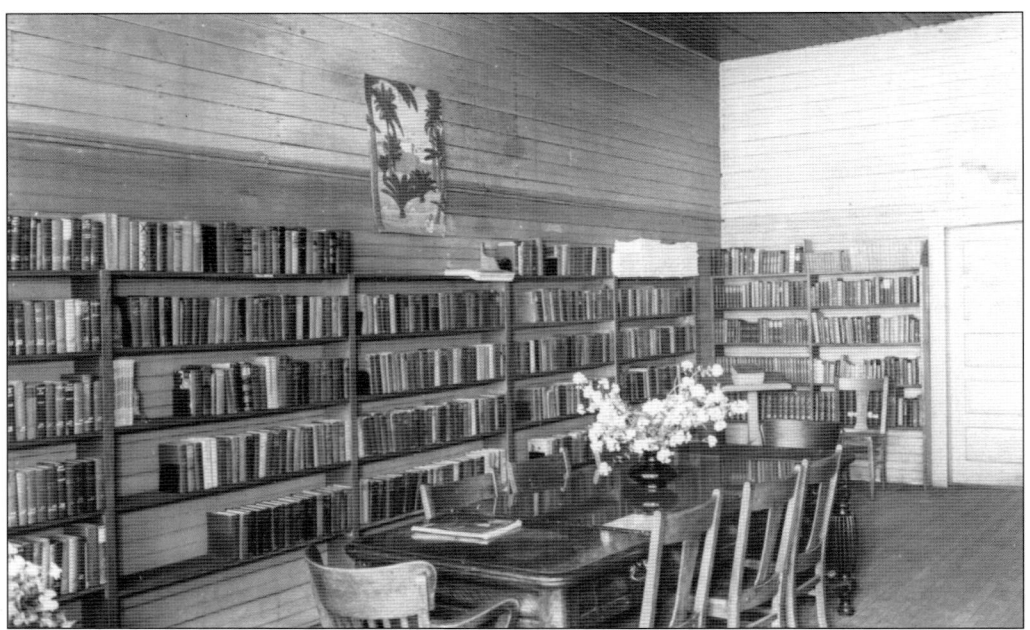

By 1920, Gladstone had grown to a population of nearly 1,100, but had no library. In 1921, three ladies of the Gladstone Euterpean Club, a woman's group that met to discuss music and art, founded the first Gladstone library in a small back room of the Gladstone Pharmacy. Gertrude Oswald served as the first librarian.

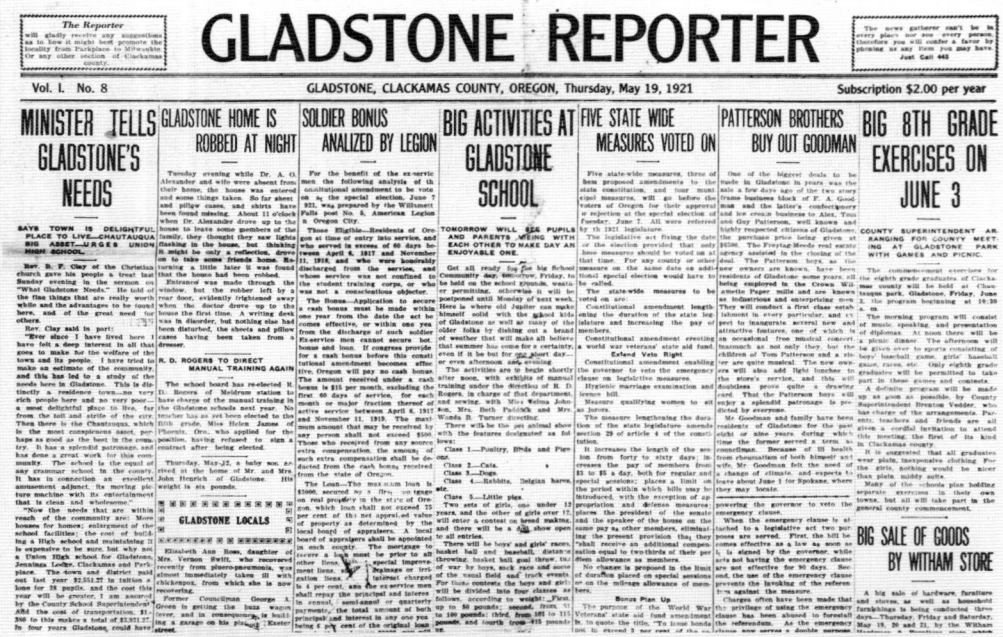

In 1921, Gladstone made news. The town's first newspaper, the *Gladstone Reporter*, was published by W.E. Hessler of Oregon City, previously of Portland's *Evening Telegram*. Considered a great addition to the community, nothing is known as to why the Gladstone newspaper stopped publication after one year.

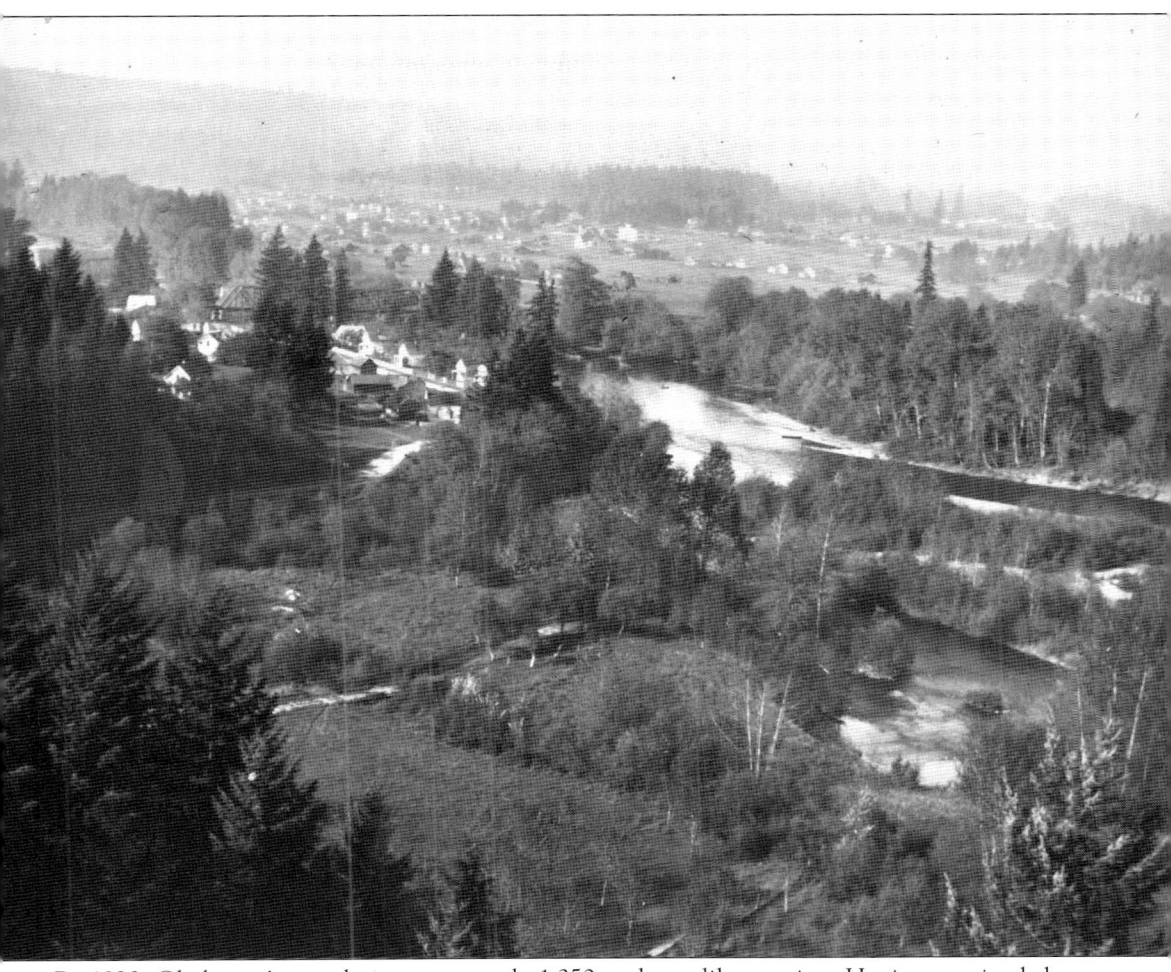

By 1930, Gladstone's population was nearly 1,350 and steadily growing. Having survived the Spanish influenza pandemic of 1918, World War I, and the Great Depression, Gladstone was now well established as the town that Judge Harvey Cross envisioned. This view from the hills above Park Place facing northeast shows the area in 1914. The Clackamas River runs through the center, with two of the three bridges that connect Gladstone (north) with Park Place (south) in view. At far left, the 1892 wagon bridge is nearly hidden in the trees, with the railroad bridge easier to see at right. In the center of Gladstone are two distinctive buildings. The large white building is the Christian church, with the square Gladstone Grade School diagonally to the right. East of town is Gladstone Park with its logged-off area once more growing trees. In the center background, behind the stand of firs, is Jennings Lodge, Gladstone's neighbor to the north. Out of view to the left lies historic Oregon City, Gladstone's parent town. (GHS.)

Bibliography

American Lumbermen: The Personal History and Public and Business Achievements of One Hundred Eminent Lumbermen of the United States. Chicago, IL: American Lumberman, 1906.

Bancroft, Hubert Howe. *The Works of Hubert Howe Bancroft, Vol XXIX: History of Oregon, Vol. 1, 1834–1848.* San Francisco, CA: The History Company, 1886.

Beals, Herbert K. *Gladstone, Oregon, a History, Part One: Earliest Times to the Civil War's Eve.* Gladstone, OR: Gladstone Historical Society, 1992.

———. *Gladstone, Oregon, a History, Part Two: Civil War to the Eve of the Great Depression.* Gladstone, OR: Gladstone Historical Society, 1998.

Blanchet, Francis Norbert. *Historical Sketches of the Catholic Church in Oregon During the Past Forty Years.* Portland, OR: 1878.

British Columbia Historical Quarterly, Vol. VI, No. 2. Victoria, BC: Archives of British Columbia in co-operation with British Columbia Historical Association, 1942.

Case, Victoria, and Robert Ormand Case. *We Called It Culture.* Garden City, NY: Doubleday and Company, 1948.

Cross, Harvey. "Gladstone Real Estate Advertisement." *Oregon City Courier,* October 20, 1903.

Dye, Eva Emery. "Answers to Yesterday's Questions." *Morning Oregonian,* March 22, 1928.

Henry, Alexander. *The Manuscript Journals of Alexander Henry, Fur Trader of the Northwest Company, and of David Thompson, Official Geographer and Explorer of the same Company. Vol. 1.* New York, NY: Francis P. Harper, 1897.

Lynch, Vera Martin. *Free Land for Free People.* Portland, OR: Artline Printing, 1973.

Organized Militia of the United States, The. Washington, DC: Government Printing Office, 1894.

White, Elijah. *Concise View of Oregon Territory, Its Colonial and Indian Relations: Compiled from Official Letters and Reports, Together with the Organic Laws of the Colony.* Washington, DC: T. Barnard, 1846.

INDEX

Beehive auditorium, 83, 90, 100, 101, 108
Blanchet, Fr. Norbert, 14
Bryan, William Jennings, 102
Buck, William, 21, 23, 24, 37–39
Camp Compson, 50, 51
Cason, Ad, 47, 53, 54, 67, 105
Cason, Fendel, 8, 21–23, 28, 30, 32, 47, 53, 67
Clackamas County Fair, 17, 19, 47, 48, 119
Clackamas Indians, 7–14, 19, 29
Clackamas Indian burial ground, 16, 17, 19
Clackamas Indian longhouses, 10, 11
Cross, Harvey, 8, 38, 39, 55, 56, 63, 67–71, 73, 81, 91, 95, 97, 100, 105–107, 111, 113–115, 120
Duncan, Isadora, 103
Dye, Eva Emery, 79, 80, 82 91–93, 103, 105
Dye, Charles, 79, 80, 91, 100, 105
Erickson, August, 108, 109
Euterpean Club, 124
First Oregon Volunteer Cavalry, Company F, 47, 49
Freytag, Oscar, 16, 115
Gladstone Improvement Club, 114, 115
Gladstone Park Trolley, 74, 75, 78, 84
Gladstone Reporter, 124
gold, 36
Hasselbrink, Henry, 98
Henderson, Joseph, 30, 31
High Rocks, 14, 15, 29, 30, 37, 60, 121
Holladay, Ben, 23, 59–62, 66
Hunsaker, Jacob, 28, 29, 32, 33, 47, 67
Indian Dave, 19, 20, 25, 36
interurban trolley, 2, 38, 51, 67, 71–78, 84
Kipling, Rudyard, 43
Lake Chautauqua, 12, 13, 81, 93, 120
LaSalle, Guy, 117
Lee, Daniel, 7, 12
Lee, Jason, 7, 12

Liberty Bell, 122
Little Red Schoolhouse, 53, 54, 56, 105
McLoughlin, John, 7, 46, 92
Miller, Joaquin, 102
Mulkey, Rev. Aaron, 112
Oregon City Hospital, 52
Oregon State Fair, 17, 47
Pickett, Charles, 21, 26–29, 32
Pow-Wow Inn, 45
Pow-Wow mound, 13
Pow-Wow tree, 17, 18, 20, 45
Rinearson, Jacob, 8, 19, 21, 24, 25, 30, 47, 49, 67
Rinearson, Peter, 8, 19, 21, 24, 25, 30, 47, 53, 67, 105
Robb, James, 22
Roosevelt, Teddy, 103
sanitarium and health homes, 52
Schuebel family, 88
Straight, Hiram, 26, 28, 30, 47, 54, 67
Southern Pacific Railroad, 42, 60, 64, 78, 84, 122
Sunday, Billy, 95, 101
Howell, T. Chambers, 46, 115, 118
Turel House, 42, 85
Waller, Rev. Alvin, 14, 15, 22
White, Elijah, 21, 22, 26

127

Discover Thousands of Local History Books Featuring Millions of Vintage Images

Arcadia Publishing, the leading local history publisher in the United States, is committed to making history accessible and meaningful through publishing books that celebrate and preserve the heritage of America's people and places.

Find more books like this at
www.arcadiapublishing.com

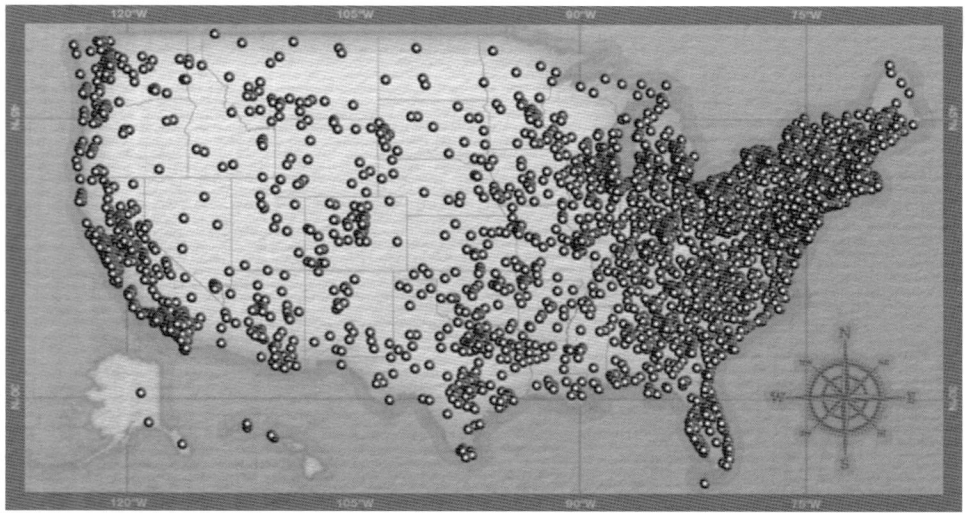

Search for your hometown history, your old stomping grounds, and even your favorite sports team.

Consistent with our mission to preserve history on a local level, this book was printed in South Carolina on American-made paper and manufactured entirely in the United States. Products carrying the accredited Forest Stewardship Council (FSC) label are printed on 100 percent FSC-certified paper.

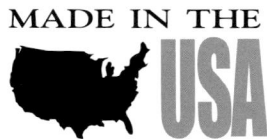